Query Answ

With

SQL Server

Volume II: In–Depth Querying

Adam Aspin

Karine Aspin

TETRAS
PUBLISHING

Query Answers with SQL Server: Volume II: In-Depth Querying

ISBN : 978-1-9996172-2-6

Tetras Publishing Ltd
Registered Office:
Gibson House
Hurricane Court
Hurricane Close.
Stafford
ST 16 1GZ
United Kingdom

Technical Reviewer: Sandra Eaton
Copyeditor: Rebecca Rider
Indexing: Tetras Publishing
Design: Tetras Publishing
Page Layout: Tetras Publishing

Contents

The Authors

Adam Aspin is an independent Business Intelligence (BI) consultant based in the United Kingdom. He has worked with SQL Server for over 20 years. During this time, he has developed several dozen database and analytical systems based on Microsoft databases. He has applied his skills for a range of clients in industry sectors across finance, utilities, telecoms, insurance, retail, and luxury goods.

A graduate of Oxford University, Adam moved into IT early in his career. Databases soon became a passion, and his experience in this arena ranges from dBase to Oracle, and Access to MySQL, with occasional sorties into the world of DB2, Informix, and PostgreSQL. He is, however, most at home in the Microsoft universe developing applications with SQL Server, SQL Server Analysis Services, SQL Server Reporting Services, SQL Server Integration Services, and Power BI.

Adam is a frequent contributor to SQLServerCentral.com and Simple Talk. He is a regular speaker at SQL Server User Groups, SQL Saturdays, and conferences such as SQL Bits. He has written numerous articles for various French IT publications. A fluent French speaker, Adam has worked in France and Switzerland for many years.

He is the author of SQL Server 2012 Data Integration Recipes (Apress, 2012), High Impact Data Visualization in Excel with Power View, 3D Maps, Get & Transform and Power BI, Second Edition (Apress, 2016), Business Intelligence with SQL Server Reporting Services (Apress, 2015), and Pro Power BI Desktop, Second Edition (Apress, 2017).

Karine Aspin is a principal consultant with Calidra Limited, a UK-based data and analytics consultancy. A mathematics graduate of the Swiss Federal Institute of Technology she previously worked for a range of IT companies including IBM Global Services.

Fluent in both French and English, Karine has worked on most of the major database systems currently available. These include SQL Server, MySQL, Oracle, PostgreSQL, Sybase and, of course, DB2 and Informix.

When not helping clients to deliver analytics and insight from their data, Karine devotes any remaining free time to equestrian pursuits

The Technical Reviewer

Sandra Eaton grew up in Birmingham, UK. After an initial career as a civil servant, Sandra took a short break to raise a family, which then turned into a long career break and a wonderful family.

While bringing up two children, Sandra gained a First Class Honors degree from the Open University. She also qualified as an ISEB software tester. She currently applies her skills testing a range of software from PC applications to ERP implementations—and anything in between.

Currently based in Telford, UK, in her spare time Sandra can usually be found walking the Shropshire hills or wild camping in the mountains of North Wales.

Acknowledgements

Writing a technical book is an arduous project at the best of times. Fortunately, the authors were lucky to have help and support from a great team.

First, we owe a deep debt of gratitude to Sandra Eaton, who kindly accepted our offer to be the technical reviewer of this book. Sandra brought a wealth of experience to this role, and her training as a software tester shone in the way that she helped us ensure that the code worked exactly as it was intended. Sandra went far beyond the call of duty in her efforts to help us deliver a book that would help readers master SQL.

We would particularly like to thank Rebecca Rider for her patience in editing the text and in making sure that our technical explanations were both clear and comprehensible. Her subtlety in polishing the prose was much appreciated, as were her rigor and attention to detail.

Finally, we have to thank the production staff at Tetras Publishing for all their help. Their professionalism in guiding us through the publication process was much appreciated.

Last—but not least—we need to thank our son, Timothy, for putting up with his parents' obsession with writing a book on a subject like SQL. His good humor and encouragement have helped us both on this particular journey.

Piracy

We take piracy of published work extremely seriously. Any unauthorised reproduction of this book will be prosecuted.

If you find, or know of any pirate copies of this book being distributed, please inform Tetras Publishing at: info@tetraspublishing.com.

On-Line Support Material

Any source code or other supplementary material referenced by the authors in this book is freely available for readers to download at www.tetraspublishing.com/sqlserver.

Questions and Feedback

We welcome any feedback that you might have. Please send your comments and queries to: info@tetraspublishing.com.

Introduction

If you are looking at this book, it is probably because you have some basic SQL ("Structured Query Language") querying knowledge and you want to raise your game and push your skillset to a higher level.

Whatever the motivation, you know that you want to build on your existing knowledge and use it to learn how to deliver the data analysis that you need. This probably means learning how to slice and filter the data in Microsoft SQL Server, as well as ensuring that you can tweak the presentation and present your results clearly and cogently.

This book is the next step on your journey. It aims to teach you in-depth SQL querying using data stored in a SQL Server database. It presumes that you have some previous knowledge of SQL and SQL Server and is designed to take you beyond the core concepts so that you are empowered to write powerful, polished, and efficient SQL queries that deliver real insight.

Why Microsoft SQL Server?

SQL Server is one of the world's bestselling and most widely used databases. It follows that learning the Microsoft flavor of SQL (called T-SQL) and the basics of the Microsoft database has the potential to be a career-enhancing move. As the data store for innumerable corporate, commercial, and web-driven databases, this mature and impressive system is used to power data analysis across the globe.

What Is T-SQL?

Every database has its own flavor of SQL, and these variants are subtly different. Microsoft uses its own dialect of SQL called T-SQL. Although the core elements are the same as those found in other databases, there are many subtle differences between T-SQL and other flavors.

This means that learning just "plain vanilla" SQL will soon leave you struggling with queries that use SQL Server. It can also mean that you will find yourself unable to extract the deeper insights that mastering T-SQL on SQL Server can provide.

Right from the start, this book takes you into the world of SQL Server and T-SQL. This way you learn to use the Microsoft dialect of SQL to its full capacity immediately, without limiting yourself to underperforming queries or missing out on T-SQL features that other flavors of SQL simply do not have.

T-SQL is, fortunately, very close to the SQL used by rival databases. So learning T-SQL sets you on the path to applying SQL query techniques in most of the available SQL databases that are currently deployed.

Why Learn SQL?

Most of the data that fuels businesses throughout the world is stored in relational databases. Nearly all of these databases are queried using a variant of Structured Query Language (SQL). So, simply put, SQL is key to data analysis. A mastery of SQL helps you delve deep into the data that is stored in corporate databases. You can apply SQL to analyze the data and then present it in a clearly understandable form.

SQL can usually serve a vital role in preparing the data for final delivery—no matter what output application you are using to present your analysis. Most end-user tools have an option for entering SQL to help derive meaning from the underlying data sources. Consequently, a good knowledge of SQL can help you analyze data faster and more clearly. The aims of this book are to give you the necessary mastery of SQL to enable you to get the most out of your data and to deliver the insights that will drive your competitive advantage.

Who This Book Is For

This book is designed to help anyone who wants to extend their knowledge of using SQL to deliver in-depth analysis. This means that you could be

- A data analyst

- A student

- A database developer

- A financial professional

- A business analyst

- A job-seeker looking to get ready for a technical interview

- A trainee preparing for a Microsoft SQL exam

or indeed anyone who needs to deliver accurate analytics from the data stored in a SQL Server database.

However, this book does presume that you have a core knowledge of querying SQL Server and that you can already write basic SQL queries. If this is not the case, then we suggest that you read the first volume in this series, *Query Answers with SQL Server, Volume I: Introduction to SQL Queries*, before you work through the examples in this book.

What This Book Will Bring You

This book was written to help you become proficient in querying databases using T-SQL. It is designed to help you master a language that can seem arcane, or even weird, at first sight. To overcome any initial reticence that you may have, it progresses step by step through all the concepts and techniques that you need to perfect the skill of writing complex SQL queries.

To make SQL comprehensible, we have chosen to introduce each new concept or keyword individually so that you can learn each new element in isolation. As the book progresses, you see how you can combine SQL keywords to extend the power of SQL as you learn to create ever-more-powerful queries.

That said, no one queries databases purely for fun, so each query that you apply in this book also has a practical purpose. As a result, you also see how to develop re-al-world queries that deliver essential data analysis. You can then adapt these queries to your own requirements using your own data.

How to Read This Book

We did not design this book only to be read from start to finish. By this we mean that you can use it in several different ways depending on your knowledge of SQL and your real-world requirements.

SQL Novices

If you are a complete beginner, we suggest that you read the first volume in this series, *Query Answers with SQL Server, Volume I: Introduction to SQL Queries*, before working through the examples in this book.

Refreshing Your Knowledge

If you are coming back to SQL after a while away, consider skimming through the sections in each chapter until you start encountering techniques and approaches that are less obvious. Then slow down and concentrate on the new elements that interest you and consolidate as well as refresh your knowledge. Of course, how you actually do this depends on your level of SQL proficiency before you start reading this book.

In-Depth Querying

This book is all about learning to query SQL Server in depth. If this is the reason that you bought this book, we suggest that you begin with the first chapter and work through all the examples in the book. The chapters are designed to build on existing knowledge as the book progresses. Consequently, you will find that the best way to build a solid set of querying skills is to proceed methodically and consolidate each level in the learning process before you proceed to the next chapter.

Transferring SQL Knowledge from Another Flavor of SQL

Even if you are already used to a different variant of SQL, you may want to read all the chapters to make sure you are clear on the differences between T-SQL and the version of SQL that you have come from. When you are writing more advanced queries, be aware that there are many subtle nuances that differentiate T-SQL from other dialects of SQL, and it is only through writing and testing SQL queries that these differences become apparent.

Solving Specific Issues

If you have been using SQL for a while but need some guidance to help you solve new kinds of query challenges, then you can use this book as a collection of "recipes."

In this case, we suggest that you look at the table of contents and jump straight to the examples that interest you.

Indeed, each chapter explains the various ways that you can use a core SQL querying technique to deliver actionable insight. So, you may choose to learn—or reacquaint yourself with—a key SQL querying concept by studying a specific chapter independently of the rest of the book.

The Structure of This Book

This book assumes a core level of SQL querying knowledge that you can build on to become proficient in writing complex SQL queries. The book follows a linear pattern of knowledge transfer, where previously acquired knowledge underpins new techniques as you progress through the book.

The chapters cover the following areas:

"Chapter 1: Subqueries". This chapter shows you how you can use independent SQL queries inside other queries.

"Chapter 2: Derived Tables". This chapter teaches you how to compare data at different levels of aggregation or carry out calculations that mix and match different ways of grouping data.

"Chapter 3: Common Table Expressions". This chapter explains a powerful way to simplify working with complex datasets.

"Chapter 4: Correlated Subqueries". This chapter shows you how you can use certain kinds of subquery to filter the data in the outer query in a specific way.

"Chapter 5: Joining and Filtering Datasets". This chapter introduces methods of handling data spread across a series of tables with identical structures.

"Chapter 6: Using SQL for More Advanced Calculations". This chapter teaches you how SQL can go much further than simple addition, subtraction, division, and multiplication and how SQL handles numbers.

"Chapter 7: Segmenting and Classifying Data". This chapter introduces ways of prioritizing and classifying lists of data in order to analyze the elements that really matter.

"Chapter 8: Rolling Analysis". This chapter covers ways of discerning trends, tracking growth, and establishing a solid factual base that you can use for your analysis.

"Chapter 9: Analyzing Data Over Time". This chapter goes deeply into techniques that you can apply to track the evolution of sales, profits, or, indeed, any metric over any time period: from years to days to hours and seconds.

"Chapter 10: Complex Data Output". This chapter concludes the book with a look at ways of shaping output so that the essence of your analysis is immediately comprehensible. These techniques will also help you to present your analysis in various ways that can make the results easier to read and understand.

The Sample Data and Sample Queries

To help you learn SQL, we have made the sample data as well as all the SQL queries in this book available on the Tetras Publishing website — www.tetraspublishing.com/SQLServer. This way you can download and install the sample data into a SQL Server database on your PC, and then you can practice SQL querying using the data that we have elaborated on to help you learn SQL.

If typing the queries is a little laborious (though we do recommend doing so as an excellent way of learning), then you can also download each query in the book and simply copy each into the querying application that you are using to see the query result.

Time to Get Started Querying SQL Server

We have said enough about the theory of SQL Server. It is now time to get up close and personal.

But first, make sure you have a working copy of the latest version of SQL Server. This book is written for SQL Server 2017, and we strongly advise you to install one of the free versions of this database as described in Appendix A.

Once you have a functioning database, you need an application that you can use to test your queries. There are many such apps available, but we advise you to use Microsoft's SQL Server Management Studio, especially since this is the application that we have used throughout this book. You can find out how to download and install this tool in Appendix B.

Finally, you need some sample data to work on. For this (and especially if you want to test your SQL using the examples in this book) you need to download and set up the sample PrestigeCars database. This is described in Appendix C.

That is it! You are now ready to start on your journey toward becoming a SQL-querying maestro.

Have fun!

Chapter 1:
Subqueries

Now that you have mastered the basics of SQL, it is time to move on and start resolving some more complex analytical challenges. The first step on this path is to learn how you can use independent SQL queries inside other queries. This technique is called using subqueries. It is particularly useful in data analysis as it allows you (among other things) to include aggregated data in detailed rowsets, for instance, or to compare a whole dataset with subsets of data.

What Are Subqueries?

Subqueries are more of a new technique than a new set of SQL keywords. In fact, you can write subqueries using only the SQL knowledge that you have acquired in *Query Answers with SQL Server, Volume I: Introduction to SQL Queries* (*Volume I* from now on). Nonetheless, learning to use subqueries to solve data challenges is a key part of your SQL apprenticeship. Once you master the art of the subquery, you are able to produce clear, concise, and in-depth analytics quickly and efficiently.

We want to convince you that subqueries are not an abstract database concept but an analytical skill that helps you dig deep into your data and unearth the insights that keep you ahead of the competition. In this chapter you learn how to

- Compare categories of data to the whole dataset and calculate percentages
- Isolate top and bottom elements in a dataset and use them as a basis for filtering records
- Filter data by comparing records to averages and overall thresholds

These—and many more analytical solutions—are made possible through the application of subqueries in your SQL. Let's now move on to some real-world examples that illustrate how subqueries can turn raw data into meaningful information.

1. Adding Aggregated Fields to Detailed Data Sets

Data analysis often means comparing individual elements to either all or a part of a dataset. As a first step, suppose that you want to count the number of cars sold per country and that you also want to see the total car sales for all vehicles, whatever their country, in the same query. Here is the SQL that lets you do this:

```
SELECT      CountryName

            ,COUNT(SD.StockID) AS CarsSold

            ,(SELECT COUNT(SalesDetailsID)

             FROM Data.SalesDetails) AS SalesTotal

FROM        Data.SalesDetails SD

INNER JOIN Data.Sales AS SA ON SA.SalesID = SD.SalesID

INNER JOIN Data.Customer CU ON SA.CustomerID = CU.CustomerID

INNER JOIN Data.Country CO ON CU.Country = CO.CountryISO2

GROUP BY    CountryName
```

Running this query gives the results that you can see in Figure 1-1.

	CountryName	CarsSold	SalesTotal
1	Belgium	10	351
2	France	69	351
3	Germany	13	351
4	Italy	18	351
5	Spain	27	351
6	Switzerland	18	351
7	United Kingdom	165	351
8	United States	31	351

FIGURE 1-1. USING A SUBQUERY

How It Works

Inevitably there are occasions in your analytical career when you want to see how a part of a set of data relates to a whole dataset. This approach frequently allows you to relativize values and to put them in a wider context.

This query exists to help you add perspective to the data. At its heart, it is a simple aggregation of sales by country. Once the Sales, SalesDetails, Customer, and Country tables have been joined, the SQL groups the data on the Country field and uses the COUNT() function to return the total number of sales for each country. Then—and this is where you are moving on to new territory—it adds a subquery to the SELECT clause to return the total number of sales without any grouping. In effect, this returns the total for all sales as a separate column alongside the number of cars sold. However, the SQL is carrying out this calculation for every row in the query output so that you can see—and possibly use—the total in every row.

To get a more visual idea of how a subquery works, take a look at Figure 1-2. The outer query "hosts" the separate inner query, yet both queries run at the same time and output their results together.

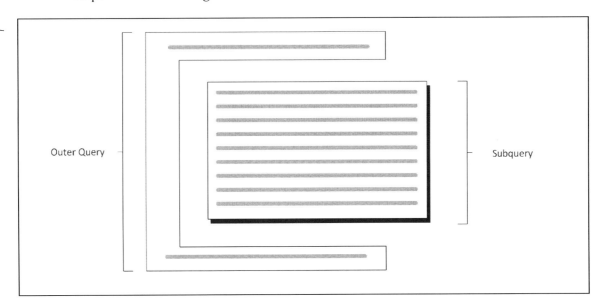

FIGURE 1-2. A CONCEPTUAL VIEW OF SUBQUERIES

The code shows you how SQL Server lets you mix separate queries in a single output using a technique called a *subquery*. The principle characteristics of a subquery are

- It is included in the SELECT, WHERE, or HAVING clause of the "main" (outer) query, just as a normal field name would be.

- It is enclosed in parentheses.
- It is a complete, separate query with—at a minimum—its own SELECT and FROM clauses.
- It can only return *one value* (that is, you cannot output more than one field from the subquery).

Tricks and Traps

A new concept like this implies a few key points that you need to remember:

- You do not have to use an alias for the name of the field returned by a subquery—but it *is* easier to understand the results if you do use aliases. You may also find that using a meaningful alias helps you understand the query better when you return to it at a later date.

- Any subquery can be executed independently of the main/outer query. This means that you can select the text that makes up the subquery (but not including the parentheses that contain it) and run it by pressing F5 or by clicking the toolbar Execute button at any time. In this example, you select the following code:

```
SELECT COUNT(SalesDetailsID) FROM Data.SalesDetails
```

Running this code returns a dataset like the one shown in Figure 1-3.

FIGURE 1-3. EXECUTING A SUBQUERY INDEPENDENTLY

- Although you can only output a single value from a subquery, you can make the value that is returned the result of a calculation in the subquery if you need to.

- The subquery can be as simple or as complex as your requirements demand and can contain its own independent WHERE or GROUP BY clauses.

2.   Displaying a Value as the Percentage of a Total

Calculating *ratios*—or percentages of a whole—is a core requirement in data analysis. Let's imagine that the sales director has put in a request for a list of sales by make of car sold that also displays the percentage of the total sales that the value for each make represents. Subqueries can help you do this easily and simply, as the following SQL snippet shows:

```
SELECT     MakeName

           ,SUM(SalePrice) AS SalePrice

           ,SUM(SalePrice) / (SELECT SUM(SalePrice)

                              FROM Data.SalesDetails) AS SalesRatio

FROM       Data.Make AS MK

INNER JOIN Data.Model AS MD ON MK.MakeID = MD.MakeID

INNER JOIN Data.Stock AS ST ON ST.ModelID = MD.ModelID

INNER JOIN Data.SalesDetails SD ON ST.StockCode = SD.StockID

GROUP BY   MakeName
```

Running this query gives the results that you can see in Figure 1-4.

	MakeName	SalePrice	SalesRatio
1	Alfa Romeo	243510.00	0.011044
2	Aston Martin	5102755.00	0.231444
3	Austin	64500.00	0.002925
4	Bentley	1689240.00	0.076618
5	BMW	60500.00	0.002744
6	Bugatti	1915500.00	0.086880
7	Citroen	101080.00	0.004584
8	Delahaye	107000.00	0.004853
9	Delorean	99500.00	0.004512
10	Ferrari	5540850.00	0.251314
11	Jaguar	882955.00	0.040047
12	Lagonda	218000.00	0.009887
13	Lamborghini	1727150.00	0.078337
14	McLaren	295000.00	0.013380
15	Mercedes	471115.00	0.021368

FIGURE 1-4. USING A SUBQUERY TO CALCULATE A RATIO

How It Works

This query works like this:

First:	It joins the tables (Make, Model, Stock, and SalesDetails) that are required to return the make as well as the selling price for each vehicle sold.
Second:	It groups on the MakeName field and selects this field as well as the SUM() of the sale price to aggregate the selling price per make.
Finally:	It adds a new calculated field that divides the sum of the sale price by the total sale price of all vehicles sold. The "grand total" for all sales is defined using a subquery. In effect, this field (SalesRatio) divides each aggregate total by the overall total and so calculates the percentage of total sales that each make represents.

Tricks and Traps

We are pushing the concept of subqueries quite a bit further in this example. Note that

- SQL frequently forces you to repeat a calculation if you need its output more than once. In this example, you can see that you need the total of vehicles sold *twice* to calculate the percentage of total sales: once for each make and once to calculate the overall total. Consequently, you have to repeat the formula

```
SUM(SalePrice)
```

This means that SQL is not like a spreadsheet where you can "chain" cells using cell references to produce ripple-through calculations. It follows that it is perfectly normal to repeat a calculation several times in a piece of SQL each time you need it.

- Percentages are expressed as a decimal value when they are calculated, just as they are in a spreadsheet. You may prefer to multiply the result by 100 to obtain a more comprehensible result:

```
SUM(SalePrice) / (SELECT SUM(SalePrice)

                  FROM Data.SalesDetails) * 100 AS SalesRatio
```

If you use SQL like this in the lines that appear in bold earlier, you get the output in Figure 1-5.

	MakeName	SalePrice	SalesRatio
1	Alfa Romeo	243510.00	1.104400
2	Aston Martin	5102755.00	23.144400
3	Austin	64500.00	0.292500
4	Bentley	1689240.00	7.661800
5	BMW	60500.00	0.274400

FIGURE 1-5. MULTIPLYING A PERCENTAGE CALCULATION TO DELIVER A MORE COMPREHENSIBLE RESULT

- If you want to format the result as a percentage, you can use the following SQL in the third line of the code snippet:

```
FORMAT(SUM(SalePrice) / (SELECT SUM(SalePrice)

FROM Data.SalesDetails), '#0.00%') AS SalesRatio
```

Doing so gives you the kind of output that you can see in Figure 1-6.

	MakeName	SalePrice	SalesRatio
1	Alfa Romeo	243510.00	1.10%
2	Aston Martin	5102755.00	23.14%
3	Austin	64500.00	0.29%
4	Bentley	1689240.00	7.66%
5	BMW	60500.00	0.27%

FIGURE 1-6. FORMATTING A PERCENTAGE OUTPUT

As you can see, if you are formatting the output, you do not need to multiply the result by 100.

- The main query in both this example and the previous one is an aggregate query. In practice the outer and inner queries can apply different levels of aggregation. This means that you can use aggregated subqueries inside simple list queries as well as in list-style subqueries inside aggregate outer queries.

Note	It is *vital* to remember that the two queries are completely independent of each other.

3. Using a Subquery to Isolate an Element

Prestige Cars' new marketing director is convinced that some colors of car sell better than others. She wants you to find the color—or colors—of the most expensive vehicles sold. Here is the SQL that can do this:

```
SELECT      ST.Color

FROM        Data.Stock AS ST

INNER JOIN  Data.SalesDetails SD ON ST.StockCode = SD.StockID

WHERE       SD.SalePrice = (SELECT MAX(SalePrice) FROM Data.SalesDetails)
```

Running this query gives the results you can see in Figure 1-7.

FIGURE 1-7. USING A SUBQUERY IN THE WHERE CLAUSE OF A QUERY

How It Works

This query is really in two parts.

A subquery	This short piece of code finds the sale price for the most expensive vehicles sold.
The main query	Uses the figure calculated by the subquery as the criterion for returning the color (or colors) of any vehicles sold at this price from the main query

The main query itself simply selects the Color field from the Stock table and joins this table to the SalesDetails table so that the sale price can be used in the WHERE clause as a filter criterion.

What this example shows is that subqueries are not restricted to being used in a SELECT clause. As you can see here, you can also use them in a WHERE clause to restrict the results returned from the main/outer query.

Tricks and Traps

We only have one comment to make about this kind of subquery:

- Technically this piece of SQL is a single query. However, we prefer to describe it as a main query and a subquery purely because we feel that this helps you understand the code more easily.

Selecting the subquery and running it gives you the result you can see in Figure 1-8.

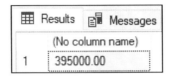

FIGURE 1-8. THE OUTPUT FROM A SUBQUERY

This is the value that is used by the main query to filter the query output.

4. Using a Subquery to Filter Data

As part of a company cost containment exercise, you have been asked to take a closer look at any vehicles whose repair cost is significantly over the average for all the vehicles in stock. Specifically, the finance director wants to see a list of all vehicles whose repair cost is more than three times the average repair cost. The following SQL snippet does just this:

```
SELECT      MK.MakeName, MD.ModelName, RepairsCost

FROM        Data.Make AS MK

INNER JOIN Data.Model AS MD ON MK.MakeID = MD.MakeID

INNER JOIN Data.Stock AS ST ON ST.ModelID = MD.ModelID

WHERE       RepairsCost > 3 * (SELECT AVG(RepairsCost) FROM Data.Stock)
```

Running this query gives the results that you can see in Figure 1-9.

	MakeName	ModelName	RepairsCost
1	Ferrari	Testarossa	6000.00
2	Ferrari	355	5500.00
3	Ferrari	355	5500.00
4	Ferrari	355	9250.00
5	Ferrari	355	9250.00
6	Ferrari	355	9250.00
7	Ferrari	Dino	5500.00
8	Ferrari	Dino	9250.00
9	Ferrari	F40	5500.00
10	Ferrari	F50	5500.00
11	Ferrari	F50	9250.00
12	Ferrari	360	9250.00
13	Ferrari	360	5500.00
14	Ferrari	Enzo	9250.00
15	Ferrari	Enzo	9250.00

FIGURE 1-9. APPLYING A CALCULATION AND A SUBQUERY IN THE **WHERE** CLAUSE

How It Works

This query shows how you can use a subquery in a calculation to highlight certain records in a dataset. The main/outer query simply selects the cost of repairs for all makes and models of vehicle in the database using the Make, Model, and Stock tables. The clever part is placing a subquery in the WHERE clause. What this subquery does is

First: It calculates the average repair cost. This is £1533.14 for the Prestige Cars dataset. You can verify this by selecting and running only the SQL for the subquery.

Then: It multiplies this average repair cost by a factor of three.

Finally: It compares this to the repair cost for each vehicle and only displays those where the repair cost is greater than three times the average repair cost—that is, over £4,599.42.

You may be thinking that it is a little strange to refer to the same table—the Stock table, in this example—twice in the same query. After all, it is already used in the outer query, so why would you need it in the subquery, too?

The reason is that you are looking at the data in two different ways:

The outer query	Looks at the data at a *detailed level*, where each record is processed individually.
The subquery	Looks at the *whole table* to calculate the average repair cost for all records in the table.

Because each query is completely independent of the other, both have separate SELECT clauses no matter which tables and fields are used.

The technical term for these two ways of looking at data is *granularity*. In effect, a SQL query can look at either the *detail* (that is, at a granular level) or *groups* of records (a higher level of granularity) or even the whole dataset—but it cannot combine multiple levels of focus at the same time in the same query. So, if you need to mix the whole with the parts, you need to use more than one query, even if the queries combine their results in a single output.

To see this more clearly, take a look at Figure 1-10. This is a visual representation of how granularity works in datasets.

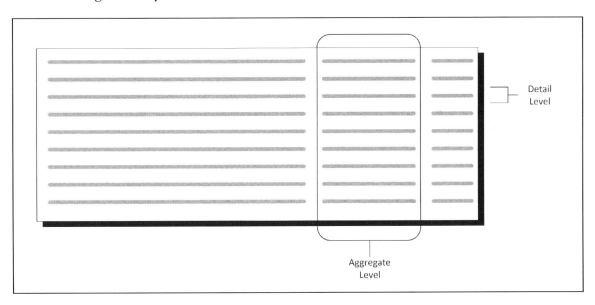

FIGURE 1-10. DATA GRANULARITY

Using subqueries enables you to look at data at two or more separate levels of detail. Indeed, you *need* subqueries to return data at different levels of granularity in a single query.

Tricks and Traps

Here are a couple of useful points that you may need to remember when applying this kind of query:

- If you want to check that the calculation of the average cost of repairs really is the figure that we quoted, all you have to do is *select the SQL in the subquery and execute it.* This means running the following short piece of code that you can see in the WHERE clause of the SQL at the start of this section:

```
SELECT AVG(RepairsCost) FROM Data.Stock
```

You should see the result shown in Figure 1-11. This is the average repair cost for all vehicles in the Stock table.

FIGURE 1-11. THE OUTPUT FROM A SUBQUERY

- It is perfectly normal to query the same table or tables in both a main query and a subquery. This only proves that the two queries are strictly independent of each other.

5. Filtering on an Aggregated Range of Data Using Multiple Subqueries

A further aspect of the finance director's corporate cost control project is to analyze all sales in which repair costs are within 10 percent of the average repair cost for all stock. The following SQL does this for you:

```
SELECT      MK.MakeName, MD.ModelName, Cost, RepairsCost

FROM        Data.Make AS MK

INNER JOIN Data.Model AS MD ON MK.MakeID = MD.MakeID

INNER JOIN Data.Stock AS ST ON ST.ModelID = MD.ModelID

WHERE       RepairsCost BETWEEN

                (SELECT AVG(RepairsCost) FROM Data.Stock) * 0.9

            AND

                (SELECT AVG(RepairsCost) FROM Data.Stock) * 1.1
```

Running this query gives the results that you can see in Figure 1-12.

	MakeName	ModelName	Cost	RepairsCost
1	Aston Martin	DB6	55600.00	1490.00
2	Bentley	Flying Spur	52712.00	1490.00
3	Porsche	959	53200.00	1490.00
4	Aston Martin	DB9	63600.00	1490.00
5	Rolls Royce	Phantom	95680.00	1490.00
6	Rolls Royce	Phantom	79600.00	1490.00
7	Rolls Royce	Silver Shadow	68000.00	1490.00
8	Delorean	DMC 12	79600.00	1490.00
9	Aston Martin	DB9	62000.00	1490.00
10	Rolls Royce	Silver Seraph	79960.00	1490.00
11	Bentley	Arnage	79960.00	1490.00
12	Aston Martin	Virage	82920.00	1490.00
13	Rolls Royce	Ghost	79160.00	1490.00
14	Porsche	959	71600.00	1490.00
15	Aston Martin	DB6	66072.00	1490.00

FIGURE 1-12. USING MULTIPLE SUBQUERIES IN THE WHERE CLAUSE

How It Works

You can use as many subqueries as you need in a SQL query. A practical use for this is when you need to isolate a dataset that falls between a range of values—such as when you are using a BETWEEN...AND in the WHERE clause.

This query selects the make, model, cost, and repair cost for all vehicles. It then filters the data in the WHERE clause. However, since the WHERE clause uses the BETWEEN... AND technique to select a range of values—and this approach requires a lower and an upper limit to the range—it needs *two* subclauses to calculate the average repair cost.

The range boundaries are defined like this:

The lower limit   Takes the overall average repair cost and multiplies by 0.9 to get the figure for 90 percent of the average value (£1,379.83).

The upper limit   Takes the overall average repair cost and multiplies by 1.1 to get the figure for 110 percent of the average value (£1,686.46).

These two range limits are then used by the BETWEEN...AND elements of the WHERE clause to filter the rows that are returned by the main query. This way only vehicles whose repair cost is plus or minus 10 percent of the average repair cost are displayed.

So, once again, you need to write a separate and independent subquery to return a specific result. You can even include multiple subqueries to apply multiple calculations across many different data tables.

Tricks and Traps

We need to make a couple of points here:

- In cases like these, you have to repeat the subquery and make sure that you have made both subqueries strictly identical.

- Remember that when using the BETWEEN ... AND technique, you *must* always begin with the lower threshold (90 percent in this example) and end with the higher threshold (110 percent in this example).

6.   Filtering on Aggregated Output Using a Second Aggregation

On certain occasions your analysis may lead you to compare an aggregate from one dataset with a completely separate aggregate. This can happen, for instance, when salespeople request a list of the average sale price of all makes whose average sale price is over twice the average sale price. SQL allows you to compare data in this way, too, as the following SQL snippet shows:

```
SELECT     MakeName, AVG(SD.SalePrice) AS AverageUpperSalePrice

FROM       Data.Make AS MK

INNER JOIN Data.Model AS MD ON MK.MakeID = MD.MakeID

INNER JOIN Data.Stock AS ST ON ST.ModelID = MD.ModelID

INNER JOIN Data.SalesDetails SD ON ST.StockCode = SD.StockID

GROUP BY   MakeName

HAVING     AVG(SD.SalePrice) > 2 * (SELECT AVG(SalePrice)

                                    FROM    Data.SalesDetails)
```

Running this query gives the results that you can see in Figure 1-13.

FIGURE 1-13. APPLYING A CALCULATION AND A SUBQUERY IN THE HAVING CLAUSE

How It Works

You can also use a subquery in the HAVING clause of an SQL query. As you might re-member from Chapter 3 of *Volume I*, the HAVING clause operates at the level of the aggregation that has been applied to a dataset rather than at the level of individual records. So, when you apply a subquery to an aggregate query's HAVING clause, you are filtering the data on a total, an average, or any other aggregated value.

In this example

First:	The outer query calculates the average sale price for each make.
Next:	The subquery calculates the overall average sale price for all vehicles sold.
Then:	The subquery then multiplies this average by two and compares it to the average sale price by make for all the makes of car sold.

The result is that any make with an average sale price over twice the overall average sale price is then listed in the query output.

Tricks and Traps

When using calculations to filter data, you need to be aware that

- There are several ways of carrying out the calculation used in the query. If you prefer, you can use arithmetic like this:

```
HAVING AVG(SD.SalePrice)  / 2 < (SELECT AVG(SalePrice)

                                 FROM    Data.SalesDetails)
```

This code gives exactly the same result as the SQL at the start of this example. It is a simple choice between two arithmetical approaches.

7. Using Multiple Results from a Subquery to Filter Data

The sales director has asked you to find all the sales for the top five bestselling makes. A request like this illustrates that some data analysis challenges require you to output a set of records that uses the result of a second set as a filter.

The (slightly more complex) SQL to solve this problem is as follows:

```
SELECT     MakeName, SalePrice

FROM       Data.Make AS MKX

INNER JOIN Data.Model AS MDX ON MKX.MakeID = MDX.MakeID

INNER JOIN Data.Stock AS STX ON STX.ModelID = MDX.ModelID

INNER JOIN Data.SalesDetails SDX ON STX.StockCode = SDX.StockID

WHERE      MakeName IN (

                       SELECT     TOP (5) MK.MakeName

                       FROM       Data.Make AS MK

                       INNER JOIN Data.Model AS MD

                                  ON MK.MakeID = MD.MakeID

                       INNER JOIN Data.Stock AS ST

                                  ON ST.ModelID = MD.ModelID

                       INNER JOIN Data.SalesDetails SD

                                  ON ST.StockCode = SD.StockID

                       INNER JOIN Data.Sales SA

                                  ON SA.SalesID = SD.SalesID

                       GROUP BY   MK.MakeName

                       ORDER BY   SUM(SA.TotalSalePrice) DESC

                       )

ORDER BY   MakeName, SalePrice DESC
```

Running this query gives the results that you can see in Figure 1-14, where you can also see the output from the subquery. Although this list contains five makes (Aston Martin, Bentley, Bugatti, Ferrari, and Lamborghini), it is, nonetheless, fairly long. You have to scroll through the output to ensure that only five makes are displayed.

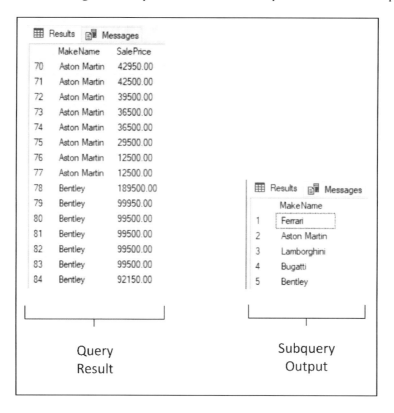

FIGURE 1-14. A COMPLEX SUBQUERY USED TO RESTRICT DATA IN THE OUTER QUERY

How It Works

Here you can see how data analysis can be a multistep process. This example shows you how to

First: Use a subquery to find the top five bestselling makes by sale value.

Then: Use this data to filter the results from a simpler "outer" query.

This example is one of those times when a subquery can be a lot more complex—and powerful—than the outer query that contains it. Indeed, most of the work is done by the subquery, so it makes sense to look at this first.

The subquery	Joins a series of tables so that you can return the make and sale price. It then aggregates sales by make, calculates the total sale price for each make, and finally returns only the top three makes.
The main query	Uses this result as the filter in its WHERE clause—which is nothing more than a list of makes and sale prices. However, since the subquery can potentially return more than one result, you have to use the IN operator in the WHERE clause, and not a simple comparison operator, such as =, <, >, <=, or >= (or even != or <>).

It is worth noting that the two queries—subquery and outer query—can be different types of query. In this example, the subquery is an aggregate query, whereas the outer query is a simple "list" (or detail-level) query.

Note	When a subquery returns more than one record you *must* use the IN operator in the WHERE clause. If you do not, you will get an error message.

Tricks and Traps

Handling complex queries like this one inevitably introduces some key points to take away:

- This example introduces something new—but it is so subtle that it is easy to miss. Here the subquery returns *more than one record*. In fact, it returns precisely *five* elements—the top five bestselling makes of car.

- When solving complex analytical problems like this one, you may well find yourself beginning with the subquery and then moving on to the outer query.

- You should be able to run any subquery independently of the outer query. So, you can select the subquery and execute it at any time, just as you would execute the entire query.

- You can begin a complex query like this by writing the subquery first, if you prefer. That way, you can be sure that it returns the data you need to filter the outer query correctly.

- You can create a subquery using many separate tables that are joined together, just as you would any "ordinary" query.

- You can see in this code that we use different aliases in the inner and outer queries, even when the same tables are used. This is not strictly necessary, because the two queries are totally separate. However, we prefer to do this for a couple of reasons:

- It highlights the fact that you are dealing with two separate queries.

- It is less confusing to read because you can easily see which field comes from which table.

- More complex subqueries like this one can take longer to run, so do not be surprised if it takes a few seconds for the results to appear.

8. Complex Aggregated Subqueries

After all the work that you did for the sales director, your reputation as an analyst has hit new heights. Now it is the CEO's turn to request some assistance. She wants to know which makes are generating the most sales, and specifically, how many cars have been sold for the top three bestselling makes. The following code snippet lets you impress her with your SQL abilities:

```
SELECT      MK.MakeName

            ,COUNT(MK.MakeName) AS VehiclesSold

            ,SUM(SD.SalePrice) AS TotalSalesPerMake

FROM        Data.Make AS MK

INNER JOIN Data.Model AS MD ON MK.MakeID = MD.MakeID

INNER JOIN Data.Stock AS ST ON ST.ModelID = MD.ModelID

INNER JOIN Data.SalesDetails SD ON ST.StockCode = SD.StockID

WHERE       MakeName IN (

                        SELECT      TOP (3) MK.MakeName

                        FROM        Data.Make AS MK

                        INNER JOIN Data.Model AS MD

                                    ON MK.MakeID = MD.MakeID

                        INNER JOIN Data.Stock AS ST

                                    ON ST.ModelID = MD.ModelID
```

```
                   INNER JOIN Data.SalesDetails SD

                           ON ST.StockCode = SD.StockID

                   INNER JOIN Data.Sales AS SA

                           ON SA.SalesID = SD.SalesID

                GROUP BY    MK.MakeName

                ORDER BY    COUNT(MK.MakeName) DESC

                )

GROUP BY   MK.MakeName

ORDER BY   VehiclesSold DESC
```

Running this query gives the results that you can see in Figure 1-15.

FIGURE 1-15. USING A COMPLEX SUBQUERY AS A FILTER IN AN AGGREGATED QUERY

How It Works

Some queries are really two queries in one. In these cases, subqueries unlock the real power of SQL to allow you to carry out complex filtering that then becomes the basis of further analysis. This example extends the code from the previous example to show that the two queries that generate the final result are—and have to be—*totally independent* of one another. Even though the subquery counts the sales per make, you cannot pass this value back to the outer query. You have to count the number of vehicles sold *twice*: once in the *subquery* to act as a filter and once in the *outer query* to display the result.

Otherwise this query is very similar to the previous one. The subquery finds the top three makes sold by quantity. Then these three makes are used as the filter by the outer query.

Tricks and Traps

There are a couple of points to note here:

- In this example, both queries (outer query and subquery) aggregate data. As you saw in the previous example, this does not necessarily need to be the case.

- This code applies the *same aliases* for the tables in both the outer query and the subquery. This reinforces the point that the two queries are *completely separate* and that the aliases in the outer query only refer to tables in the outer query and the aliases in the inner query only refer to tables in the inner query—even if the same aliases are used in both queries.

9. Using a Subquery to Filter a Percentage of a Dataset

Investigating trends and patterns in data often means looking at the data that makes up a specific area of data. Finding attributes of least (and most) profitable sales is an example of this kind of analysis. As a specific example, the sales director wants you to find all colors for cars sold for the least profitable 5 percent of sales. Take a look at the following SQL snippet to see how this is done:

```
SELECT      DISTINCT Color

FROM        Data.Stock STX

INNER JOIN  Data.SalesDetails SDX

            ON STX.StockCode = SDX.StockID

WHERE       SalesID IN (

                    SELECT      TOP 5 PERCENT SalesID

                    FROM        Data.Stock AS ST

                    INNER JOIN Data.SalesDetails SD

                            ON ST.StockCode = SD.StockID
```

```
ORDER BY    (SD.SalePrice -

                 (Cost + ISNULL(RepairsCost, 0)

                 + PartsCost + TransportInCost)

            ) ASC

       )
```

Running this query gives the results that you can see in Figure 1-16.

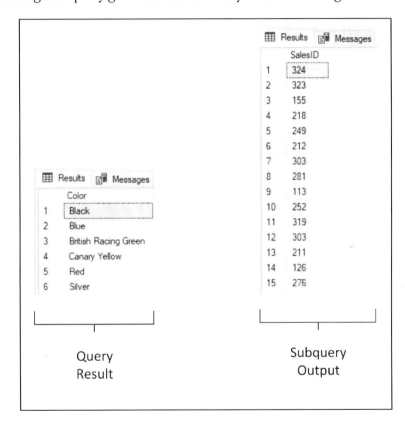

FIGURE 1-16. USING A SUBQUERY TO FILTER A PERCENTAGE OF A DATASET

How It Works

Once again, the subquery is the central part of this overall piece of SQL. It joins the Stock table to the SalesDetails table so that only cars sold are taken into consideration by the query. Then it calculates the net profit per car sold. Finally, it sorts this data set from lowest to highest—that is, from the smallest to the greatest profit. Adding the TOP 5 PERCENT to the SELECT clause ensures that only the initial 5 percent of sales records are returned.

The outer query then lists the colors of the vehicles whose SalesIDs are passed up to the outer query's WHERE clause as a filter. As a final touch, the outer query's SELECT clause uses the DISTINCT keyword to avoid duplication of colors, even if the same color appears several times in the top 5 percent of sales per make.

This query looks quite dense, yet it delivers some extremely efficient analysis. The art (as is so often the case) is to work out how to break down the requirement into its component parts so that you can then design and write the appropriate SQL.

Tricks and Traps

When using subqueries as filters, you need to remember that

- Even though the subquery uses the TOP keyword, it is really returning the *bottom* percentage. This is because the sort order is set to *ascending*—that is, from smallest to largest. So, the top 5 percent, starting at the smallest figure, in effect returns the lowest sales figures—that is, the *bottom* five percent.

10. Nested Subqueries

The only downside to making senior managers happy is that it generates even more work for you. This time the sales director wants you find the top five vehicles sold for the bestselling color by value. The following piece of SQL does exactly this:

```
SELECT      TOP 5 MK.MakeName, MD.ModelName, SD.SalePrice

FROM        Data.Make AS MK

INNER JOIN Data.Model AS MD ON MK.MakeID = MD.MakeID

INNER JOIN Data.Stock AS ST ON ST.ModelID = MD.ModelID

INNER JOIN Data.SalesDetails SD ON ST.StockCode = SD.StockID

INNER JOIN Data.Sales AS SA ON SA.SalesID = SD.SalesID
```

```
WHERE        Color IN (SELECT      ST.Color

                      FROM         Data.Model AS MD

                      INNER JOIN Data.Stock AS ST

                                   ON ST.ModelID = MD.ModelID

                      INNER JOIN Data.SalesDetails SD

                                   ON ST.StockCode = SD.StockID

                      WHERE        SD.SalePrice =

                                   (

                                     SELECT      MAX(SD.SalePrice)

                                     FROM        Data.SalesDetails SD

                                     INNER JOIN  Data.Sales SA

                                     ON SA.SalesID = SD.SalesID

                                   )

                      )
ORDER BY    SD.SalePrice DESC
```

Running this query gives the results that you can see in Figure 1-17.

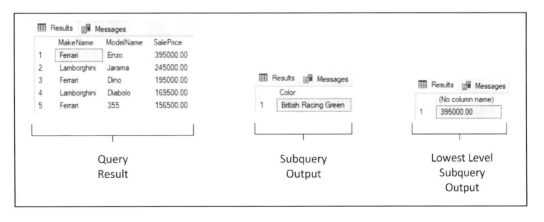

FIGURE 1-17. A QUERY CONTAINING NESTED SUBQUERIES

How It Works

Answering some questions can require more complex queries. This is where SQL Server's ability to "nest" subqueries inside subqueries can help you find a solution to even quite tricky problems. This query is an example of this kind of approach because it contains a subquery inside another subquery. As is often the case with subqueries, it is easiest to start on the inside with the deepest nested subquery and then work outward to explain the SQL.

The innermost query:	Joins the Sales and SalesDetails tables and returns the highest sale price for a vehicle sold.
The middle subquery:	Uses the sale price from the deepest nested subquery as a filter (in its WHERE clause) to find any vehicles that have been sold at this price. It then returns the colors of this vehicle, or vehicles. Note that the WHERE clause uses IN and not = (equals) because there is potentially *more than one vehicle* at this price.
The outer query:	Lists the Make, Model, and Sale Price for all the vehicles sold in the color returned by the middle subquery.

When faced with a challenge such as "Find the Top Five Vehicles Sold for the Best-selling Color by Value," the hard part can be to analyze the question and then break the solution down into separate parts that can then be answered as separate SQL queries. In these cases, our advice is to look hard at the question before starting to write any SQL. Often the code itself is easier than the analysis—and if the initial analysis is correct, then you are likely to write simpler and better SQL.

Because the concept of using nested subqueries can seem a little daunting at first glance, take a look at Figure 1-18. Here you can see how each query uses the output from the query at a lower level to filter the data that it, in turn, passes up to the query above it. Finally, the topmost query returns the required result.

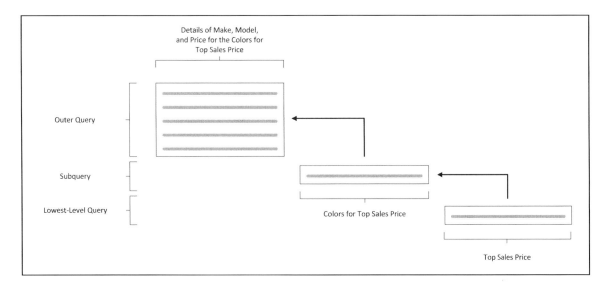

FIGURE 1-18. USING SUBQUERIES TO FILTER DATA PROGRESSIVELY

Tricks and Traps

This approach is best applied when you bear the following points in mind:

- There is a theoretical limit of 32 levels of nested subqueries in SQL Server. In practice, however, it is rare when you need to use more than 3 or 4 levels, so it is unlikely that you will hit the limit.

- As you can see in this example, you can easily end up repeating table joins in nested subqueries. This is perfectly normal considering that—as we have mentioned—*each query is completely independent of the others.*

11. Using Subqueries to Exclude Data

Some analysis requires you to examine data that lies *outside* a certain range or category. For instance, at Prestige Cars, the CEO wants a report that shows sales by make for all vehicles sold that are *not* in the sales made to the bottom four countries by value. Subqueries can often be the solution to these requirements, as the following SQL illustrates:

```
SELECT      MakeName, SUM(SA.TotalSalePrice) AS TotalSales

FROM        Data.Make AS MK INNER JOIN Data.Model AS MD

            ON MK.MakeID = MD.MakeID

INNER JOIN Data.Stock AS ST ON ST.ModelID = MD.ModelID

INNER JOIN Data.SalesDetails SD ON ST.StockCode = SD.StockID

INNER JOIN Data.Sales AS SA ON SA.SalesID = SD.SalesID

INNER JOIN Data.Customer CU ON SA.CustomerID = CU.CustomerID

INNER JOIN Data.Country CO ON CU.Country = CO.CountryISO2

WHERE       CountryName NOT IN (

                        SELECT     TOP 4 CO.CountryName

                        FROM       Data.Sales AS SA

                        INNER JOIN Data.Customer CU

                                   ON SA.CustomerID =

                                                 CU.CustomerID

                        INNER JOIN Data.Country CO

                                   ON CU.Country = CO.CountryISO2

                        GROUP BY   CountryName

                        ORDER BY   SUM(SA.TotalSalePrice) ASC

                        )

GROUP BY    MakeName
```

Running this query gives the results that you can see in Figure 1-19.

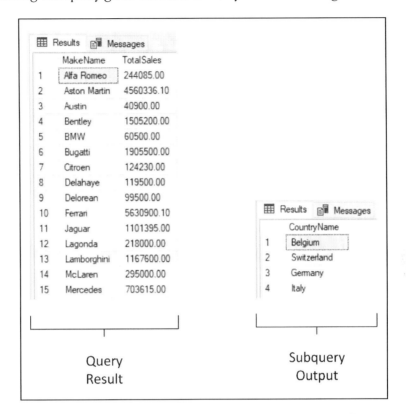

FIGURE 1-19. EXCLUDING DATA FROM A DATASET USING A SUBQUERY AND NOT IN

How It Works

This query extends the concepts that you have seen so far in this chapter. It also tries to show that what appears to be complex or convoluted SQL is, in fact, quite simple.

If you look at the preceding SQL, you can see that it breaks down into two main elements:

First: Create a subquery that uses the tables required to aggregate sales by countries. This subquery then isolates the bottom four countries by sales by sorting the resulting data from lowest to highest

Second:	The outer query joins a series of tables so that you can use the make, customer country, and sales price fields. Even if you are only displaying the make and sales price fields, you are using the customer country field in the WHERE clause to use the subquery as a filter. So, the code must make the country field accessible by joining the table that contains this data to the query.

Once you have defined these queries, it is simply a question of using the output from the subquery (the top four countries for vehicle sales) and *excluding* it from the result that the outer query returns. You do this by using the NOT IN operator in the WHERE clause of the outer query. So, what you have done is say, "find me makes and sales where the sales are *not* made to the bottom four least-performing countries."

So, a query that seems long and complex is, in fact, relatively simple once you break it down into its constituent parts. Here, as in most SQL, it is largely a question of ensuring that a query or subquery can access *all* the required fields by ensuring that all the necessary tables are joined in the FROM clause of each query.

Tricks and Traps

To finish this introduction to subqueries, you should take note of the following:

- Once again, if a subquery is returning potentially more than one element—and because we are asking for four countries, we hope that more than one element is returned—you *cannot* use equals or not equals (=, !=, or <>); you have to use the IN keyword. Then you make it negative by adding NOT to the IN. This way you are excluding from the outer query an element returned from the subquery.

12. Filtering across Queries and Subqueries

In your analytical career you will probably have to produce reports that do not look at a dataset in its entirety. The following SQL snippet returns each make sold in 2015, along with the total sales figure per make for 2015, and the percentage that this represents of the total sales for that year only.

```
SELECT      MakeName

            ,SUM(SD.SalePrice) AS SalePrice

            ,SUM(SD.SalePrice) /

                    (SELECT      SUM(SD.SalePrice)

                     FROM        Data.SalesDetails SD

                     INNER JOIN Data.Sales AS SA

                            ON SA.SalesID = SD.SalesID

                     WHERE       YEAR(SaleDate) = 2015

                    ) AS SalesRatio

FROM        Data.Make AS MK

INNER JOIN Data.Model AS MD ON MK.MakeID = MD.MakeID

INNER JOIN Data.Stock AS ST ON ST.ModelID = MD.ModelID

INNER JOIN Data.SalesDetails SD ON ST.StockCode = SD.StockID

INNER JOIN Data.Sales AS SA ON SA.SalesID = SD.SalesID

WHERE       YEAR(SaleDate) = 2015

GROUP BY    MakeName
```

Running this query gives the results that you can see in Figure 1-20—where you can also see the result of the subquery.

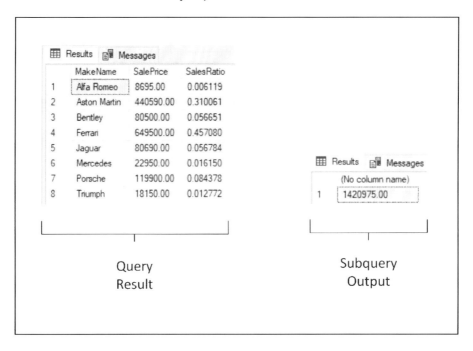

FIGURE 1-20. APPLYING FILTERS TO SUBQUERIES

How It Works

As you saw earlier in this chapter, a classic analytical requirement is comparing the whole with its constituent parts. Sometimes, however, you need to compare a subset of data with another subset. You do this by applying separate filters to both the main/outer query *and* the subquery (which some people call the inner query). So even if this query does provoke a sense of Déjà vu (it is quite similar to the query that you saw in Section 1.2), nonetheless, there is a major difference. Each query has a *separate* WHERE clause.

The subquery   Finds the figure for the total sales for 2015.

The outer query   Finds the sales per make for 2015. It then divides this by the total sales figure for the same year to display the percentage sales per make for the year.

We prefer to explain the subquery first, since SQL queries nearly always work from the inside to the outside, and not the other way around. The subquery is calculated first, and it returns the *total* sales for 2015. This query merely provides the total figure with no subaggregation at all. It joins the necessary tables (only Sales and SalesDetails are needed to find the annual total) and calculates the SUM() of the sale price field. The outer query finds the sales for each make for the same year and then divides the sales for each make by the yearly total, giving the percentage of sales by value for each make. The outer query needs to return not only the sales total (from the SalesDetails table) but also the year (from the Sales table); it also needs to return the makes of car sold. Consequently, it needs to add joins to the Stock and Make tables.

The really important thing to take away from this example is that each query is truly independent of the other. So, if you want to compare the sales by make for a given year with the total sales for the same year, you must apply an *identical* filter (that is, set the year to be 2015) in both queries.

Tricks and Traps

Obviously, you need to bear a few key points in mind when filtering multiple data sets like this:

- The subquery shown here follows all the same rules and restrictions as the subqueries that you saw earlier in this chapter.

- The fact that the queries are completely independent can work to your advantage by making querying really fluid. For instance, if you want to compare the sales per make for a given year to the total for all vehicles ever sold, all you have to do is omit the WHERE clause from the subquery. The subquery then calculates the value of all cars ever sold by the company, which you still use in the outer query to calculate the percentages of sales per make.

- Remember to test the subquery and to ensure that it gives the result that you expect before you rely blindly on the output that it sends up to the outer query.

- If you are filtering inner and outer queries, you need to pay particular attention to the filters that you apply and ensure that you are using similar filters in both queries if you are attempting to compare comparable datasets.

13.   Applying Separate Filters to the Subquery and the Main Query

"Like for Like" comparisons are a mainstay of business analysis. Like most companies that make their margin by buying and selling, Prestige Cars needs to see if sales are up or down compared to previous years. Specifically, the CEO wants to see the difference in sale price for each car sold compared to the average price for the previous year. As the following SQL snippet shows, year-on-year sales comparisons are not overly difficult:

```
SELECT      MK.MakeName

            ,MD.ModelName

            ,SD.SalePrice AS ThisYearsSalePrice

            ,SD.SalePrice

              - (SELECT  AVG(SD.SalePrice)

                  FROM        Data.Stock ST

                  INNER JOIN Data.SalesDetails SD

                              ON ST.StockCode = SD.StockID

                  INNER JOIN Data.Sales AS SA

                              ON SA.SalesID = SD.SalesID

                  WHERE       YEAR(SaleDate) = 2015)

                                          AS DeltaToLastYearAverage

FROM        Data.Make AS MK INNER JOIN Data.Model AS MD

            ON MK.MakeID = MD.MakeID

INNER JOIN Data.Stock AS ST ON ST.ModelID = MD.ModelID

INNER JOIN Data.SalesDetails SD ON ST.StockCode = SD.StockID

INNER JOIN Data.Sales AS SA ON SA.SalesID = SD.SalesID

WHERE       YEAR(SA.SaleDate) = 2016
```

Running this query gives the results that you can see in Figure 1-21.

	MakeName	ModelName	ThisYearsSalePrice	DeltaToLastYearAverage
1	Ferrari	Testarossa	165000.00	114250.892858
2	Ferrari	Testarossa	195000.00	144250.892858
3	Ferrari	355	156500.00	105750.892858
4	Ferrari	355	159500.00	108750.892858
5	Ferrari	355	205000.00	154250.892858
6	Ferrari	Mondial	102950.00	52200.892858
7	Ferrari	360	99500.00	48750.892858
8	Porsche	911	29500.00	-21249.107142
9	Porsche	911	17500.00	-33249.107142
10	Porsche	911	22150.00	-28599.107142
11	Porsche	911	33600.00	-17149.107142
12	Porsche	911	66500.00	15750.892858
13	Porsche	911	20950.00	-29799.107142
14	Porsche	911	68900.00	18150.892858
15	Porsche	911	45950.00	-4799.107142

	(No column name)
1	50749.107142

Query Result
(detailed sales for 2016)

Subquery Output
(average sales for 2015)

FIGURE 1-21. USING DIFFERENT AGGREGATION FUNCTIONS IN OUTER AND INNER QUERIES

How It Works

Being able to use completely independent queries together is particularly useful when you want to compare data over time. This time the subquery (or the inner query, if you prefer) calculates the average vehicle sale price for *2015*. The outer query, however, filters on *2016*—the following year.

When the outer query returns the list of makes sold in 2016, it calculates for each make the difference between the sale price for 2016 (returned by the outer query) and the average sale price for 2015 (returned by the inner query). This way you can compare data from two separate years.

The fact that the two queries can work together, while remaining completely independent, allows you to see how sales evolve over time from one year to the next.

Tricks and Traps

One important point to remember when applying different filters to queries and subqueries is this:

- Another indication of the fact that subqueries are completely independent of the query that contains them is given by the fact that you can use different aggregations in each query. In this example, for instance, the outer query uses the SUM() function, whereas the subquery uses the AVG() function.

Conclusion

In this chapter, you saw how you can nest queries inside queries to deliver far-reaching analytics. As you have learned, a subquery is nothing more than a standard SQL query in its own right. However, the ability to return two or more independent datasets inside a single query opens up the road to much more advanced comparative analysis of your data. You can compare data at different levels of aggregation and calculate percentages of a total with a minimum of effort. Subqueries also let you isolate data in many subtle and surprising ways and can, consequently, help you deliver deeper insights into your data.

Core Knowledge Learned in This Chapter

The concepts that you have seen in this chapter are

- A subquery is completely independent of the outer query.
- You can refer to the subquery in the SELECT, WHERE, or HAVING clauses of the outer query.
- You must enclose a subquery in parenthesis.
- A subquery must include a SELECT clause and a FROM clause.
- A subquery can include optional WHERE, GROUP BY, and HAVING clauses.
- You can include an ORDER BY clause only when a TOP clause is included.
- If a subquery returns more than one record, then you *have* to use the IN operator in the WHERE or HAVING clause of the outer query.
- You can nest subqueries in other subqueries.

Chapter 2:
Derived Tables

Some analytical challenges require you to combine different types of query to get the result that you are looking for. You may need to compare data at different levels of aggregation or carry out calculations that mix and match different ways of grouping data. For these types of problem, SQL has a clear answer—derived tables.

What Is a Derived Table?

Derived tables let you focus on producing complex datasets inside a single query. You can then use this data to solve your analytical conundrum. As you see during the course of this chapter, whenever you are faced with a challenge that seems to require different types of SQL queries at the same time, it can help to think in terms of derived tables. This is not only because they deliver a technical answer; they also help you analyze a problem by breaking it down into smaller, separate components. This, in turn, assists you in constructing the code that can produce the result that you need.

A derived table is, in many ways, a subquery. However, it is also often the "engine room" where most of the hard work is done. After the work is complete, the derived query may pass its output to the outer query that shapes and presents the final dataset.

Indeed, trying to carry out certain kinds of calculations and aggregations without a derived table is extremely difficult—both conceptually and practically. So, in this chapter, you learn how to use derived tables to

- Define calculated metrics that you can reuse several times without having to redefine the calculation each time
- Create your own ad-hoc classifications that you can use to group data
- Analyze ratios for subgroups of data
- Mix different data sources that have differing levels of data aggregation, such as monthly budgets and daily sales
- Compare values across years

- Isolate maximum, minimum, and average values and use them to analyze data that you have classified

The aim of this chapter is to enhance and extend the knowledge that you have already acquired so far in this book. We also hope to introduce you to ways of juggling data that not only extend your SQL skills but also start you on the road to thinking in datasets as a way of solving analytical challenges.

1. Using a Derived Table to Create Intermediate Calculations

There is no point in being in business unless you are making a profit—at least that is what the boss of Prestige Cars maintains. She wants a printout of the sales, costs, and gross and net profit for every car sold. Fortunately, SQL Server makes delivering this kind of output easy, as the following code shows:

```
SELECT

 MakeName

,ModelName

,SaleDate

,SalePrice

,Cost

,SalePrice - DirectCosts AS GrossProfit

,SalePrice - DirectCosts - LineItemDiscount AS NetProfit

FROM

(

  SELECT

   MK.MakeName

  ,MD.ModelName

  ,SA.SaleDate

  ,SD.SalePrice

  ,ST.Cost
```

```
,LineItemDiscount

,(ISNULL(ST.RepairsCost, 0) + ST.PartsCost

+ ST.TransportInCost) AS DirectCosts

FROM        Data.Make AS MK INNER JOIN Data.Model

            AS MD ON MK.MakeID = MD.MakeID

            INNER JOIN Data.Stock AS ST ON ST.ModelID = MD.ModelID

            INNER JOIN Data.SalesDetails SD ON ST.StockCode =
SD.StockID

            INNER JOIN Data.Sales AS SA ON SA.SalesID = SD.SalesID

) DT
```

Running this query gives the results that you can see in Figure 2-1.

	MakeName	ModelName	SaleDate	SalePrice	Cost	GrossProfit	NetProfit
1	Ferrari	Testarossa	2015-01-02 00:00:00.000	65000.00	52000.00	60575.0000	57875.0000
2	Ferrari	355	2015-01-25 00:00:00.000	220000.00	176000.00	210350.0000	150350.0000
3	Porsche	911	2015-02-03 00:00:00.000	19500.00	15600.00	18690.0000	NULL
4	Porsche	924	2015-02-16 00:00:00.000	11500.00	9200.00	10100.0000	NULL
5	Porsche	944	2015-01-02 10:33:00.000	19950.00	15960.00	17940.0000	NULL
6	Aston Martin	DB4	2015-03-14 00:00:00.000	29500.00	23600.00	28100.0000	26850.0000
7	Aston Martin	DB5	2015-03-24 00:00:00.000	49500.00	39600.00	44950.0000	42500.0000
8	Aston Martin	DB6	2015-03-30 00:00:00.000	76000.00	60800.00	71250.0000	65750.0000
9	Porsche	911	2015-04-06 00:00:00.000	19600.00	15680.00	18060.0000	NULL
10	Aston Martin	DB5	2015-04-04 00:00:00.000	36500.00	29200.00	33500.0000	31000.0000
11	Porsche	944	2015-04-30 00:00:00.000	8500.00	6800.00	7875.0000	7825.0000
12	Aston Martin	DB6	2017-03-31 00:00:00.000	45000.00	36000.00	42450.0000	NULL
13	Bentley	Flying Spur	2015-04-30 00:00:00.000	80500.00	64400.00	78500.0000	78000.0000
14	Ferrari	355	2015-05-10 00:00:00.000	169500.00	135600.00	159850.0000	NULL
15	Porsche	944	2015-05-20 00:00:00.000	8950.00	7160.00	7550.0000	7525.0000

FIGURE 2-1. A DERIVED TABLE THAT CREATES INTERMEDIATE CALCULATIONS

How It Works

It sometimes gets a little laborious to carry out financial analysis using SQL. The speed at which SQL Server can perform calculations on a large set of data is rarely a problem. However, as you have probably seen when practicing SQL, because you are required to repeat field names over and over as you create intermediate and final calculations, the process can get rather wearing.

Fortunately, there is a convenient way to minimize the repetitive use of field names. Start by creating a core query that carries out any basic analysis. You can then use the results of these calculations in the outer query without having to repeat the initial arithmetic.

In this example, the derived table (which has the alias DT in the preceding code) calculates the direct costs associated with a sale by adding up the total for the cost of repairs, parts, and transport. This inner query also ensures that any NULLs in the data are handled at the source to avoid them falsifying the results. The derived table joins all the tables that we need to output the make, model, date of sale, selling price, and vehicle cost. To see this more clearly, take a look at Figure 2-2, which displays part of the output from the derived table.

	MakeName	ModelName	SaleDate	SalePrice	Cost	LineItemDiscount	DirectCosts
1	Ferrari	Testarossa	2015-01-02 00:00:00.000	65000.00	52000.00	2700.00	4425.00
2	Ferrari	355	2015-01-25 00:00:00.000	220000.00	176000.00	60000.00	9650.00
3	Porsche	911	2015-02-03 00:00:00.000	19500.00	15600.00	NULL	810.00
4	Porsche	924	2015-02-16 00:00:00.000	11500.00	9200.00	NULL	1400.00
5	Porsche	944	2015-01-02 10:33:00.000	19950.00	15960.00	NULL	2010.00
6	Aston Martin	DB4	2015-03-14 00:00:00.000	29500.00	23600.00	1250.00	1400.00
7	Aston Martin	DB5	2015-03-24 00:00:00.000	49500.00	39600.00	2450.00	4550.00
8	Aston Martin	DB6	2015-03-30 00:00:00.000	76000.00	60800.00	5500.00	4750.00
9	Porsche	911	2015-04-06 00:00:00.000	19600.00	15680.00	NULL	1540.00
10	Aston Martin	DB5	2015-04-04 00:00:00.000	36500.00	29200.00	2500.00	3000.00

Figure 2-2. The output from a derived table

As you can see, the columns that are returned are not the same in the derived table as they are in the outer query. Nonetheless, the columns in the derived table are the basis for any data that is output by the outer query.

In cases like this, a derived table is a *query in a query*. More precisely, it is a completely independent piece of SQL that feeds its output into an outer query that wraps around the derived table. In this example, you can see that the outer query has a FROM clause that does not directly use a table or a set of joined tables. Instead, the code uses a self-sufficient query (the derived table or inner query) to isolate a dataset. This dataset is then used as the data source for the outer query.

The outer query is a straightforward list of the fields that are in the SELECT clause of the derived table. These fields are then extended with a couple of simple calculations to deliver both the gross profit and the net profit.

You could achieve the final calculation of gross and net profit without using a derived table. However, in this case, the query that returns the gross and net profit looks like this:

```
,SD.SalePrice  -  (ISNULL(ST.RepairsCost, 0)

            + ST.PartsCost + ST.TransportInCost) AS GrossProfit

,SD.SalePrice  -  (ISNULL(ST.RepairsCost, 0) + ST.PartsCost

            + ST.TransportInCost + LineItemDiscount) AS NetProfit
```

Although this code is not difficult to write, it is more laborious and certainly more repetitive; it is also possibly a greater source of potential errors precisely because of its repetitive nature. Defining a derived table not only removes the need to repeat fields (as well as their NULL handling code), it also makes any additional calculations you have to apply to these fields easier.

This technique is similar to the way you might use a spreadsheet to perform financial arithmetic. In a spreadsheet, you carry out basic arithmetic in multiple cells to get an intermediate result that you then use for other calculations. The principle is similar when you use a derived table in SQL:

First:	You carry out any essential calculations in a derived table and give the result an alias.
Then:	You use the derived table as the basis for any further calculations in the outer query.

The derived table we use in this example shows the two basic techniques used to define a derived table:

Enclosed in parentheses	A derived table *must* be enclosed in parentheses. If you forget the parentheses, you get an error message. Think of them as isolating and enclosing the derived table and making it into a separate self-contained table.

Must have an alias

A derived table *must* have an alias. In this example, the derived table is given the alias DT. You can use this alias just as you would use the alias for any "normal" table in a SQL query.

Visualizing a concept can often make it easier to understand, so take a look at Figure 2-3 to see how a derived table works from a high level.

FIGURE 2-3. THE CONCEPT OF A DERIVED TABLE

Tricks and Traps

Derived tables are a fundamental concept in SQL, so there are, perhaps inevitably, several key points to remember when you begin to use them in your analysis:

- When you use a derived table in a FROM clause, you *must include all the fields that you wish to return from the outer query in the SELECT clause of the inner derived table*. This is because the derived table is the source of all the data that is accessible to the outer query. Consequently, you must ensure that every field that you want to output from the overall code is part of the inner SELECT clause. If you forget to include a field in the derived table and then try to select it in the main query, SQL Server returns an error message. Adding the field to the derived table normally solves this problem.

- Another advantage of beginning with a derived table when calculating metrics is that you only have to handle potential NULLs once—in the derived table at the heart of the query.

- Another factor that argues in favor of using a derived table to simplify calculations is that if a core calculation changes, you only make the change *once* in the derived table (just like in a spreadsheet). Any modifications ripple up through the rest of the query. Without a derived table, you have to make the change every time the calculation is repeated in the query.

- It is important to ensure that every field in a derived table has a name. SQL Server does *not* add a name (such as "Column 1") if you forget to add an alias. Indeed, the query does *not work* if any calculated fields (such as SalePrice and CustomerClassification in this example) are *not* given aliases.

- The AS keyword that introduces the derived table alias is not strictly necessary, but it is good practice to use it, so we have kept it, even if the query would work without it.

2. Grouping and Ordering Data Using a Custom Classification

Suppose the CEO decides that she wants you to classify all your customers by spend. You realize that what she really wants is five categories of customer (tiny, small, medium, large, and mega-rich) according to a series of thresholds of total sales per customer. Then she wants the total spend for customers in each of these spending brackets.

This sounds complicated. Yet we can do it with only a few lines of SQL and the clever use of a derived table:

```
SELECT     DT.CustomerClassification

           ,COUNT(DT.CustomerSpend) AS CustomerSpend

FROM

           (

           SELECT     SUM(SD.SalePrice) AS CustomerSpend

           ,SA.CustomerID

           ,CASE

           WHEN SUM(SD.SalePrice) <= 100000 THEN 'Tiny'

           WHEN SUM(SD.SalePrice) BETWEEN 100001 AND 200000

                THEN 'Small'

           WHEN SUM(SD.SalePrice) BETWEEN 200001 AND 300000

                THEN 'Medium'

           WHEN SUM(SD.SalePrice) BETWEEN 300001 AND 400000

                THEN 'Large'

           WHEN SUM(SD.SalePrice) > 400000 THEN 'Mega Rich'

           END AS CustomerClassification

           FROM       Data.SalesDetails SD

                      INNER JOIN Data.Sales AS SA

                      ON SA.SalesID = SD.SalesID
```

```
        GROUP BY    SA.CustomerID

    ) AS DT

GROUP BY   DT.CustomerClassification

ORDER BY   CustomerSpend DESC
```

Running this query gives the results that you can see in Figure 2-4.

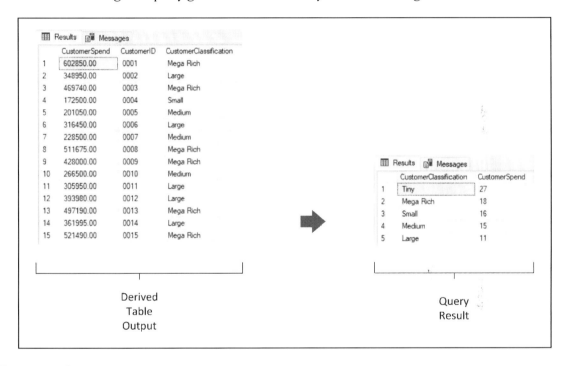

FIGURE 2-4. AN AGGREGATED DERIVED TABLE FEEDING INTO A SEPARATE OUTER AGGREGATION

How It Works

It is said that a problem shared is a problem halved. In the case of SQL queries, a problem broken down into smaller parts is often a problem that has become much easier to solve. Using derived tables is a fundamental technique for breaking down seemingly complex challenges into smaller and more comprehensible solutions. This piece of SQL is an example of how a derived table can help you break down analytical tasks into their component parts.

Consequently (as is the case with much SQL), the logic of this code begins at the center and works its way outward. The overall query does two things:

The inner query	Takes the data from the Sales and SalesDetails tables and finds the total value of sales per customer. This query then uses a CASE statement to test the total value of sales for each customer and places each one in one of five custom categories—from the tiny customers to the mega-rich ones. In this kind of statistical query, we do not need to see the customer name because we are not interested in detail-level analysis. We can group on the CustomerID field from the SalesDetails table, and we do not need to refer to the Customer table for any customer data.
The outer query	Aggregates the results of the derived table by counting the number of customers in each category and grouping on the category itself (the field that has been given the alias CustomerClassification). Finally, it sorts the categories in descending order of the number of customers per classification.

As you can see, the main element in this piece of code is the derived table (the inner query), where the core aggregation is carried out. Indeed, you can run the derived table separately if you wish. You can do this by selecting *only* the SQL inside the parentheses, from SELECT SUM(SA.SalePrice) to GROUP BY SA.CustomerID. This way, you can check that the inner query gives you the result that you expect—something like the output from the derived table shown earlier in Figure 2-4.

Now that you can see the output from the derived table, hopefully you have a clearer understanding of the way that the overall query works. The derived table has let you create a classification of your entire customer base where each customer is categorized. The main query then groups and sorts this data to produce the final result set that shows the spend for customers in each classification "bucket."

3.   Joining Derived Tables to Other Tables

When you are buying and selling, it can help to see how an article compares to others in its category. Specifically, say you have decided that you want to look at the purchase and selling price of each vehicle that has been sold and see how this data maps to the average cost and sale price for every similar model. This is all in a day's work for SQL.

```
SELECT    ST.DateBought, MK.MakeName, MD.ModelName, ST.Color

          ,ST.Cost, SD.SalePrice, DT.AveragePurchasePrice

          ,DT.AverageSalePrice

FROM

     (

       SELECT      MakeName

                   ,ModelName

                   ,AVG(Cost) AS AveragePurchasePrice

                   ,AVG(SalePrice) AS AverageSalePrice

       FROM        Data.Make AS MK1

                   INNER JOIN Data.Model AS MD1 ON MK1.MakeID = MD1.MakeID

                   INNER JOIN Data.Stock AS ST1 ON ST1.ModelID =

                                                              MD1.ModelID

                   INNER JOIN Data.SalesDetails SD1

                   ON ST1.StockCode = SD1.StockID

       GROUP BY    MakeName, ModelName

     ) AS DT

     INNER JOIN Data.Make AS MK

     INNER JOIN Data.Model AS MD ON MK.MakeID = MD.MakeID

     INNER JOIN Data.Stock AS ST ON ST.ModelID = MD.ModelID

     INNER JOIN Data.SalesDetails SD ON ST.StockCode = SD.StockID

     ON MK.MakeName = DT.MakeName
```

```
        AND MD.ModelName = DT.ModelName

ORDER BY    DateBought, MakeName, ModelName
```

Running this query gives the results that you can see in Figure 2-5.

	DateBought	MakeName	ModelName	Color	Cost	SalePrice	AveragePurchasePrice	AverageSalePrice
1	2015-01-01	Ferrari	Testarossa	Red	52000.00	65000.00	139200.00	174000.000000
2	2015-01-10	Ferrari	355	Blue	176000.00	220000.00	136165.7142	170207.142857
3	2015-01-29	Porsche	911	British Racing Green	15600.00	19500.00	29357.1428	36696.428571
4	2015-02-14	Porsche	924	British Racing Green	9200.00	11500.00	12448.00	15560.000000
5	2015-02-27	Porsche	944	Red	15960.00	19950.00	9818.4615	12273.076923
6	2015-03-05	Aston Martin	DB4	Night Blue	23600.00	29500.00	32194.2857	40242.857142
7	2015-03-15	Aston Martin	DB5	Black	39600.00	49500.00	40045.3333	50056.666666
8	2015-03-26	Aston Martin	DB6	Canary Yellow	60800.00	76000.00	58234.00	72792.500000
9	2015-04-04	Porsche	911	Blue	15680.00	19600.00	29357.1428	36696.428571
10	2015-04-12	Aston Martin	DB5	Blue	29200.00	36500.00	40045.3333	50056.666666
11	2015-04-15	Porsche	944	Blue	6800.00	8500.00	9818.4615	12273.076923
12	2015-04-30	Aston Martin	DB6	Night Blue	36000.00	45000.00	58234.00	72792.500000
13	2015-05-04	Bentley	Flying Spur	British Racing Green	64400.00	80500.00	60350.2222	75437.777777
14	2015-05-15	Ferrari	355	Black	135600.00	169500.00	136165.7142	170207.142857
15	2015-05-26	Porsche	944	Green	7160.00	8950.00	9818.4615	12273.076923

FIGURE 2-5. A DERIVED TABLE THAT IS PART OF A COMPLEX JOIN CLAUSE

How It Works

SQL Server considers derived tables to be just like any "ordinary" tables that exist in a database. This means that you can collate or aggregate data from one or more tables to obtain a derived table and then join the result to another table, or tables, just as you would for any table.

This is particularly useful when you need to aggregate data and include the aggregated result in a query that contains *nonaggregated* data. This example shows how a single query can show—for every sale—the average selling price for that model of car. This opens up a whole spectrum of analytical possibilities that allow you to put each sale into perspective and see how it compares to other, similar sales.

This example differs from those that you have seen so far in this chapter in that it does not have an inner and outer query structure. Instead, it contains a series of table joins, which are

| *Standard joins* | Using regular database tables to return the cost and sale price for every model of car sold. |
| *A derived table join* | Where a derived table is joined to the existing tables in the query. |

The derived table is interesting because it operates on a different level of data granularity than the other tables. More precisely, the derived table is an aggregation that calculates the average cost and selling price of each model of car. The derived table is then joined to the other tables in the query perfectly normally.

Because the SQL that underlies this example is a little complex at first sight, take a look at Figure 2-6, which is a visual representation of the joins—including the join to the derived table.

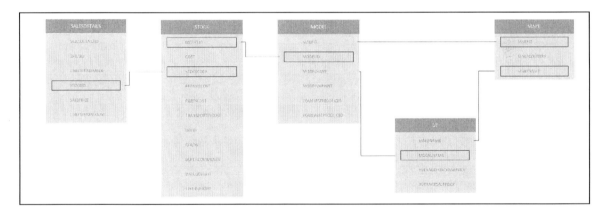

FIGURE 2-6. VISUALIZING A COMPLEX JOIN USING A DERIVED TABLE

To help you understand how this works, take a look at Figure 2-7. In it, you can see the output from the derived table (aliased as DT in the SQL code that you used to obtain this output).

FIGURE 2-7. THE OUTPUT FROM AN AGGREGATED DERIVED TABLE

What is really interesting here is that because the derived table isolates data by *two* fields (make *and* model), it needs to join to the other tables using *both* these fields. Consequently, the derived table *has* to contain both these fields in its SELECT clause; otherwise you cannot join the derived table to the outer query.

The trick, in these cases, is to establish the join as you normally would. However, when you link a table to two tables at the same time, you start with an ON clause, as you would normally, and then you continue adding further field joins using the AND keyword.

The query then outputs fields from any or all of the tables that make up the FROM clause. It is in all other respects a perfectly standard query. However, using the derived table to calculate the average cost and average sale price allows you to show these aggregated figures in the query output and make some interesting comparisons.

Tricks and Traps

When joining derived tables, you need to remember the following:

- We chose to use independent table aliases in the derived query (ST1 for the Stock table, for instance) even if it is possible to use the same aliases in the derived table subquery as those we used in the main query's FROM clause. This is because it is generally easier to understand and debug queries when all the component elements are identifiable separately and uniquely.

4. Joining Multiple Derived Tables

Continuing with the theme of comparisons, let's suppose that you want to see which colors sell the most. Indeed, you want not only to produce this kind of analysis but also find the percentage of cars purchased by value for each color of vehicle. The following SQL does this for you:

```
SELECT

TOT.PurchaseYear

,AGG.Color

,(AGG.CostPerYear / TOT.TotalPurchasePrice) * 100 AS
PercentPerColorPerYear

FROM

    (

    SELECT          STX.Color

                    ,SUM(STX.Cost) AS CostPerYear

                    ,YEAR(STX.DateBought) AS YearBought

    FROM            Data.Make AS MKX

    INNER JOIN   Data.Model AS MDX ON MKX.MakeID = MDX.MakeID

    INNER JOIN   Data.Stock AS STX ON STX.ModelID = MDX.ModelID

    GROUP BY     STX.Color

                    ,YEAR(STX.DateBought)

    ) AGG

INNER JOIN

    (

    SELECT          YEAR(DateBought) AS PurchaseYear, SUM(Cost)

                    AS TotalPurchasePrice

    FROM            Data.Stock

    GROUP BY     YEAR(DateBought)
```

```
)  TOT

ON TOT.PurchaseYear = AGG.YearBought

ORDER BY PurchaseYear, PercentPerColorPerYear DESC
```

Running this query gives the results that you can see in Figure 2-8.

	Purchase Year	Color	Percent PerColorPerYear
1	2015	Black	24.38
2	2015	Red	16.76
3	2015	British Racing Green	12.68
4	2015	Blue	11.56
5	2015	Night Blue	10.56
6	2015	Silver	10.28
7	2015	Green	8.53
8	2015	Canary Yellow	5.20
9	2016	Black	29.10
10	2016	Red	12.04
11	2016	Blue	11.32
12	2016	British Racing Green	9.25
13	2016	Green	9.05
14	2016	Silver	7.66
15	2016	Dark Purple	6.58

FIGURE 2-8. USING TWO SEPARATE DERIVED TABLES IN A QUERY

How It Works

This query requires you to produce two completely different aggregations and then use them together to deliver the final result.

The first aggregation	Is the total cost of vehicles purchased for each year for each color
The second aggregation	Is the total cost of purchases per year

Using derived tables allows you to handle each aggregation as a separate derived table. Before going any further, it is probably worth taking a look at the output from each of the derived tables so that you can see what each one is doing. Figure 2-9 illustrates how multiple derived tables relate to an outer query. Once again, we hope that this simple illustration makes the concept clearer.

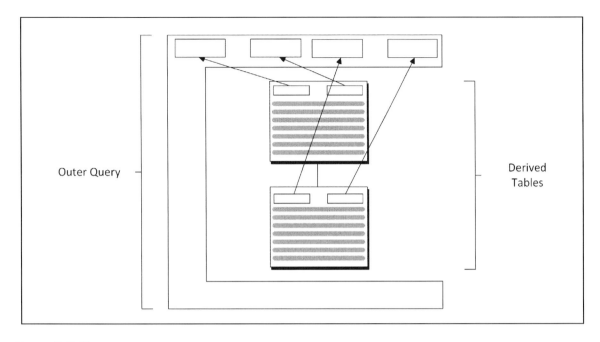

FIGURE 2-9. DERIVED TABLES AND THE OUTER QUERY

The first derived table (aliased as AGG in this example) shows the year, color, and cost per year for each color of vehicle bought. If you select just the SQL for the first of the two derived tables, you see output similar to that in Figure 2-10.

	Color	CostPerYear	YearBought
1	Black	494944.00	2015
2	Blue	234720.00	2015
3	British Racing Green	257400.00	2015
4	Canary Yellow	105600.00	2015
5	Green	173280.00	2015
6	Night Blue	214392.00	2015
7	Red	340196.00	2015
8	Silver	208800.00	2015
9	Black	1275128.00	2016
10	Blue	496240.00	2016

FIGURE 2-10. THE OUTPUT FROM AN AGGREGATED DERIVED TABLE

Data Visibility

As we have already noted—but it bears repeating—one important aspect of derived tables is that they only allow access to the data that you specify. So, if you want the outer query to be able to access a field from the derived table, you *must* include the field name in the SELECT clause of the derived table.

"Self-contained" also means "locked away" as far as the data in a derived table is concerned. It does not matter if a table is part of the derived table definition; none of its fields are accessible to the rest of the code if they are not made visible in the SELECT clause.

This derived table needs three database tables to be joined to return the required data: Make, Model, and Stock. Then all it does is aggregate the result by year and color and return the total vehicle cost for all available combinations of these two fields.

Running the second of the derived table queries (aliased as TOT in the SQL code for this section) shows you the data that you can see in Figure 2-11.

	Purchase Year	Total Purchase Price
1	NULL	NULL
2	2015	2029332.00
3	2016	4380988.00
4	2017	7083824.00
5	2018	6265020.00

FIGURE 2-11. THE OUTPUT FROM A HIGH-LEVEL AGGREGATED DERIVED TABLE

This high-level aggregated derived table only needs the Stock table to produce the annual cost of cars that have been purchased. Indeed, it contains NULL values because some vehicles have not yet been purchased, and so they do not have a purchase year.

These two derived tables both output the Year field. Consequently, the overall query can use this field to join the two derived tables. Once the derived tables are constructed and joined, you can treat this query just like any other query and use the fields it contains to analyze your data.

In this specific example, the year and color fields are output and the cost per color for each year is divided by the total cost for the same timeframe to return the percentage cost of each color for each year.

Finishing the query with an ORDER BY clause allows you to list the result first by year and second in descending order of sales per color. This makes it easy to see which color tops the sales charts over several years.

Once again, we use derived tables to break down the problem into component parts. The challenge is to produce two sets of data that aggregate at different "levels." One requires the year and the color, the other only the year. We build the query to handle these different requirements using the flexibility that derived tables bring to analysis with SQL.

What is interesting here is that the query uses nothing but derived tables to carry out its analysis. Once again, each derived table is a completely separate entity that works independently of the other parts of the overall query.

Tricks and Traps

One point needs to be made about joining derived tables:

- Because derived tables are *always* independent entities in a query, you can reuse tables in separate derived tables. Here, for instance, the Stock table is used twice—once in each derived table. Each derived table makes use of the Stock table separately and in different ways.

5. Using Multiple Derived Tables for Complex Aggregations

Good analysis is about seeing the wood for the trees. This is where SQL really shines. The following code lets you create a report for the CEO that lists sales per customer by volume and value. Not only that, but the output is broken down by country and sorted to make it clear who the best customers are in each country. All of this is possible in a single query that produces an analysis of sales ratios per customer per country—as you can see in the following code:

```
SELECT

 DT2.CountryName

,CustomerName
```

```
,NumberOfCustomerSales

,TotalCustomerSales

,CAST(NumberOfCustomerSales AS NUMERIC)

  / CAST(NumberOfCountrySales AS NUMERIC) AS PercentageOfCountryCarsSold

,TotalCustomerSales / TotalCountrySales

  AS PercentageOfCountryCarsSoldByValue

FROM

(

    SELECT      CO.CountryName

                ,COUNT(*) AS NumberOfCountrySales

                ,SUM(SD.SalePrice) AS TotalCountrySales

    FROM        Data.Stock AS ST

    INNER JOIN Data.SalesDetails SD ON ST.StockCode = SD.StockID

    INNER JOIN Data.Sales AS SA ON SA.SalesID = SD.SalesID

    INNER JOIN Data.Customer CU ON SA.CustomerID = CU.CustomerID

    INNER JOIN Data.Country CO ON CU.Country = CO.CountryISO2

    GROUP BY    CO.CountryName

) AS DT1


INNER JOIN

(

    SELECT       CO.CountryName

                ,CU.CustomerName

                ,COUNT(*) AS NumberOfCustomerSales

                ,SUM(SD.SalePrice) AS TotalCustomerSales

    FROM        Data.Stock AS ST
```

```
    INNER JOIN Data.SalesDetails SD ON ST.StockCode = SD.StockID


    INNER JOIN Data.Sales AS SA ON SA.SalesID = SD.SalesID

    INNER JOIN Data.Customer CU ON SA.CustomerID = CU.CustomerID

    INNER JOIN Data.Country CO ON CU.Country = CO.CountryISO2

    GROUP BY    CO.CountryName, CU.CustomerName

) AS DT2

ON DT1.CountryName = DT2.CountryName

ORDER BY CountryName, NumberOfCustomerSales DESC
```

Running this query gives the results that you can see in Figure 2-12.

	CountryName	CustomerName	NumberOfCustomerSales	TotalCustomerSales	PercentageOfCountryCarsSold	PercentageOfCountryCarsSoldByValue
1	Belgium	Stefan Van Helsing	6	80900.00	0.6000000000000000000	0.259419
2	Belgium	Diplomatic Cars	3	224000.00	0.3000000000000000000	0.718294
3	Belgium	Flash Voitures	1	6950.00	0.1000000000000000000	0.022286
4	France	Vive La Vitesse	13	1269600.00	0.1884057971014492753	0.215815
5	France	Laurent Saint Yves	11	1343950.00	0.1594202898550724637	0.228453
6	France	SuperSport S.A.R.L.	9	509630.00	0.1304347826086956521	0.086630
7	France	M. Pierre Dubois	8	511675.00	0.1159420289855072463	0.086977
8	France	Capots Reluisants S.A.	6	583115.00	0.0869565217391304347	0.099121
9	France	La Bagnole de Luxe	6	497190.00	0.0869565217391304347	0.084515
10	France	Casseroles Chromes	4	201050.00	0.0579710144927536231	0.034175
11	France	Mme Anne Duport	3	162650.00	0.0434782608695652173	0.027648
12	France	Khader El Ghannam	2	50500.00	0.0289855072463768115	0.008584
13	France	Wladimir Lacroix	2	55100.00	0.0289855072463768115	0.009366
14	France	Le Luxe en Motion	1	255950.00	0.0144927536231884057	0.043508
15	France	Jean-Yves Truffaut	1	1950.00	0.0144927536231884057	0.000331

FIGURE 2-12. A COMPLEX USE OF DERIVED TABLES TO APPLY DIFFERENT LEVELS OF AGGREGATED CALCULATION

How It Works

Given the size of this query, it is probably easier to understand what it does if you begin by looking at the output from the two derived tables that are the core of the SQL.

The first derived table (DT1) shows the number of sales per country and the total value of sales, as you can see in Figure 2-13.

FIGURE 2-13. AN AGGREGATE DERIVED TABLE TO PRODUCE HIGH-LEVEL TOTALS

The second derived table (DT2) goes into greater detail and shows the value and number of sales per customer for each country, as you can see (partially, at least) in Figure 2-14.

FIGURE 2-14. AN AGGREGATE DERIVED TABLE THAT PRODUCES DETAIL-LEVEL TOTALS

As a whole, the query builds on the data that is returned from the two derived tables. It joins the derived tables on the country field so that it can then list countries, clients, the number of sales made per client, and the value of those sales. So far, then, it is just an extension of the derived table DT2. However, once the aggregate data at country level is added to the query, it allows you to see the percentage of both the value of sales and the number of sales that each customer represents. This is done simply by dividing the totals for number of sales and sale value) by country in the derived table DT1 by the number of sales and sale value for each customer in the derived table DT2.

Because the SQL that creates and uses an aggregated derived table can seem a little dense at first sight, taking a look at a more graphic representation, like the one shown in Figure 2-15, might help you understand how it works.

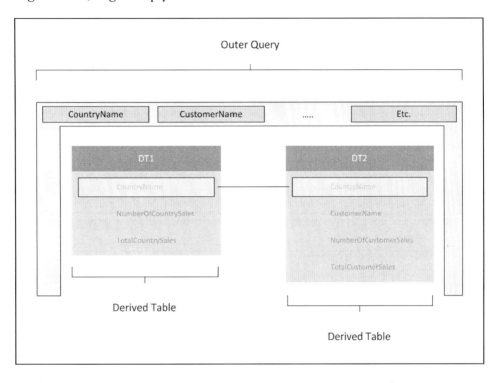

FIGURE 2-15. JOINING ON DERIVED TABLES

Tricks and Traps

When creating complex analyses using multiple derived tables, you need to remain aware of the following key points:

- In this example, we left the figures as "raw" numbers without any formatting. You can use the FORMAT() function to display the percentages in a more readable way if you prefer.

- When calculating the percentage of cars sold per country, we had to force the count function to treat its output as NUMERIC—and, consequently, to include the decimals (we explain this in greater detail in Chapter 8). This is because the COUNT() function always returns a whole number, and SQL takes this to be an INTEGER data type. This is not a problem until you divide an integer by an integer. When this happens, the result is considered to be an integer as well. This means that the percentage is then displayed as an integer, too—a zero. This is not only counterintuitive, it is highly disconcerting. However, if you use the CAST() function to force SQL Server to consider the result of the COUNT() a decimal number, then it can display the percentage as a decimal number as well.

6. Using Derived Tables to Join Unconnected Tables

A well-managed business almost certainly defines budgets and then tracks them over time. Fortunately, SQL can be very efficient at monitoring budgets and comparing and forecasts. So, when the financial director comes to your desk requesting a report that compares sales to the budget for each country by year and month, you know there is nothing to worry about. The following SQL is an example of this:

```
SELECT      CO.CountryName

            ,SUM(SD.SalePrice) AS Sales

            ,SUM(CSQ.BudgetValue) AS BudgetValue

            ,YEAR(SaleDate) AS YearOfSale

            ,MONTH(SaleDate) AS MonthOfSale

            ,SUM(CSQ.BudgetValue)

            - SUM(SD.SalePrice) AS DifferenceBudgetToSales
 FROM       Data.SalesDetails SD
INNER JOIN Data.Sales AS SA ON SA.SalesID = SD.SalesID

INNER JOIN Data.Customer CU ON SA.CustomerID = CU.CustomerID

INNER JOIN Data.Country CO ON CU.Country = CO.CountryISO2

INNER JOIN              (

                SELECT      BudgetValue, BudgetDetail, Year,

                            Month

                FROM        Reference.Budget

                WHERE       BudgetElement = 'Country'

            ) CSQ

        ON CSQ.BudgetDetail = CO.CountryName
```

```
        AND CSQ.Year = YEAR(SaleDate)

        AND CSQ.Month = MONTH(SaleDate)

GROUP BY CO.CountryName, YEAR(SaleDate), MONTH(SaleDate)

ORDER BY CO.CountryName, YEAR(SaleDate), MONTH(SaleDate)
```

Running this query gives the results that you can see in Figure 2-16.

	CountryName	Sales	BudgetValue	YearOfSale	MonthOfSale	DifferenceBudgetToSales
1	Belgium	125000.00	100000.00	2016	8	-25000.00
2	Belgium	12500.00	15500.00	2017	2	3000.00
3	Belgium	86500.00	100000.00	2017	3	13500.00
4	Belgium	45950.00	137850.00	2017	7	91900.00
5	Belgium	34000.00	68000.00	2017	11	34000.00
6	Belgium	950.00	950.00	2018	1	0.00
7	Belgium	6950.00	6950.00	2018	6	0.00
8	France	19600.00	19600.00	2015	4	0.00
9	France	8950.00	8950.00	2015	5	0.00
10	France	22950.00	22950.00	2015	6	0.00
11	France	75500.00	151000.00	2015	7	75500.00
12	France	2550.00	2550.00	2016	1	0.00
13	France	39500.00	39500.00	2016	2	0.00
14	France	49580.00	49580.00	2016	5	0.00
15	France	180150.00	720600.00	2016	6	540450.00

FIGURE 2-16. A DERIVED TABLE USED TO JOIN OTHERWISE UNCONNECTED TABLES

How It Works

Even a well-thought-out database model can have some tables that simply do not link in any conventional way to the core data tables that you are using. Budget data is frequently an example of this. Yet you can use the budget data stored in your database and compare it to the other data that you use to compare sales and budget data and highlight any differences. This only works, however, if you shape the data in a way that allows it to be joined to other tables.

This query joins the tables that contain the essential data for make, model, stock sales details, and sales that you have used so far in this book. Then it also joins data from a new table—the Budget table—to the query so that you can also display data from this source.

The Budget table cannot be joined directly to the other tables that contain sales and stock data, however. This is because it contains budget data for many different elements (countries, makes of vehicle, etc.). As a result, you have to query this table and select only the data that you need. In this example, you need to filter the table on the Budget element to limit it to budgets for country sales. If you highlight and run the SELECT query for the derived table, then you will see what the data is like (it is shown in Figure 2-17).

	Budget Value	Budget Detail	Year	Month
1	100000.00	Belgium	2016	8
2	15500.00	Belgium	2017	2
3	100000.00	Belgium	2017	3
4	45950.00	Belgium	2017	7
5	34000.00	Belgium	2017	11
6	950.00	Belgium	2018	1
7	6950.00	Belgium	2018	6
8	19950.00	France	2015	2
9	19600.00	France	2015	4
10	8950.00	France	2015	5
11	22950.00	France	2015	6
12	75500.00	France	2015	7
13	2550.00	France	2016	1
14	39500.00	France	2016	2
15	49580.00	France	2016	5

FIGURE 2-17. A DERIVED TABLE THAT FILTERS SOURCE DATA

As you can see from Figure 2-17 the budget data is for country, year, and month. To join the derived table to the other tables in the query, you must perform a complex join using three fields—country, year, and month of sale. This is why the join for the derived table uses the YEAR() and MONTH() functions to isolate these elements from the SaleDate field in the SalesDetails table.

Finally, the elements that are output from the outer query have to be grouped and aggregated. This is because the data from the tables used in the outer query is at a much more detailed level than the budget data used in the subquery. Mixing data at different levels of detail (or granularity, as it is also called) almost never produces coherent results. It is up to you to ensure that the data from all your tables is at the same level of detail.

Tricks and Traps

We have a couple of points to stress here:

- It is interesting that in the outer query, you have to aggregate the budget value that is returned from the derived query (that is, the figure for each month's projected sales per country), even if the value is already at an aggregate level. This is because the outer query is an aggregate query, and so every value that is used must be used as part of an aggregate function such as SUM(), even if this does not alter the value since there is only one value per country per month.

- Unless you extract the year and month elements from the SalesDate field, the join to the derived tables cannot work correctly because it attempts to match a year (or a month) to a full date. This means that no data matches between the two tables and, consequently, no records are returned by the query.

7. Compare Year-on-Year Data Using a Derived Table

As part of a relentless focus on profitability, the CEO wants to look at all vehicle sales in 2016 and see how each sale compares to the best price achieved in the previous year for the same model of car. All this can be done with one piece of SQL:

```
SELECT       MK.MakeName

         ,MD.ModelName

         ,SD.SalePrice

         ,CSQ.MaxSalePrice - SD.SalePrice AS
PriceDifferenceToMaxPrevYear

FROM       Data.Make AS MK

INNER JOIN Data.Model AS MD ON MK.MakeID = MD.MakeID

INNER JOIN Data.Stock AS ST ON ST.ModelID = MD.ModelID

INNER JOIN Data.SalesDetails SD ON ST.StockCode = SD.StockID

INNER JOIN Data.Sales AS SA ON SA.SalesID = SD.SalesID

INNER JOIN  (

             SELECT      MAX(SDX.SalePrice) AS MaxSalePrice
```

```
                            ,YEAR(SAX.SaleDate) AS SaleYear

                            ,MKX.MakeName
            FROM        Data.Make AS MKX
            INNER JOIN Data.Model AS MDX
                        ON MKX.MakeID = MDX.MakeID
            INNER JOIN Data.Stock AS STX
                        ON STX.ModelID = MDX.ModelID
            INNER JOIN Data.SalesDetails SDX
                        ON STX.StockCode = SDX.StockID
            INNER JOIN Data.Sales AS SAX

                        ON SAX.SalesID = SDX.SalesID
            WHERE       YEAR(SAX.SaleDate) = 2015
            GROUP BY    YEAR(SAX.SaleDate)
                        ,MKX.MakeName
        ) CSQ
    ON CSQ.MakeName = MK.MakeName
WHERE       YEAR(SA.SaleDate) = 2016
```

Running this query gives the results that you can see in Figure 2-18.

	MakeName	ModelName	SalePrice	PriceDifferenceToMaxPrevYear
1	Ferrari	Testarossa	165000.00	55000.00
2	Ferrari	Testarossa	195000.00	25000.00
3	Ferrari	355	156500.00	63500.00
4	Ferrari	355	159500.00	60500.00
5	Ferrari	355	205000.00	15000.00
6	Ferrari	Mondial	102950.00	117050.00
7	Ferrari	360	99500.00	120500.00
8	Porsche	911	29500.00	-6550.00
9	Porsche	911	17500.00	5450.00
10	Porsche	911	22150.00	800.00
11	Porsche	911	33600.00	-10650.00
12	Porsche	911	66500.00	-43550.00
13	Porsche	911	20950.00	2000.00
14	Porsche	911	68900.00	-45950.00
15	Porsche	911	45950.00	-23000.00

FIGURE 2-18. APPLYING DIFFERENT FILTERS TO A QUERY AND A DERIVED TABLE

How It Works

In this chapter, you have seen that a derived table is a completely independent dataset relative to the rest of the query. You can use this to your advantage when comparing virtually identical datasets.

In this code the main query is the part of the query that is not a derived table. It lists the makes and models of car sold in 2016 along with their sale price.

The derived table does something fairly similar. It, too, finds makes, models, and sale price, only it finds the maximum sale price for each model for a *different year* to the outer query—the previous year (2015), in fact. The output from this inner query (if you run it separately) is shown in Figure 2-19.

FIGURE 2-19. OUTPUT FROM A DERIVED TABLE QUERY

As you can see, the derived table shows the maximum sale price per model for one year, yet a close examination of the code shows that the outer query looks at the data for another year. The trick is to join the derived table to the rest of the query using the make as the join element.

You can then output not only the details for sales in 2016, but also the maximum value of each make sold in the previous year. In this example, the current sale price is subtracted from the maximum sale price for the previous year. You can then analyze the difference to compare sales growth from year to year.

Tricks and Traps

We have a single comment for you to take away when using derived tables for data comparison:

- This type of query is extremely extensible and can become a basis for many varied types of comparative analysis. For instance, you cannot ever use a year in the WHERE clause of the derived table and compare the current sale price to the maximum sale price. The fact that the derived table and the outer query are completely independent makes derived queries ideal for comparing certain types of data over time.

8. Synchronizing Filters between a Derived Table and the Main Query

Clever buying strategies can make or break a business. Because of this, the finance director wants to ensure that Prestige Cars is not spending too much when buying stock. The following piece of SQL compares the purchase price of every car bought in 2016 with the average price of cars of the same color in 2015.

```
SELECT      ST.Color, ST.DateBought, ST.Cost, CSQ.MinPurchaseCost

FROM        Data.Stock ST

INNER JOIN

            (

            SELECT      Color, MIN(Cost) AS MinPurchaseCost

                        ,YEAR(DateBought) AS PurchaseYear

            FROM        Data.Stock

            WHERE       YEAR(DateBought) = 2016

            GROUP BY    Color, YEAR(DateBought)

            ) CSQ

            ON ST.Color = CSQ.Color

            AND YEAR(ST.DateBought) = CSQ.PurchaseYear - 1
```

Running this query gives the results that you can see in Figure 2-20; you can also see the output from the derived table.

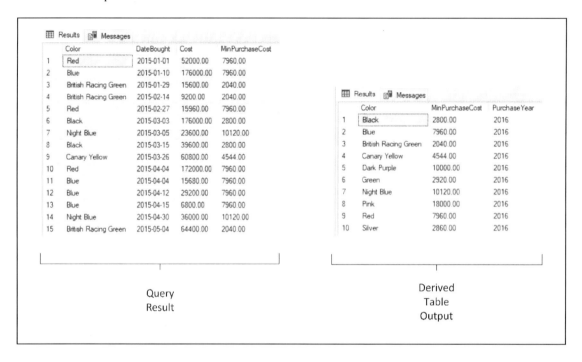

FIGURE 2-20. EXTENDING THE JOIN CLAUSE FOR A DERIVED TABLE

How It Works

This SQL is essentially two pieces of code:

A derived table	That calculates the minimum price for each car bought for every year of available data
An outer query	That displays the key stock information for all the cars bought in 2016

The interesting tweak is the way that the outer query and the inner derived table are joined. As the grouping for the derived table is by color and year, these are the fields that must be used in the JOIN clause. However, as the derived table contains data for all years, you can tweak the JOIN clause so that the data from the derived table is mapped not to the year that is specified in the WHERE clause of the outer query, but to the previous year. This is done simply by specifying

```
AND YEAR(ST.DateBought) = CSQ.PurchaseYear - 1
```

This filters the data returned from the derived table so that only data for the previous year is returned to the outer query.

Of course, you could have specified the year to filter on in the derived table, but this approach is more fluid and extensible because it automatically finds data from the *previous* year in the derived table—whatever year is defined in the WHERE clause of the outer query.

Tricks and Traps

To end your introduction to derived tables, we suggest that you remember the following point:

- This particular technique can be used in JOIN clauses whenever the fields that are used in a join are numeric. It is particularly useful when comparing data across years. It also makes the point that the fields used in a JOIN can themselves be calculated if necessary.

Conclusion

In this chapter, we introduced you to ways of combining data that allow you to answer some tough analytical questions. We did all of this using derived tables—a technique that lets you assemble complex datasets "on the fly" inside other queries.

These virtual tables let you aggregate, filter, and slice data in-depth and then use the results to carry out all sorts of queries. Moreover, derived tables help you think in terms of sets of data and, consequently, learn to adapt your way of tackling data-based problems so that you can handle more complex data analysis.

Core Knowledge Learned in This Chapter

The concepts that you have seen in this chapter are

Concept	Description
Derived tables	*When creating complex joins, you can define any or all of the component tables to be derived tables—that is, SQL that returns a dataset.*
Multiple join fields	*You can join tables using several fields if you need to.*

Chapter 3:
Common Table Expressions

The previous two chapters have shown you that SQL is all about creating the datasets that allow you to deliver the analysis that you need. As you have probably surmised while reading this book, SQL imposes on its practitioners a particular way of thinking. More specifically, it is a language that wants you to adopt its world view and to think in terms of sets of data that become the building blocks of your analysis. "Thinking in datasets" can, nonetheless, be a skill that takes a while to acquire. Moreover, the way that some SQL solutions nest queries inside other queries can make for complex code that seems to hide—rather than expose—the true simplicity of the approach. The time has come to demonstrate a powerful way to simplify working with complex datasets.

Simplifying Complex Queries with Common Table Expressions

Once again SQL Server can come to the rescue if an analytical challenge seems too daunting at first sight. This is because SQL can not only help you create the code that delivers the analysis, it can also help you define the analytical approach and focus on how you structure the datasets based on the underlying tables. This can be accomplished using a technique known as *Common Table Expressions* (CTEs).

We admit that the name sounds cryptic and gives little indication of the power of this approach. Yet CTEs (as they are normally called) can help you

- Create datasets outside the core of a query to help you think a problem through.
- Reuse datasets so that you do not have to rewrite or copy SQL code several times.
- Create CTEs that use the output from other CTEs. This allows you to break down an analytical challenge into a sequence of coherent steps in which the results created by one CTE ripple through other CTEs in a query to deliver the final output.

Let's now see how CTEs can help you tame even the most complex SQL queries.

1. A Basic Common Table Expression

In sales and marketing, it is essential that you understand what your customers want. A first step to this knowledge can be analyzing what they have bought in the past. The following code snippet lets you prepare a report for the CEO of Prestige Cars that displays the make, model, and color combinations of every vehicle sold in 2015.

```
WITH Sales2015_CTE

AS

(

SELECT     MK.MakeName, MD.ModelName, ST.Color

FROM       Data.Make AS MK

INNER JOIN Data.Model AS MD ON MK.MakeID = MD.MakeID

INNER JOIN Data.Stock AS ST ON ST.ModelID = MD.ModelID

INNER JOIN Data.SalesDetails SD ON ST.StockCode = SD.StockID

INNER JOIN Data.Sales AS SA ON SA.SalesID = SD.SalesID

WHERE      YEAR(SaleDate) = 2015

)

SELECT     MakeName, ModelName, Color

FROM       Sales2015_CTE

GROUP BY   MakeName, ModelName, Color
```

Running this query gives the results that you can see in Figure 3-1.

	MakeName	ModelName	Color
1	Alfa Romeo	Giulia	Red
2	Aston Martin	DB4	Night Blue
3	Aston Martin	DB5	Black
4	Aston Martin	DB5	Blue
5	Aston Martin	DB6	Canary Yellow
6	Aston Martin	DB6	Silver
7	Aston Martin	Virage	Black
8	Bentley	Flying Spur	British Racing Green
9	Ferrari	355	Black
10	Ferrari	355	Blue
11	Ferrari	Testarossa	Green
12	Ferrari	Testarossa	Red
13	Jaguar	XJS	Red
14	Jaguar	XJS	Silver
15	Jaguar	XK120	Red

FIGURE 3-1. A SIMPLE CTE

How It Works

This code snippet takes a two-phased approach to finding all the existing make, model, and color combinations of cars sold in 2015.

First: An independent initial query—a *CTE*—joins the Make, Model, Stock, SalesDetails, and Sales tables. It then selects the Make, Model, and Color fields from these tables. Since the query contains joins to the two tables that contain all the sales information, the output only shows the detailed list of the cars that have been sold.

Then: The output from this CTE is then used as the data source in the FROM clause of the subsequent SQL statement.

A CTE is really nothing more than a kind of derived table, like those that you saw in the previous chapter. It is a perfectly normal SELECT query that you build to isolate a subset of data. As you can see from this example, a CTE is composed of the following:

A CTE name A CTE must have a name. In this example, it is called "Sales2015_CTE." The name can be a single character or something more complex that explains more clearly what the CTE does.

A WITH clause	Begins the CTE.
A query	This is the core of the CTE. It must be a valid SQL SELECT query. It can be as complex as your needs require. The query *must* be enclosed in parentheses.
A use for the CTE	By this we mean that you must do something using the CTE—such as using the SELECT data from it as we do in this example.

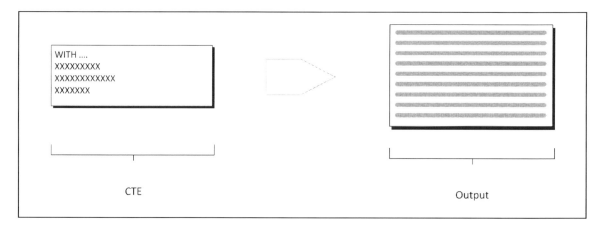

FIGURE 3-2. CONCEPTUALIZING A CTE

If you are looking at this example a little quizzically and thinking, "I am sure that I could have done this just by grouping the data without even needing a CTE," then you are right. The CTE that we apply here is not *strictly* necessary. Either approach delivers the required result. However, as you will see in this chapter, CTEs can be extremely useful in many different ways. We prefer to make the first one as easy as possible so it is as comprehensible as possible. However, there is more to using CTEs than just resolving coding challenges. A CTE like this helps you break down a problem into its component parts. In this specific example, this means

First:	Defining the list of data that you want to aggregate (this is the query inside the CTE).
Finally:	Grouping the data subset from the CTE to achieve the desired result.

So using CTEs is more than merely a variation on a theme; it can also help you think through a problem and enable you to separate out the building blocks that SQL uses to provide a solution in a clear and sequential way.

Tricks and Traps

With a new concept come a few key points to remember:

- You do not have to include the acronym CTE in a Common Table Expression name; however, we have chosen to adopt this approach in this book so that you can identify CTEs more easily among all the other SQL objects that we use.

- If you decide to use a CTE to isolate a subset of data, then you have to apply the CTE in some way. In other words, you cannot "declare" a CTE (as they say in the world of SQL programming) and then not use it. Indeed, if you do not use a CTE that you have created, then your code will *not* work.

- The query that makes up a CTE is completely independent of the rest of the query that uses the CTE, so you can always test the CTE by first selecting the SQL inside the parentheses that enclose the query that makes it up, and by then executing it. Figure 3-3 shows the results for the code in the CTE in this example.

FIGURE 3-3. THE INDEPENDENT QUERY CONSTITUTING A CTE

2. Calculating Averages across Multiple Values Using a CTE

One simple metric can tell many businesses if they are on the path to profitability. This is the average profit for each type of product. A CTE helps you produce this analysis for the CEO of Prestige Cars:

```
WITH Sales_CTE

AS

(

SELECT      MakeName

            ,SalePrice - (

                        ST.Cost

                        + ST.RepairsCost

                        + ST.PartsCost

                        + ST.TransportINCost

                        ) AS Profit

FROM        Data.Make AS MK

INNER JOIN Data.Model AS MD ON MK.MakeID = MD.MakeID

INNER JOIN Data.Stock AS ST ON ST.ModelID = MD.ModelID

INNER JOIN Data.SalesDetails SD ON ST.StockCode = SD.StockID

)


SELECT      MakeName, AVG(Profit) AS AverageProfit

FROM        Sales_CTE

GROUP BY    MakeName
```

If you run this query, you see the results that are shown in Figure 3-4.

	MakeName	AverageProfit
1	Alfa Romeo	758.272727
2	Aston Martin	10433.064935
3	Austin	197.142857
4	Bentley	13831.400000
5	BMW	2500.000000
6	Bugatti	53890.500000
7	Citroen	1962.333333
8	Delahaye	3473.250000
9	Delorean	16910.000000
10	Ferrari	29664.107142
11	Jaguar	4997.360000
12	Lagonda	18175.000000
13	Lamborghini	27957.000000
14	McLaren	44650.000000
15	Mercedes	4572.214285

FIGURE 3-4. CALCULATING AVERAGES ACROSS MULTIPLE VALUES USING A CTE

How It Works

Calculating averages is fundamental to much data analysis, and this is something that SQL does well. The preceding piece of SQL uses multiple fields to calculate the profit for each car sold, and then it returns the average profit per make.

You may be wondering why you even need a CTE to carry out this calculation. After all, surely you could just average the sale price and the various cost elements and then perform the math?

Indeed, you can do this; however, adding and subtracting overall averages is not the same thing as calculating the average profit. To get this information, you really need to calculate the profit per car and then work out the average of this figure. This is a prime example of how a CTE can prove invaluable. It allows you

First: To calculate the profit figure for each car in the Stock table. This metric is worked out at the most detailed level possible—that of each car in the Stock table.

Finally: To return the average of the profit figure, aggregated by Make in the main query.

3. Reusing CTEs in a Query

When you are trying to control costs, it can help to compare various metrics to a multiple of an average value in order to focus on higher-than-expected values. This is exactly what the finance director wants. In fact, he has asked for a report that finds all makes and models sold where the discount was more than twice the average discount for any vehicle sold in that year. The following piece of SQL is an example of this type of analysis.

```
;
WITH Discount2015_CTE (Make, Model, Color, SalePrice, LineItemDiscount)

AS

(

SELECT      MK.MakeName, MD.ModelName, ST.Color

            ,SD.SalePrice, SD.LineItemDiscount

FROM        Data.Make AS MK

INNER JOIN Data.Model AS MD ON MK.MakeID = MD.MakeID

INNER JOIN Data.Stock AS ST ON ST.ModelID = MD.ModelID

INNER JOIN Data.SalesDetails SD ON ST.StockCode = SD.StockID

INNER JOIN Data.Sales AS SA ON SA.SalesID = SD.SalesID

WHERE       YEAR(SaleDate) = 2015

)

SELECT      Make, Model, Color, LineItemDiscount, SalePrice

            ,(SELECT AVG(LineItemDiscount) * 2 FROM Discount2015_CTE)

            AS AverageDiscount

FROM        Discount2015_CTE

WHERE       LineItemDiscount > (SELECT AVG(LineItemDiscount) * 2

                                FROM Discount2015_CTE)
```

Running this query gives the results that you can see in Figure 3-5.

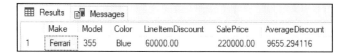

FIGURE 3-5. REUSING A CTE IN A QUERY

How It Works

This piece of analytical SQL uses a CTE to produce a list of the makes and models of car sold in 2015. It also displays the color, sale price, and sales discount (a column named LineItemDiscount) for each model.

Once the CTE has defined the data subset that will be used by the main query, a few interesting things happen:

First:	The rest of the query selects the fields passed into it by the CTE.
Then:	A WHERE clause in the main query reuses the CTE to calculate the average sales discount for 2015. This is then doubled and used as a filter so that only sales where a discount greater than twice the average sales discount for the year has been applied appear in the final output.
Finally:	The average sales discount for 2015 is recalculated and added to the SELECT clause as a subquery.

The key point here is that a CTE can be reused *several times* in the main query. This approach is based on two fundamental ideas:

- You only have to write the SQL that defines a subset of data *once*, because you can reuse it over and over again. In this example, the main advantage of this approach is that the filter (the WHERE clause that limits the data to the sales for a specific year) is only applied once—in the CTE.

- Whenever the CTE is reused to calculate or to display the average value, the filter that it contains is applied *every time*.

CTE or Derived Table?

When you see how a CTE works, you may be struck by its similarity to the derived tables that you saw in a previous chapter.

Well, this similarity should come as no surprise, as they are largely identical. Both are independent of the query that they are used by, both must specify the fields that can be read by the outer query, and both must have an alias.

CTEs, however, can help when you are developing a SQL solution. This is because they help you isolate sections of a data challenge. Indeed, they can help considerably when you are conceptualizing a solution because they guide you toward separating out data subsets as CTEs. This approach can also make SQL queries less intimidating and easier to extend and maintain.

If you have a challenging query that lends itself to using a derived table or a CTE, simply choose the approach that suits you. There is probably no "best" way—only the way that you feel most at ease with will solve your analytical problem.

There are several clear advantages to this way of working:

Less complexity	Subqueries can sometimes be fairly complex, so having to rewrite the same piece of SQL (or adapt it without making any errors) to use in a subquery can become laborious and time-consuming. Reusing a CTE means that you only write the core query *once* to get a reusable dataset.
Avoid repetition	This means you are less likely to make a SQL syntax error or enter a wrong value in one of the multiple WHERE clauses that would otherwise be necessary when you reuse the data in the data subset.
Forgetting is harder	You do not have to remember to add or update a WHERE clause in multiple subqueries.
Modification is easier	If you want to filter the data on a different year, all you have to do is to change the WHERE clause in the CTE. This change cascades through to the main query everywhere the CTE is used, so you only have to change filter values in one place.

Tricks and Traps

A set of key points are worth noting here:

- The CTE used in this example begins with a semicolon (;). Although this mark is only really necessary if your code contains other elements before you add the CTE, we begin CTEs with a semicolon from now on because it is better practice, and because it avoids the error message that arises if we forget the semicolon and then add more code before the CTE.

- As was the case with derived tables, the SELECT clause of the CTE *must* include all the fields that you want to use in the main query. If you do not select a field in the CTE, then it is completely invisible downstream in the main query that returns the final recordset based on the CTE.

- Although you absolutely *must* use a CTE if you have added one to your code, you are not obligated to use *all* the fields that you have selected in the CTE elsewhere in your query. In practice, however, it is probably best *only* to select the fields that you *need* when creating a CTE.

- You can make sure a CTE contains the list of fields that it returns—as the CTE in this example does—by placing a list of fields in parentheses after the CTE name. However, this is not compulsory. Doing so is really nothing more than a way of giving aliases to the fields that the CTE outputs. This can be useful when you are making the column names in underlying tables easier to understand for users.

4. Using a CTE in a Derived Table to Deliver Two Different Levels of Aggregation

The sales director for Prestige Cars wants a slightly subtler analysis of who the most valuable customers are. In this case, he wants a list of customers who bought the most expensive model of car for each make in 2015. The following piece of SQL lets you deliver this information.

```
;

WITH ExpensiveCar_CTE (

                  MakeName, ModelName, SalePrice

                  ,Color, TransportInCost, SaleDate
```

```
                          ,InvoiceNumber, CustomerName

)

AS

(

SELECT     MK.MakeName, MD.ModelName, SD.SalePrice, ST.Color,
ST.TransportInCost, SA.SaleDate, SA.InvoiceNumber, CU.CustomerName

FROM       Data.Make AS MK

INNER JOIN Data.Model AS MD ON MK.MakeID = MD.MakeID

INNER JOIN Data.Stock AS ST ON ST.ModelID = MD.ModelID

INNER JOIN Data.SalesDetails SD ON ST.StockCode = SD.StockID

INNER JOIN Data.Sales AS SA ON SA.SalesID = SD.SalesID

INNER JOIN Data.Customer CU ON SA.CustomerID = CU.CustomerID

WHERE      YEAR(SaleDate) = 2015

)

SELECT     SLS.MakeName, ModelName, SLS.Color, CustomerName

           ,TransportInCost, SaleDate, InvoiceNumber

FROM       ExpensiveCar_CTE SLS

           INNER JOIN (

                      SELECT     MakeName

                                 ,MAX(SalePrice) AS MaxSalePrice

                      FROM       ExpensiveCar_CTE

                      GROUP BY MakeName

                      ) MX

           ON SLS.MakeName = MX.MakeName

           AND SLS.SalePrice = MX.MaxSalePrice
```

Running this query gives the results that you can see in Figure 3-6.

	MakeName	ModelName	Color	CustomerName	TransportInCost	SaleDate	InvoiceNumber
1	Ferrari	355	Blue	Snazzy Roadsters	1950.00	2015-01-25 00:00:00.000	GBPGB002
2	Porsche	911	Black	Convertible Dreams	150.00	2015-11-10 00:00:00.000	GBPGB025
3	Aston Martin	Virage	Black	Theo Kowalski	750.00	2015-10-30 00:00:00.000	USDUS024
4	Bentley	Flying Spur	British Racing Green	Wonderland Wheels	750.00	2015-04-30 00:00:00.000	GBPGB011
5	Mercedes	280SL	Red	La Bagnole de Luxe	150.00	2015-06-04 16:37:00.000	EURFR015
6	Alfa Romeo	Giulia	Red	Convertible Dreams	150.00	2015-07-12 00:00:00.000	GBPGB016
7	Jaguar	XK150	Night Blue	Alexei Tolstoi	150.00	2015-07-15 00:00:00.000	GBPGB017
8	Triumph	TR5	Green	Peter McLuckie	150.00	2015-09-05 00:00:00.000	GBPGB020

FIGURE 3-6. USING A CTE IN A DERIVED TABLE TO DELIVER TWO DIFFERENT LEVELS OF AGGREGATION

How It Works

The challenge here is to isolate the highest-value car sold for each make as well as return all the important details for each sale. Fortunately, a CTE can really help here:

First:	You define a CTE that contains all the key sales information (customer, sale price, make, model, etc.).
Second:	You select all the important data from this CTE.
Third:	You use the CTE a second time in a derived table that groups and aggregates the data from the CTE by make and maximum sale price.
Finally:	You join the derived table to the main query on the MakeName and SalePrice fields (or, rather, you join the maximum sale price field from the derived table to the sale price field from the main query).

This way the derived table filters out all cars from the main query where the sale price is not equal to the greatest sale price—in effect isolating the most expensive car sold for each make.

Once again you have reused a CTE. This time, rather than rewrite complex joins in a derived table, you used the CTE as the basis for a simple aggregation. This allowed you to concentrate on getting the initial query (the one used in the CTE) correct and then focus separately on how to use this data twice:

- Once to find the most expensive car for each make
- Once to list the details of that particular sale

To more easily understand this, take a look at Figure 3-7, which provides a visual breakdown of the query used in this example.

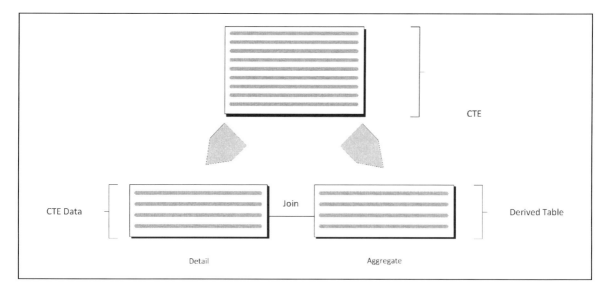

Figure 3-7. Analyzing a complex CTE

Tricks and Traps

When creating more complex CTEs, you need to remember

- If you have created a CTE that outputs many fields, then you need to pay attention to the list of column names that you add inside the parentheses that follow the name of the CTE. This involves doing the following:

  - First, make sure that you have the same number of fields as those in the SELECT clause of the CTE.

  - Second, ensure that all the fields are in the same order both in the SELECT clause and inside the parentheses. It is all too easy to mix up the order of the fields—and produce some really bizarre output as a result.

5. Using a CTE to Isolate Data from a Separate Dataset at a Different Level of Detail

The sales director has asked you to produce a regular report that ensures that the sales-people are meeting their targets. To do so, you need to compare sales figures to budget projections. The SQL that follows is one way of doing this.

```
;
WITH SalesBudget_CTE
AS
(
SELECT     BudgetValue, BudgetDetail, Year, Month
FROM       Reference.Budget
WHERE      BudgetElement = 'Country'
)


SELECT     CountryName, YEAR(SaleDate) AS YearOfSale
           ,MONTH(SaleDate) AS MonthOfSale
           ,SUM(SD.SalePrice) AS SalePrice
           ,SUM(CTE.BudgetValue) AS BudgetValue
           ,SUM(CTE.BudgetValue)
           - SUM(SD.SalePrice) AS DifferenceBudgetToSales
FROM       Data.Make AS MK
INNER JOIN Data.Model AS MD ON MK.MakeID = MD.MakeID
INNER JOIN Data.Stock AS ST ON ST.ModelID = MD.ModelID
INNER JOIN Data.SalesDetails SD ON ST.StockCode = SD.StockID
INNER JOIN Data.Sales AS SA ON SA.SalesID = SD.SalesID
INNER JOIN Data.Customer CU ON SA.CustomerID = CU.CustomerID
```

```
INNER JOIN Data.Country CO ON CU.Country = CO.CountryISO2

INNER JOIN SalesBudget_CTE CTE

        ON CTE.BudgetDetail = CO.CountryName

        AND CTE.Year = YEAR(SaleDate)

        AND CTE.Month = MONTH(SaleDate)

GROUP BY   CountryName, YEAR(SaleDate), MONTH(SaleDate)
```

Running this query gives the results that you can see in Figure 3-8.

	CountryName	YearOfSale	MonthOfSale	SalePrice	BudgetValue	DifferenceBudgetToSales
1	Belgium	2016	8	125000.00	100000.00	-25000.00
2	Belgium	2017	2	12500.00	15500.00	3000.00
3	Belgium	2017	3	86500.00	100000.00	13500.00
4	Belgium	2017	7	45950.00	137850.00	91900.00
5	Belgium	2017	11	34000.00	68000.00	34000.00
6	Belgium	2018	1	950.00	950.00	0.00
7	Belgium	2018	6	6950.00	6950.00	0.00
8	France	2015	4	19600.00	19600.00	0.00
9	France	2015	5	8950.00	8950.00	0.00
10	France	2015	6	22950.00	22950.00	0.00
11	France	2015	7	75500.00	151000.00	75500.00
12	France	2016	1	2550.00	2550.00	0.00
13	France	2016	2	39500.00	39500.00	0.00
14	France	2016	5	49580.00	49580.00	0.00
15	France	2016	6	180150.00	720600.00	540450.00

FIGURE 3-8. USING A CTE TO ISOLATE DATA FROM A SEPARATE DATASET AT A DIFFERENT LEVEL OF DETAIL

How It Works

Once again you are probably thinking, "this is using a CTE like it is a derived table." You are right—this is exactly what we are doing.

More precisely, we are using the CTE to isolate the budget data from the Budget table so that it can be joined to a query in a way that allows us to compare actual and budget data. Now, the budget data does not really fit into the tightly structured "relational" model of the main tables of the Prestige Cars database. However, it *is* possible to produce budget data that returns a list of makes along with the predicted sales for each month and year. The SELECT query that makes up the CTE does exactly this. To get a clearer idea of how this works, take a look at Figure 3-9, which shows you the output from the CTE if you select the SQL and run it independently.

FIGURE 3-9. THE RECORDS RETURNED BY A CTE THAT FILTERS DATA

As you can see, this is nothing more than a "virtual table" of selected budget data. However, you can now join this data to sales data in the following three fields:

MakeName	Which maps to the BudgetDetail field in the Budget table (once the BudgetDetail table is filtered to show the makes)
Year of Sale	Which requires you to use the YEAR() function to extract the year from the SaleDate field
Month of Sale	Which requires you to use the MONTH() function to extract the month from the SaleDate field

The main query in this code snippet then joins the CTE to the other tables as if it is just another table—which it almost is. The main query can then select any necessary fields as well as carry out any required calculations.

Tricks and Traps

When using a CTE to join data from separate data areas at different levels of granularity, be sure to remember that

- In the CTE, all the numeric values in the query have to be aggregated (using SUM() functions in this example) and the text fields have to appear in a GROUP BY clause. This is because you are comparing budget data that is aggregated by country, year, and month with data that is at a more detailed level. So, to make the figures meaningful, the detailed sales data also has to be aggregated to country, year, and month, or it cannot be joined to the CTE.

6.   Multiple Common Table Expressions

It may be near the end of the day, but the sales director has appeared at your desk with an urgent request. She wants to see how her budget predictions for sales by color stack up against actual sales for 2016. Fortunately, you can answer this request in a few minutes with the kind of SQL that you can see here:

```
WITH

ColorSales_CTE

AS

(

SELECT      Color

            ,SUM(SD.SalePrice) AS TotalSalesValue

FROM        Data.Stock ST

INNER JOIN Data.SalesDetails SD

            ON ST.StockCode = SD.StockID

INNER JOIN Data.Sales SA

            ON SD.SalesID = SA.SalesID

WHERE       YEAR(SA.SaleDate) = 2016

GROUP BY    Color

)

,

ColorBudget_CTE

AS

(

SELECT  BudgetDetail AS Color, BudgetValue

FROM    Reference.Budget

WHERE   BudgetElement = 'Color'
```

```
            AND YEAR = 2016
)


SELECT      BDG.Color, SLS.TotalSalesValue, BDG.BudgetValue
            ,(SLS.TotalSalesValue - BDG.BudgetValue) AS BudgetDelta


FROM        ColorSales_CTE SLS
INNER JOIN  ColorBudget_CTE BDG
            ON SLS.Color = BDG.Color
```

Running this code gives you the result that you can see in Figure 3-10. In this figure, you can also see the output of the two separate CTEs.

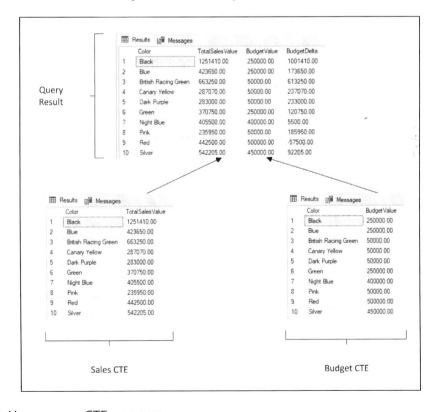

FIGURE 3-10. USING MULTIPLE CTES IN A QUERY

How It Works

This query uses two separate CTEs to isolate two different datasets that are then joined in the final "output" query.

The first CTE	Joins the Sales, Stock, and SalesDetails tables to return all the required sales values per color of vehicle sold for 2016. This CTE is called ColorSales_CTE.
The second CTE	Isolates the budget data for colors for 2016 from the Budget table. If you remember, the budget table contains data for many budget elements, and so it needs to be filtered on both the budget element (color, in this example) and the year that you want to get data for. This CTE is called ColorBudget_CTE.
The output query	Joins the two "source" CTEs on the shared color field and returns both the sales and budget values for all the available colors. As a final flourish, it uses the values to calculate any sales that are over—or under—budget values.

This example illustrates how you can use CTEs to generate completely independent datasets that you can then use together to deliver insight. In the Prestige Cars database, budget data is held completely independently from sales data, and moreover, has its own unique structure. However, using CTEs to isolate the two datasets before you join them shows you that

First:	You can isolate separate data elements from each other before attempting to combine them.
Second:	The two CTEs are totally separate—neither has any effect on the other.

Indeed, using multiple separate CTEs like this can prove to be a valuable analytical technique. This is because you can concentrate on each dataset individually (and even test the output of each CTE in isolation). Often this can be a valuable way to break down your analysis into smaller, more digestible pieces that you then combine for a final result.

Tricks and Traps

If you decide to use multiple independent CTEs in your queries be aware that

- You can use multiple independent CTEs as a way of testing various approaches to solving data analysis challenges.

- You only need to introduce CTEs with a single WITH keyword. After that, you merely separate each CTE from the others with a comma.

7. Nested Common Table Expressions

As part of your analytical quest to deliver the insight that will lead to increased sales and profits, you want to take a look at the cars that sell more than a minimum quantity. More specifically, you want to display all the makes of car sold in a given year where more than two cars are sold per make. After all, perhaps these are the ones that the company should be pitching to potential buyers. The following SQL shows you how to do this:

```
;
WITH Outer2015Sales_CTE

AS

(

SELECT      MK.MakeName

FROM        Data.Make AS MK

INNER JOIN Data.Model AS MD ON MK.MakeID = MD.MakeID

INNER JOIN Data.Stock AS ST ON ST.ModelID = MD.ModelID

INNER JOIN Data.SalesDetails SD ON ST.StockCode = SD.StockID

INNER JOIN Data.Sales AS SA ON SA.SalesID = SD.SalesID

WHERE       YEAR(SaleDate) = 2015

)

,

CoreSales_CTE (MakeName, NumberOfSales)

AS

(

SELECT      MakeName

            ,COUNT(*)

FROM        Outer2015Sales_CTE

GROUP BY    MakeName

HAVING      COUNT(*) >= 2
```

```
)

SELECT      CTE.MakeName, MK2.MakeCountry AS CountryCode

            ,NumberOfSales

FROM        CoreSales_CTE CTE

INNER JOIN Data.Make MK2

            ON CTE.MakeName = MK2.MakeName
```

Running this query gives the results that you can see in Figure 3-11.

	MakeName	CountryCode	NumberOfSales
1	Ferrari	ITA	4
2	Porsche	GER	8
3	Aston Martin	GBR	7
4	Jaguar	GBR	4
5	Triumph	GBR	2

FIGURE 3-11. NESTED CTE OUTPUT

How It Works

This query shows how you can create a short sequence of two CTEs where the second uses the output from the first as its source of data. This way, CTEs can be used as a way of breaking down the initial requirement into a series of successive steps that lead to the solution. What the query does is take a three-phased approach:

First: The initial CTE joins all the tables that are required to produce a list of all makes of vehicle sold in 2015. Even though only two fields are actually used by this query (MakeName and SaleDate), these fields are in the Sales and Make tables, and so several "intermediate" tables must be part of the FROM clause to link the source data tables correctly.

Then:	The second CTE (CoreSales_CTE) is built using the first CTE (Outer2015Sales_CTE) as its data source. This query is an aggregate query that only returns makes of car where more than two have been sold. Because this CTE is based on the first CTE, only sales for 2015 are analyzed.
Finally:	A regular query lists the makes of vehicle returned by the second CTE. It joins this result to the Make table to add further columns to the output.

Once again, it might be easier to grasp this concept with the aid of a more visual representation. Figure 3-12 explains nested CTEs graphically.

FIGURE 3-12. THE DATA FLOW IN NESTED CTEs

Although you could probably arrive at the same result using different approaches, this example shows you that CTEs can be "linked" in a way that lets you make your SQL reflect the analytical challenge that you are faced with. It has the advantage of being more sequential than some other approaches since it lets you see these steps, which are required to produce the final output, more clearly:

First:	Filter the data.
Second:	Aggregate the data.
Finally:	Extend the data selection.

Tricks and Traps

Here are a couple of points to take away:

- When you are writing SQL that uses multiple CTEs, the core principles to using any CTE still apply. Remember that you have to begin with a semicolon (;) if there is any other code before the CTE, and you *must* use all of the CTEs that you write. This means you still need a SQL query after the final CTE to output the data.

- When writing dependent CTEs like this, you only need to use a single WITH keyword. This serves to introduce any number of CTEs. The CTEs can be independent from one another or derived from one another—it makes no difference.

8. Using Multiple Common Table Expressions to Compare Disparate Datasets

When a customer contacts Prestige Cars, the sales director wants to know if customers they contact are profitable. Consequently, she wants to see how much each customer has spent in 2017, and how this relates to Prestige Cars' total annual sales. What is more, she wants to see a percentage of total sales per customer as well. The following SQL snippet gives you precisely this information:

```
;

WITH Initial2017Sales_CTE

AS

(

SELECT      SD.SalePrice, CU.CustomerName, SA.SaleDate

FROM        Data.Make AS MK

INNER JOIN Data.Model AS MD ON MK.MakeID = MD.MakeID

INNER JOIN Data.Stock AS ST ON ST.ModelID = MD.ModelID

INNER JOIN Data.SalesDetails SD ON ST.StockCode = SD.StockID

INNER JOIN Data.Sales AS SA ON SA.SalesID = SD.SalesID

INNER JOIN Data.Customer CU ON SA.CustomerID = CU.CustomerID
```

```
WHERE        YEAR(SaleDate) = 2017
)

,

AggregateSales_CTE (CustomerName, SalesForCustomer)
AS
(
SELECT       CustomerName, SUM(SalePrice)
FROM         Initial2017Sales_CTE
GROUP BY     CustomerName
)

,

TotalSales_CTE (TotalSalePrice)
AS
(
SELECT       SUM(SalePrice)
FROM         Initial2017Sales_CTE
)


SELECT
 IT.CustomerName
,IT.SalePrice
, IT.SaleDate
,FORMAT(IT.SalePrice / AG.SalesForCustomer, '0.00%')
         AS SaleAsPercentageForCustomer
,FORMAT(IT.SalePrice / TT.TotalSalePrice, '0.00%') AS SalePercentOverall
```

```
FROM        Initial2017Sales_CTE IT

            INNER JOIN AggregateSales_CTE AG

            ON IT.CustomerName = AG.CustomerName

            CROSS APPLY TotalSales_CTE TT

ORDER BY   IT.SaleDate, IT.CustomerName
```

Running this query gives the results that you can see in Figure 3-13.

	CustomerName	SalePrice	SaleDate	SaleAsPercentageForCustomer	SalePercentOverall
1	Eat My Exhaust Ltd	85000.00	2017-01-01 00:00:00.000	60.71%	1.08%
2	Peter Smith	125000.00	2017-01-01 00:00:00.000	43.48%	1.59%
3	Vive La Vitesse	22500.00	2017-01-01 00:00:00.000	2.47%	0.29%
4	La Bagnole de Luxe	1250.00	2017-01-10 00:00:00.000	100.00%	0.02%
5	Le Luxe en Motion	22500.00	2017-01-11 00:00:00.000	7.61%	0.29%
6	Magic Motors	125950.00	2017-01-12 00:00:00.000	28.01%	1.60%
7	Le Luxe en Motion	8850.00	2017-01-13 00:00:00.000	2.99%	0.11%
8	Posh Vehicles Ltd	9950.00	2017-01-14 00:00:00.000	18.11%	0.13%
9	Vive La Vitesse	56500.00	2017-01-30 00:00:00.000	6.21%	0.72%
10	Honest Pete Motors	56950.00	2017-01-31 00:00:00.000	10.79%	0.72%
11	Screamin' Wheels	55000.00	2017-01-31 00:00:00.000	32.63%	0.70%
12	Vive La Vitesse	365000.00	2017-02-07 00:00:00.000	40.13%	4.64%
13	Laurent Saint Yves	395000.00	2017-02-08 00:00:00.000	44.71%	5.02%
14	Screamin' Wheels	21500.00	2017-02-09 00:00:00.000	12.76%	0.27%
15	Screamin' Wheels	6500.00	2017-02-10 00:00:00.000	3.86%	0.08%

FIGURE 3-13. USING MULTIPLE CTES TO COMPARE DISPARATE DATASETS

How It Works

We imagine that when you first see this piece of SQL, you think, "Wow, this is complicated!" After all, this example uses no less than three CTEs to deliver the required analysis. However, before looking at the code, let's see exactly what we are trying to deliver. In essence, the request is for the following pieces of information:

Individual Customer Sales   We need the detail of each sale for each customer for the given period (2017).

Total Customer Sales   We want the total sales figure for each customer for the given period.

Total Sales   We also require the total overall sales for the sales period.

Each of the three CTEs used in this query corresponds to one of these analytical requirements.

Initial2017Sales_CTE	Provides the sales data at a detail level. It joins all the necessary tables needed to output the date of each sale, the customer, and the amount of the sale. This CTE also filters the data to restrict it to a specified year.
AggregateSales_CTE	Takes the data supplied by the initial CTE (Initial2017Sales_CTE) and aggregates it by customer. This way you also can obtain the total sales per customer.
TotalSales_CTE	Also takes the data supplied by Initial2017Sales_CTE and aggregates it, only this time, only the total figure for the dataset is returned, without any grouping.

Once the CTEs have been defined (or "declared" as the techies say), the final query can then assemble the data from all of them. It does this in two ways:

First:	Initial2017Sales_CTE (the detailed list of sales) is joined to AggregateSales_CTE (the total sales per customer). As both contain the CustomerName field, they are joined on this field. This join allows you to return the total sales per customer as well as the detail of each sale for every sale. Dividing the total sales per customer by the value of each sale gives you the percentage of total customer sales that each individual sale represents.
Second:	The total overall sales figure is added to the query. This is done using the CROSS APPLY operator. What this does is add the total sales figure to each row that is output. Once the total is there, it can be used to provide the percentage of total sales that each individual sale represents.

This example shows you just how versatile CTEs can be. As you can see, the initial detailed CTE (Initial2017Sales_CTE) is used not only in the final query but also in the other two CTEs. This makes the code much simpler, as it means that you do not have to repeat a series of table joins several times. Instead, you define a source dataset *once* that you then *reuse* on multiple occasions to help deliver different levels of aggregation. Not only that, but if you need to change the filter that underlies the analysis (the year, in this case), you only need to alter it once in the top CTE for the filter to be cascaded down through the subsequent, dependent CTEs.

Tricks and Traps

Despite its apparent complexity, this CTE needs only one principal comment:

- In the SQL, we have formatted the percentage output using the FORMAT() function. This makes the output more readable. If you are feeding this data into another application, you may want to remove this function from the code because it can cause the percentages to be interpreted as text by some programs.

Conclusion

This chapter showed you how to harness the power of SQL to rise to the most daunting data analysis challenges. You did this using Common Table Expressions (CTEs)—a technique that lets you break down data analysis problems into smaller, more manageable parts that you can then join together to obtain the result that you want.

CTEs not only solve technical problems, they also help you handle data analysis one step at a time. This combination makes them one of the most useful SQL techniques available—and, almost certainly, a valuable tool in your armory.

Core Knowledge Learned in This Chapter

The concepts and keywords that you have seen in this chapter are

Concept	Description
Common Table Expressions (CTEs)	*A CTE is a separate derived table that allows you to define a dataset outside the main query for use—and reuse—in the body of the query. Multiple CTEs can be used in the same query, CTEs can be chained so that one CTE depends on the output of another CTE and CTEs can be independent from each other.*
WITH	*This keyword introduces one or more CTEs in a query.*

Chapter 4:
Correlated Subqueries

We realize that the title of this chapter may seem a little hard to understand when you first read it. After all, the term correlated subqueries is more than a little technical—if not incomprehensible—at first sight. However, since it is the term that database people use, we have to use it, too. What this expression means is, quite simply, that certain kinds of subquery can be used to filter the data in the outer query in a specific way. This is done by applying a specific method to join the subquery to the outer query, which means that each query depends on the other. Using correlated subqueries can often enable you to deliver some uniquely powerful data analysis.

Why Use Correlated Subqueries?

As with so many database concepts, this is easier to understand if you see it in action. In this chapter, you see how to

- Calculate ratios and percentages of parts relative to a whole.
- Filter data in a table only if corresponding data exists in another table.
- Filter data based on a calculation that relates to a specific aspect of the data.
- Isolate data according to certain characteristics of another linked dataset.

Since an example is worth a thousand words, let's take a look at a few correlated subqueries that will extend your knowledge of SQL. You can then take your analytical abilities to a higher level so that you can solve ever more challenging requests.

1. Simple Correlated Subqueries

Most of the clients of Prestige Cars only buy one vehicle at a time; however, some do buy two or more at once. To this end, the sales director wants a list of all invoice items as well as the total for the invoice so that she can do some further analysis. The following SQL provides this:

```
SELECT

SalesDetailsID

,SalePrice

,(SELECT TotalSalePrice FROM Data.sales

  WHERE SalesId = SD.SalesId) AS TotalSales

FROM Data.SalesDetails SD
```

Running this SQL returns the data that you can see in Figure 4-1. Although the sale price is equal to the total sales in most cases, on occasion—such as in lines 11 and 12—two lines make up a single invoice and the sale price is only part of the total sales.

FIGURE 4-1. A SIMPLE CORRELATED SUBQUERY

How It Works

This query is created from an outer query and an inner query, just like many of the examples that you saw in the previous three chapters. Nonetheless, this example has one really important difference. The two queries are not independent of each other; they are linked. More specifically, they both contain the SalesID field, and this field is used in the WHERE clause of the subquery to connect the inner and outer queries.

Once the subquery is "connected" to the outer query (or once it becomes a correlated subquery, as it is called in the world of SQL), then the way that the whole query works alters radically. The *outer query now depends on the inner query*, and the inner query is run once for each record in the outer query.

Once again, we prefer to illustrate this concept graphically to help you to understand what exactly a correlated subquery is doing. You can see this in Figure 4-2.

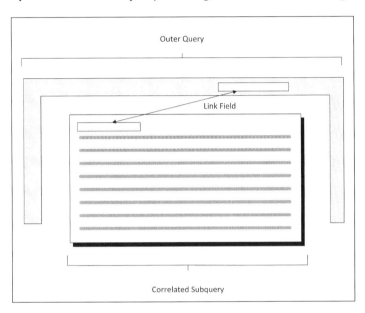

FIGURE 4-2. THE CONCEPT OF A CORRELATED SUBQUERY

This graphic illustrates how the inner and outer queries relate one to the other.

The outer query	Returns the first record that it finds from the SalesDetails table (which is the list of line items in every invoice) and passes a "link" field (SalesID) to the correlated subquery (the inner query).
The inner query	Reads the Sales table (the invoice header table) and returns the total sales price **only** for records containing the SalesID passed in from the outer query.

This is, admittedly, a simple example where we are not doing very much with the data that is returned. In the real world you would probably use this information to calculate the percentage of line items per invoice. Just read on and see how to apply the concept of correlated subqueries to deliver precisely this kind of analysis.

Tricks and Traps

There is one fundamental point to memorize when creating correlated subqueries:

- You cannot execute the correlated subquery independent of the outer query because the correlated subquery depends on the outer query in its WHERE clause. You can, however, remove the WHERE clause from the correlated sub-query and then execute the SQL for the inner query.

2. Correlated Subqueries to Display Percentages of a Specific Total

When she is negotiating each sale, the sales director wants to see a history of all previous sales for every client as well as the percentage of the total value of vehicles sold to the client that each individual sale represents. She says that this will help her develop a discount strategy. The next piece of SQL uses a correlated subquery to deliver this insight:

```
SELECT

 CustomerName

,SA.INVOICENUMBER

,SD.SalePrice

,SD.SalePrice

/

(

SELECT      SUM(SDC.SalePrice)

FROM        Data.SalesDetails SDC

INNER JOIN Data.Sales SAC

            ON SDC.SalesID = SAC.SalesID

INNER JOIN Data.Customer CSC

            ON SAC.CustomerID = CSC.CustomerID

WHERE       SAC.CustomerID = CS.CustomerID
```

```
)  *  100 AS PercentSalesPerCustomer


FROM       Data.SalesDetails SD

INNER JOIN Data.Sales SA

       ON SD.SalesID = SA.SalesID

INNER JOIN Data.Customer CS

       ON SA.CustomerID = CS.CustomerID

ORDER BY   CustomerName
```

Running this piece of SQL displays the percentage of each sale for each client relative to the total sales for the client, as you can see in Figure 4-3. If you add up the total sales records for each client, you will see that they equate to 100 percent per client.

	CustomerName	INVOICENUMBER	SalePrice	PercentSalesPerCustomer
1	Alex McWhirter	GBPGB308	17850.00	100.0000000000000000
2	Alexei Tolstoi	GBPGB055	205000.00	39.3104374005254176
3	Alexei Tolstoi	GBPGB063	102500.00	19.6552187002627088
4	Alexei Tolstoi	GBPGB046	9950.00	1.9079944006596483
5	Alexei Tolstoi	GBPGB046	39500.00	7.5744501332719707
6	Alexei Tolstoi	GBPGB026	69500.00	13.3271970699342269
7	Alexei Tolstoi	GBPGB023	22600.00	4.3337360256188997
8	Alexei Tolstoi	GBPGB017	22990.00	4.4085217357955090
9	Alexei Tolstoi	GBPGB081	3500.00	0.6711538092772632
10	Alexei Tolstoi	GBPGB092	45950.00	8.8112907246543558
11	Alicia Almodovar	EURES098	12500.00	3.2714805412337407
12	Alicia Almodovar	EURES109	39500.00	10.3378785102986207
13	Alicia Almodovar	EURES244	45950.00	12.0259624695752310
14	Alicia Almodovar	EURES237	15950.00	4.1744091706142532
15	Alicia Almodovar	EURES232	5690.00	1.4891779423695988

FIGURE 4-3. USING A CORRELATED SUBQUERY TO CALCULATE PERCENTAGES OF A SUBSET

How It Works

This query extends the correlated subquery principle that you saw in the previous example to more complex data sets. More specifically, the code consists of

An outer query	That joins the Sales, SalesDetails, and Customer tables to return the details—the customer name and sale amount—for every sale made by the company.
A correlated subquery	That calculates the total sales per customer. This uses the same tables as the outer query (Sales, SalesDetails, and Customer); however, it groups the data by customer to give the total sales for each customer. The correlated subquery is joined to the outer query by the CustomerID field, so the total returned is only for the customer from the outer list and *not* for the whole SalesDetails table.

The overall query essentially works as a whole. When each record of the outer query is returned, the correlated subquery calculates the total sales *only for the relevant customer*. This figure is then used in the percentage calculation of the sales ratio for this particular sale.

Tricks and Traps

There is one point to note here:

- Since the correlated subquery is linked to the outer query, you cannot just select the SQL for the subquery and run it. Should you wish to test the subquery, we advise that you copy the correlated subquery into a new query window and replace the reference to the outer query (CS.CustomerID in this example) with a real customer ID. Indeed, you may find it helpful to develop and test a correlated subquery in this way *before* adding it to the outer query.

3. Comparing Datasets Using a Correlated Subquery

Once again, the finance director is determined to reduce the cost of repairs. This time he has asked you to produce a list of vehicle repair costs that are 50 percent higher than the average for each make. The following code lets you deliver this for him:

```
SELECT      MKX.MakeName, STX.RepairsCost, STX.StockCode

FROM        Data.Make AS MKX INNER JOIN Data.Model AS MDX

            ON MKX.MakeID = MDX.MakeID

INNER JOIN Data.Stock AS STX ON STX.ModelID = MDX.ModelID

INNER JOIN Data.SalesDetails SDX ON STX.StockCode = SDX.StockID

WHERE       STX.RepairsCost >

                (

                    SELECT      AVG(ST.RepairsCost) AS AvgRepairCost

                    FROM        Data.Make AS MK

                    INNER JOIN Data.Model AS MD

                            ON MK.MakeID = MD.MakeID

                    INNER JOIN Data.Stock AS ST

                            ON ST.ModelID = MD.ModelID

                    WHERE       MK.MakeName = MKX.MakeName

                ) * 1.5
```

Running this query gives the results that you can see in Figure 4-4.

	MakeName	RepairsCost	StockCode
1	Porsche	1360.00	2189D556-D1C4-4BC1-B0C8-4053319E8E9D
2	Aston Martin	2500.00	E6E6270A-60B0-4817-AA57-17F26B2B8DAF
3	Aston Martin	3250.00	CEDFB8D2-BD98-4A08-BC46-406D23940527
4	Aston Martin	1950.00	D63C8CC9-DB19-4B9C-9C8E-6C6370812041
5	Aston Martin	2175.00	18E980AB-452D-42EF-8728-12822AD20C60
6	Porsche	1360.00	3F3BED8D-1203-4D3E-8AC0-3ACAC73BDE17
7	Lamborghini	5500.00	88AFBF67-13A6-4BC5-AE50-8C64F0F25453
8	Porsche	2000.00	B165CAEF-FF77-4E63-98C1-59D97F97E7C9
9	Alfa Romeo	1360.00	07F0D746-085B-4FB9-9F82-6CEAC851FBC3
10	Jaguar	2000.00	8F278478-CA0B-4CDB-8F02-1A054AAE88A9
11	Porsche	1360.00	518125AE-9A67-45A6-B3FD-557C785796FC
12	Ferrari	9250.00	66C9034C-23A3-44F1-B946-2DDA65E684D8
13	Porsche	1490.00	E00D10E9-7F7F-49A9-BDC0-4C2611580B4E
14	Porsche	1360.00	AAF61ECC-0BAC-4EAF-9E50-01749253329A
15	Triumph	970.00	0B0E0FC2-E72B-4BD4-9C46-1AF98F17BEC4

FIGURE 4-4. A CORRELATED QUERY USED FOR COMPARISON

How It Works

Finding exceptions—especially costly exceptions—is a core requirement in data analysis. Correlated subqueries are especially useful when you need to compare values to an average for a particular category of items. This query begins by calculating the average repair cost for all vehicles in stock and then multiplying this figure by 150 percent. However, since it is a correlated subquery where the inner and outer queries are linked using the MakeName field, this average is calculated for *every record in the outer query*. The result is that the repair cost is evaluated not for *all* vehicles in stock, but as the average for *each make* of vehicle in stock. This changes the calculation completely. Now, for each record in the outer query, the average repair cost is only calculated relative to that particular make of car. If the repair cost for a car is over 1.5 times the average repair cost for that make, then the query output shows the repair cost for the car.

Tricks and Traps

Exception reporting can prove tricky in practice. Be sure to take note of the following points if you want to get better results:

- The "filter" effect of a correlated subquery is not limited to finding records that are (or are not) in a dataset as was the case with the three previous examples. You can use a correlated subquery to compare values using all the traditional comparison operators—greater than (>), less than (<), greater than or equal to (>=), less than or equal to (<=), or not equal to (<>). This example

Avoid Correlated Subqueries—Sometimes

Correlated subqueries can be incredibly useful when you need to mix data from two or more datasets; however, they can be overused—and can complicate otherwise simple SQL solutions.

Before you decide that a correlated subquery is the only answer to a particular problem, we advise you to see if you can achieve your objectives using simple table joins, or even derived tables.

If your requirement boils down, one way or another, to a classic WHERE query, then it can be easier to avoid a subquery.

Also, if your particular challenge does not require different levels of aggregation between the outer query and the correlated subquery, then it may be a good candidate for a (much simpler) traditional series of table joins and a WHERE clause.

This is not to say that any code that works is to be avoided. It is just that a more "classic" SQL approach can often help you both analyze your needs and deliver a solution faster and more easily.

only shows how to compare using less than, but all the others are available if your analysis requires them.

- You are also not limited to comparing results to an average. You can just as easily use the MAX() or MIN() functions to find records that are close to the upper and lower limits of a dataset for a specific element.

- In this example, the two queries—inner and outer—use very similar datasets. This is not always the case with correlated subqueries. It can, however, be a frequent occurrence.

- In a correlated subquery it is vital to create individual aliases for any tables that are used in both the inner and outer tables of the query. Because many of the same tables are used in both the outer query and the correlated subquery, we distinguished them by adding an "X" for each outer query table alias.

4. Duplicating the Output of a Correlated Subquery in the Query Results

The finance director was pleased with the data that you just sent him; however, he now wants the average repair cost per make to appear in the resulting data while keeping the filter on the average repair cost per make that you set up previously.

If you want to be absolutely certain that this query is working, the best way to find out is to display the average repair cost per make in the output. This means you need to duplicate the correlated subquery that you use in the WHERE clause in the actual SELECT clause of the query. If you do this, the code looks like the following:

```
SELECT      MKX.MakeName, STX.RepairsCost, STX.StockCode
, (

    SELECT      AVG(ST.RepairsCost) AS AvgRepairCost

    FROM        Data.Make AS MK
    INNER JOIN Data.Model AS MD

                ON MK.MakeID = MD.MakeID

    INNER JOIN Data.Stock AS ST

                ON ST.ModelID = MD.ModelID

    WHERE       MK.MakeName = MKX.MakeName

  ) AS MakeAvgRepairCost


FROM        Data.Make AS MKX

INNER JOIN Data.Model AS MDX

            ON MKX.MakeID = MDX.MakeID

INNER JOIN Data.Stock AS STX ON STX.ModelID = MDX.ModelID

INNER JOIN Data.SalesDetails SDX ON STX.StockCode = SDX.StockID
```

```
WHERE        STX.RepairsCost >

             (

                 SELECT     AVG(ST.RepairsCost) AS AvgRepairCost

                 FROM       Data.Make AS MK

                 INNER JOIN Data.Model AS MD

                        ON MK.MakeID = MD.MakeID

                 INNER JOIN Data.Stock AS ST

                        ON ST.ModelID = MD.ModelID

                 WHERE      MK.MakeName = MKX.MakeName

             ) * 1.5
```

The output looks like that shown in Figure 4-5.

	MakeName	RepairsCost	StockCode	MakeAvgRepairCost
1	Porsche	1360.00	2189D556-D1C4-4BC1-B0C8-4053319E8E9D	848.0208
2	Aston Martin	2500.00	E6E6270A-60B0-4817-AA57-17F26B2B8DAF	1236.6666
3	Aston Martin	3250.00	CEDFB8D2-BD98-4A08-BC46-406D23940527	1236.6666
4	Aston Martin	1950.00	D63C8CC9-DB19-4B9C-9C8E-6C6370812041	1236.6666
5	Aston Martin	2175.00	18E980AB-452D-42EF-8728-12822AD20C60	1236.6666
6	Porsche	1360.00	3F3BED8D-1203-4D3E-8AC0-3ACAC73BDE17	848.0208
7	Lamborghini	5500.00	88AFBF67-13A6-4BC5-AE50-8C64F0F25453	3481.00
8	Porsche	2000.00	B165CAEF-FF77-4E63-98C1-59D97F97E7C9	848.0208
9	Alfa Romeo	1360.00	07F0D746-085B-4FB9-9F82-6CEAC851FBC3	673.0434
10	Jaguar	2000.00	8F278478-CA0B-4CDB-8F02-1A054AAE88A9	1002.9032
11	Porsche	1360.00	518125AE-9A67-45A6-B3FD-557C785796FC	848.0208
12	Ferrari	9250.00	66C9034C-23A3-44F1-B946-2DDA65E684D8	4645.00
13	Porsche	1490.00	E00D10E9-7F7F-49A9-BDC0-4C2611580B4E	848.0208
14	Porsche	1360.00	AAF61ECC-0BAC-4EAF-9E50-01749253329A	848.0208
15	Triumph	970.00	0B0E0FC2-E72B-4BD4-9C46-1AF98F17BEC4	628.1818

FIGURE 4-5. USING A CORRELATED QUERY IN TWO PARTS OF A QUERY

How It Works

This query extends the SQL from the previous section by repeating the entire content of the subquery in the main query's SELECT clause. Both the identical correlated subqueries are linked to the outer query using the MakeName field.

5.   **Aggregated Correlated Subqueries**

The sales director has appeared at your desk. She has a new challenge—a report that shows the top two customers per country by sales.

This kind of challenge proves that there are times when you need to look at multiple categories of data in order to get a better idea of the relative importance of certain data items. Isolating the top (or bottom) few records for a specific category is a case in point. The following SQL is an example of this—for each country, it isolates the top two customers:

```
SELECT     CUX.CustomerName

           ,CUX.Town

           ,COX.CountryName

FROM       Data.Customer CUX
INNER JOIN Data.Country COX ON CUX.Country = COX.CountryISO2
WHERE      CUX.CustomerID IN

                (

                SELECT     TOP (2) CU.CustomerID

                FROM       Data.Make AS MK

                INNER JOIN Data.Model AS MD

                           ON MK.MakeID = MD.MakeID

                INNER JOIN Data.Stock AS ST

                           ON ST.ModelID = MD.ModelID

                INNER JOIN Data.SalesDetails SD

                           ON ST.StockCode = SD.StockID

                INNER JOIN Data.Sales AS SA

                           ON SA.SalesID = SD.SalesID

                INNER JOIN Data.Customer CU
```

```
                          ON SA.CustomerID = CU.CustomerID

               INNER JOIN Data.Country CO

                          ON CU.Country = CO.CountryISO2

               WHERE      CUX.Country = CU.Country

               GROUP BY   CU.CustomerID

               ORDER BY   SUM(SD.SalePrice) DESC

               )

ORDER BY    COX.CountryName, CUX.CustomerName
```

Running this query gives the results that you can see in Figure 4-6.

	CustomerName	Town	CountryName
1	Diplomatic Cars	Brussels	Belgium
2	Stefan Van Helsing	Brussels	Belgium
3	Laurent Saint Yves	Marseille	France
4	Vive La Vitesse	Marseille	France
5	Glitz	Stuttgart	Germany
6	WunderKar	Berlin	Germany
7	Smooth Rocking Chrome	Milan	Italy
8	Stefano DiLonghi	Rome	Italy
9	Antonio Maura	Madrid	Spain
10	Prestige Imports	Barcelona	Spain
11	Le Luxe en Motion	Geneva	Switzerland
12	Matterhorn Motors	Lausanne	Switzerland
13	Honest Pete Motors	Stoke	United Kingdom
14	Magic Motors	Birmingham	United Kingdom
15	Sondra Horowitz	Los Angeles	United States

FIGURE 4-6. AN AGGREGATE CORRELATED SUBQUERY

How It Works

This example is an extension of the previous one, but if you look carefully, you see that the correlated subquery is an aggregate query—it uses the GROUP BY clause to find the top two customers by value per country. It does this by sorting the data in the subquery in descending order of sales.

Let's take a closer look at how this query works:

The outer query	Creates a list of customers by town and country. It does this by joining the Customer and Country tables.
The inner query	Then takes the country field for each customer and uses this as the filter for a query that joins the Make, Model, Stock, SalesDetails, Sales, Customer, and Country tables to obtain a complete dataset of sales information. This dataset groups the data using the CustomerID field to aggregate the total sales for each customer in the specific country that was passed in from the outer query. Because the correlated subquery orders the data by the sales amount, only the top two records are returned.
The outer query	Then detects whether the customer ID returned by the correlated subquery matches the customer for the record that is being analyzed. If it does, then the record from the outer query is displayed.

To resume, because the subquery is linked to the outer query on the Country field, it now finds the top two customers per country when the whole query is run. This is because, once again, the inner query runs once for each record in the outer query. Because the country field links the two queries, the inner query only aggregates customers per country.

Once the IDs of the top two customers by country have been identified by the subquery—and passed up to the outer query via its WHERE clause—the outer query can select all required fields and order the result just as you would for any standard query.

Note	It is important to remember that although the outer query is filtering on customer IDs, the *correlation* is on the country. This makes the point that the filter and the correlation can be completely separate.

Tricks and Traps

There are a few points that you may want to take note of when using aggregated correlated subqueries:

- A correlated subquery can be an aggregate query if your query logic requires it to be so. This is also the case for ordinary subqueries. In this respect, the outer and inner queries are structurally independent. Either can be a simple detail query or an aggregate query, no matter what type the other query is.

- Because the correlated subquery is passing two elements back to the outer query for each make of car, it is important to use the IN operator for the outer query WHERE clause, and not the equal (=) operator. Remember that you can only use the equal operator if a *single value* is used in a WHERE clause.

- This example shows that the inner and outer queries can be quite different query types. However, they do share a field that allows them to be linked as well as some way of using the result from the subquery to filter the outer query, and this is all that is really necessary to create a correlated subquery.

6. Using Correlated Subqueries to Filter Data on an Aggregate Value

No firm wants to spend too much when buying goods, so it follows that you have to be able to analyze purchases that exceed certain calculated thresholds. As the finance director is homing in on purchasing costs as part of his drive to control spending, he wants you to create a report that shows all models of car where the maximum purchase cost is more than one and a half times the average purchase price for that model. The following SQL is an example of how to do this:

```
SELECT      MKX.MakeName, MDX.ModelName

FROM        Data.Make AS MKX

            INNER JOIN Data.Model AS MDX ON MKX.MakeID = MDX.MakeID

            INNER JOIN Data.Stock AS STX ON STX.ModelID = MDX.ModelID

GROUP BY    MKX.MakeName, MDX.ModelName

HAVING      MAX(STX.Cost) >=

                (

                SELECT      AVG(ST.Cost) * 1.5 AS AvgCostPerModel

                FROM        Data.Make AS MK

                INNER JOIN Data.Model AS MD

                    ON MK.MakeID = MD.MakeID

                INNER JOIN Data.Stock AS ST

                    ON ST.ModelID = MD.ModelID
```

```
WHERE       MD.ModelName = MDX.ModelName

            AND MK.MakeName = MKX. MakeName

    )
```

Running this query gives the results that you can see in Figure 4-7.

	MakeName	ModelName
1	Peugeot	205
2	Mercedes	280SL
3	Peugeot	404
4	Porsche	911
5	Porsche	924
6	Porsche	944
7	Lamborghini	Countach
8	Aston Martin	DB2
9	Aston Martin	DB6
10	Aston Martin	DB9
11	Alfa Romeo	Giulia
12	Alfa Romeo	Giulietta
13	Austin	Lichfield
14	Jaguar	Mark X
15	Rolls Royce	Phantom

FIGURE 4-7. USING A CORRELATED SUBQUERY IN THE HAVING CLAUSE OF THE OUTER QUERY

How It Works

For a change, let's begin by looking at the outer query in this example.

The outer query generates a list of vehicle makes and models based on the Make, Model, and Stock tables. It uses a GROUP BY to make this into an aggregate list where the make and model name only appear once.

Then the outer query gets interesting. Since it is an aggregate query, it can have a HAVING clause (if you remember, this clause filters data at the level of the aggregation, not at the level of individual records). It applies a HAVING clause to say, "only if the maximum cost for any make and model is greater than or equal to 150 percent of the average cost for this make and model."

It is the correlated subquery that calculates 150 percent of the average cost. Yet again, since this is a correlated subquery, it is filtered on data passed in from the outer query—in this case, the make and model. The subquery calculates the average cost for a specific make and model, then multiplies it by 1.5. This result is, in turn, passed back up to the outer query so it can be compared to the greatest vehicle cost for each make and model combination. Finally, the comparison operator (>=, or greater than or equal to) allows *only those records that meet the filter criterion* to pass through into the final output. That is, only makes and models are shown if any car of this type costs more than one and a half times the average for that particular car.

Tricks and Traps

There are only a couple of points to take away from this section:

- Correlated subqueries are, at their heart, a filtering mechanism, so you need to analyze what kind of filter you are looking for. If you are filtering data row by row, then you will probably use the correlated subquery in the WHERE clause. If, however, you are filtering records to compare a value with an aggregate result (such as the maximum cost for a vehicle model here), then you will almost inevitably want to apply the correlated subquery to the HAVING clause of the outer query.

- If the outer query is an aggregation query, then you can use any of the classic aggregation functions—SUM(), AVG(), MIN(), or MAX(), for instance—in the HAVING clause. This allows you to compare a result from the subquery to the total, the average, the highest, or the lowest aggregate value for a specific data group.

7. Using Correlated Subqueries to Detect If Records Exist

"Know your customer" is the mantra that resounds throughout businesses across every continent. For many firms, however, the refrain could just as well be "know who your customer is." The following SQL shows you how to create a list of all the active clients of Prestige Cars in 2017:

```
SELECT DISTINCT    CU.CustomerName

FROM               Data.Customer CU

WHERE              EXISTS

                   (

                     SELECT    *

                     FROM      Data.Sales SA

                     WHERE     SA.CustomerID = CU.CustomerID

                               AND YEAR(SA.SaleDate) = 2017

                   )

ORDER BY           CU.CustomerName
```

The list that you can see in Figure 4-8 shows only the customers that have bought a vehicle from Prestige Cars in a specific year—2017, in this example. Any potential customer in the Customer table who did *not* buy a car in 2017 is not displayed.

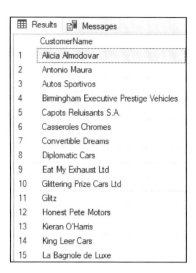

FIGURE 4-8. A SIMPLE CORRELATED SUBQUERY USING EXISTS

How It Works

Correlated subqueries are not just for calculations. They can also be very useful in determining whether data should be included in a result set. In practice, what this means is that you need to apply the EXISTS keyword to the query. When you use this new keyword, the outer query checks to see if any records exist for this specific customer ID. If one does, then the customer name is output. The flip side to this is that if *no records exist* then data for this customer is *not* displayed.

This means that *if* the correlated subquery contains any records for this particular CustomerID, then the customer name is returned by the outer query. This is because the filter in the outer query says, "Where a record exists in the inner query." If there is no corresponding record in the correlated subquery, then no customer name is output. This way the query as a whole only returns data from one dataset when a criterion applied to a second set of data is met.

Tricks and Traps

When using correlated subqueries, you need to be aware that

- Correlated subqueries depend on a link existing between the inner and outer queries, so, if you can use a JOIN to link tables in a query, then you can use the same tables in a correlated subquery.

- When you use the EXISTS keyword, you are looking simply for the existence of a record in the subquery. This means that you can make the SELECT clause of the correlated subquery really simple and not even specify any particular column names. After all, column names in the subquery will not be used in this type of correlated subquery since you are only looking to see if records exist.

- You have already seen queries in the previous two chapters that compare data in tables. However, the use of correlated subqueries is specifically tailored to tables that can be joined.

8. Using a Correlated Subquery to Exclude Data

No business wants to carry excess stock. Consequently, we are sure that you understand why the company finance director wants to know which vehicles have not yet been sold and are paralyzing valuable cash in the parking lot. The following SQL code shows you how to produce this list for him:

```
SELECT      MakeName + ', ' + ModelName AS VehicleInStock, ST.STOCKCODE

FROM        Data.Make AS MK

INNER JOIN Data.Model AS MD ON MK.MakeID = MD.MakeID

INNER JOIN Data.Stock AS ST ON ST.ModelID = MD.ModelID

WHERE       NOT EXISTS

                    (SELECT   *

                     FROM     Data.SalesDetails SD

                     WHERE    ST.StockCode = SD.StockID)
```

What Makes a Query Correlated?

A correlated query is not one query, but two interdependent queries. The inner query is filtered on a field that it shares with the outer query. The outer query filters its results based on the calculation carried out by the inner query.

Each query, then, uses something shared with the other query as a filter. Each record in the outer query passes a value into the subquery (often for some kind of calculation). The outer query only returns rows that match the results of the inner query.

This mutual interdependence can appear complicated at first. In practice, however, it opens up whole vistas of analysis that would be difficult any other way.

Running this query gives the results that you can see in Figure 4-9. You can see all the results if you scroll down this list.

	VehicleInStock	STOCKCODE
1	Ferrari, Testarossa	DE3096AD-76F9-4AAF-B2E1-49FA8E2C377F
2	Ferrari, Testarossa	8BD326B3-8DE8-4DC9-9F96-FD132C5E1BF2
3	Ferrari, 355	C82D133F-3442-464B-A16A-D5419A9E1CDF
4	Ferrari, 308	FBF39066-2C13-469D-B913-EBCF22CCFD63
5	Ferrari, Dino	F187F74F-3909-4291-A15B-F793AB88DE3B
6	Ferrari, 360	579AD98F-B7A5-456A-8F17-5B77A5479767
7	Porsche, 944	74F717DA-B4DA-44F2-857A-F062AC60052E
8	Porsche, 944	52F665EA-2D6D-4ECA-8A14-553522A45B04
9	Aston Martin, DB2	62611547-0F2D-41B1-BA32-E34AB67E10A3
10	Aston Martin, DB2	532B985F-94AC-45DF-AE17-431FBCC66D0C
11	Aston Martin, DB2	51451AC8-A35F-4597-B4BC-94E92C150C3D
12	Aston Martin, DB4	4831A9DA-09BD-4AC3-8984-947F284CD4A8
13	Aston Martin, DB5	2309FF52-564A-4A2C-B6EB-D94AA321D687
14	Aston Martin, DB6	26A3D067-DCEA-4FF1-9A97-E7AEE0D2BC14
15	Aston Martin, DB6	373B7D39-B5A3-4018-883C-AC81EF3B5D8F

FIGURE 4-9. A CORRELATED SUBQUERY USING NOT EXISTS

How It Works

Just as you may need to know when data exists (as was the case in the previous example), there could be cases when you need to find out when data is *not* present in related tables. In the Prestige Cars data model, the Stock table contains all the vehicles ever bought. The SalesDetails table contains all the vehicles ever sold. A correlated subquery can compare the data in one table with the data in the other.

When you want to run this kind of analysis, it is probably easier to use the table that contains the most data as the outer query and the table that contains a mode-limited set of data as the correlated (or inner) subquery. The code above does exactly this.

The outer query	Joins the Make, Model, and Stock tables so that the required fields can be output—as well as ensuring access to a field that can be shared with the subquery (the StockCode field in this example).
The inner query	Selects all the data from the SalesDetails table, but as this is a correlated subquery, it only finds records where the StockID matches the StockCode of the outer query.

Once again, the subquery is rerun for every record that the outer query finds. If there is a match on the StockCode/StockID fields, then the WHERE clause of the outer query comes into play. This filter says, "tell me if there is not a match," which is the colloquial way of saying WHERE NOT EXISTS. If the two tables do *not match* for a record in the outer query, this record is returned by the query.

Tricks and Traps

It takes a little practice to successfully use the NOT EXISTS function, so when you are applying this concept to your queries, be sure to remember the following key points:

- A correlated subquery that uses NOT EXISTS is also only looking for the existence of data in the subquery—the actual fields selected by the subquery are irrelevant.

- A correlated subquery like this can run much more slowly than a simpler query does. This should not worry you; it is precisely because the inner query has to run once for every record in the outer query. However, you need to be aware that a query like this can take quite a while to run for a large dataset.

9.   Complex Joins in Correlated Subqueries

Diligent purchasing can require an in-depth knowledge of your products, so it follows that the buyers for Prestige Cars want to track any vehicles that seem unduly expensive compared to similar models. The following piece of SQL helps you keep tabs on your costs by listing all makes where the maximum purchase cost is over twice the average purchase cost for that make for the year:

```
SELECT      MKX.MakeName, YEAR(STX.DateBought) AS PurchaseYear

FROM        Data.Make AS MKX INNER JOIN Data.Model AS MDX

            ON MKX.MakeID = MDX.MakeID

            INNER JOIN Data.Stock AS STX ON STX.ModelID = MDX.ModelID

WHERE       YEAR(STX.DateBought) IN (2015, 2016)

GROUP BY    MKX.MakeName, YEAR(STX.DateBought)

HAVING      MAX(STX.Cost) >=

                    (

                        SELECT   AVG(ST.Cost) * 2 AS AvgCostPerModel

                        FROM     Data.Make AS MK

                                 INNER JOIN Data.Model AS MD

                                 ON MK.MakeID = MD.MakeID

                                 INNER JOIN Data.Stock AS ST

                                 ON ST.ModelID = MD.ModelID

                        WHERE    MK.MakeName = MKX.MakeName

                                 AND YEAR(ST.DateBought)

                                     = YEAR(STX.DateBought)

                    )
```

Running this query gives the results that you can see in Figure 4-10.

	MakeName	PurchaseYear
1	Aston Martin	2015
2	Aston Martin	2016
3	Bentley	2016
4	Jaguar	2016
5	Lamborghini	2016
6	Porsche	2016

FIGURE 4-10. A CORRELATED SUBQUERY WITH A COMPLEX JOIN

How It Works

Some questions require you to be more restrictive in your analysis. You might want to add multiple elements to the calculated comparison, not just one, as was the case in the previous couple of examples. Correlated subqueries allow you to join the inner and outer queries on more than one field. Consequently, this query *also* calculates an average value for a subset of data. This time the value that is passed in to the correlated subquery from the outer query is a calculation—double the average cost for each make. This figure is then compared to the aggregate maximum cost per make in the HAVING clause of the outer query.

What makes this query a little subtler is the use of a more complex link between the outer and inner queries. This time there are two elements:

- The make of vehicle
- The year that the car was bought

A double connection like this has the effect of limiting the comparison even further. Now it is the *maximum cost per make per year* that is used as the comparison element. The net result is that certain makes of car can appear in the final result more than once, because at least one item in stock costs more than twice the average for that make in more than a single year.

The outer query also adds a filter in the form of a WHERE clause. Since the field that is used in the WHERE clause is also used to join the outer query to the correlated subquery, the choice of years is applied in *both* queries, even though it is only added *once*—to the outer query.

Tricks and Traps

When applying complex joins you need to take away a fundamental point concerning correlated subqueries:

- Being able to join the inner and outer queries on several fields is, in fact, a powerful tool for simplifying certain types of analysis. In Chapter 1, you saw that if you filtered an ordinary query that contained a subquery, you *also* had to filter the subquery in certain cases to get the result that you wanted. If you are filtering the outer query on a field that is used to create the correlation between the two queries, then you are automatically applying the WHERE clause of the outer query to the inner query. This avoids repetition—and minimizes the risk of error.

10. Using a Correlated Subquery to Verify Values across Tables

No organization wants erroneous data. This is especially true where invoices are concerned. Fortunately SQL is a perfect tool when it comes to data validation. Specifically, let's suppose that you want to check that invoice header totals correspond to invoice line aggregation. The following short piece of SQL shows how to do this:

```
SELECT      SalesID

            ,TotalSalePrice

            ,CASE WHEN

                  (

                      SELECT SUM(SalePrice)

                      FROM    Data.SalesDetails

                      WHERE   SalesID = Data.Sales.SalesID

                  ) = TotalSalePrice

                        THEN 'OK'

                        ELSE 'Error in Invoice'

                  END AS LineItemCheck

FROM        Data.Sales
```

Running this query gives the results that you can see in Figure 4-11.

	SalesID	TotalSalePrice	LineItemCheck
1	1	65000.00	OK
2	2	220000.10	Error in Invoice
3	3	19500.00	OK
4	4	11500.00	OK
5	5	19900.00	Error in Invoice
6	6	29500.00	OK
7	7	49500.20	Error in Invoice
8	8	76000.90	Error in Invoice
9	9	19600.00	OK
10	10	36500.00	OK
11	11	89000.00	OK
12	12	169500.00	OK
13	13	8950.00	OK
14	14	195000.00	OK
15	15	22950.00	OK

FIGURE 4-11. USING A CORRELATED SUBQUERY TO VERIFY VALUES ACROSS TABLES

How It Works

Despite the best efforts of programmers and data entry staff everywhere, errors can creep into data. Fortunately, SQL can also carry out automated checks and balances on your data. This code works because the two tables that it uses—Sales and SalesDetails—are part of a relational structure. More specifically, the Sales table is in a one-to-many relationship with the SalesDetails table. That is, several sales details records can be linked to a single Sales record. What is more, the Sales table contains a field—Sale-Price—that should contain the total sales value of all the corresponding detail records for that particular sale in the SalesDetails table.

This query begins with a subquery that returns the sum of the SalePrice for the SalesDetails table. However, to prevent the query from merely returning the total for every record, a correlation is set up between the subquery and an outer query that lists the SalePrice for every record in the Sales table. This forces the inner query to calculate only the total sales for the records that are linked to the Sales table.

The trick in this query is how the output from the correlated subquery is used. Rather than just returning the total sales for each sale from the SalesDetails table, this aggregate figure is compared—using a CASE statement—with the sales figure from the Sales table. If the two are identical, the query returns "OK." Should they not match, it returns "Error in Invoice."

This way the query can verify that the data is as it should be, and if not, bring any erroneous records to your attention for further investigation.

Conclusion

This short chapter introduced you to a new tool to extend your SQL skillset—correlated subqueries. Correlated subqueries let you link subqueries to main queries and filter the data in the outer query by checking every record that it contains against the result of a subquery.

Core Knowledge Learned in This Chapter

The keywords and concepts that you have seen in this chapter are

Concept	Description
Correlated subqueries	*Correlated subqueries let you link subqueries to main queries and filter the data in the outer query by checking every record that it contains against the result of a subquery.*
EXISTS	*This keyword tests for the existence of a record in a subquery that is linked to the outer query.*
NOT EXISTS	*This keyword tests for the absence of a record in a subquery that is linked to the outer query.*

Chapter 5:
Joining and Filtering Datasets

Sometimes that data that you use may not be in a single table (as you might expect it to be) but can be spread across a series of tables with identical structures. Moreover, since much data analysis is comparative, you may want to compare one specific set of data with another and isolate any differences. You can accomplish this by seeing if two sets of data overlap, for instance. Yet another potential requirement can consist of isolating the data that exists in one dataset but not in another. These challenges involve handling entire datasets.

Using Datasets to Mix and Match Data

This short chapter takes you further into the domain of comparative analysis of data using SQL Server. It builds on the techniques that you saw in the previous chapters and teaches you how to mix and match datasets in order to delve deep into the information they contain.

More specifically, in this chapter you learn how to

- Read data from several identically structured tables simultaneously.

- Create separate subsets of data that you can use for comparison purposes.

- Compare the data in two tables and only display data that is common to both tables.

- Compare the data in two tables and only display data that is in one table but not the other.

1. Read Data from Multiple Identical Tables Using the UNION Operator

Data comes in a multitude of shapes and forms and is not always available as a relational set of tables that can be joined. Sometimes you may have to query data from two or more tables that have identical structures—meaning each table contains a slice of a total dataset. As an example of this, imagine that you have been asked to look at *three tables* of sales information, one for sales in each of the years 2015, 2016, and 2017. All three tables contain the *same columns of data in the same order*.

The SQL to query the three tables at once looks like this:

```
SELECT   MakeName, ModelName, CustomerName, CountryName

         ,Cost, RepairsCost, PartsCost, TransportInCost

         ,SalePrice, SaleDate

FROM     DataTransfer.Sales2015

UNION

SELECT   MakeName, ModelName, CustomerName, CountryName

         ,Cost, RepairsCost, PartsCost, TransportInCost

         ,SalePrice, SaleDate

FROM     DataTransfer.Sales2016

UNION

SELECT   MakeName, ModelName, CustomerName, CountryName

         ,Cost, RepairsCost, PartsCost, TransportInCost

         ,SalePrice, SaleDate

FROM     DataTransfer.Sales2017
```

Running this query gives the results in Figure 5-1. As you can see, the data is returned for any of the three years, whereas each table only contains data for a single year.

	MakeName	ModelName	CustomerName	CountryName	Cost	RepairsCost	PartsCost	TransportInCost	SalePrice	SaleDate
1	Alfa Romeo	Giulia	Convertible Dreams	United Kingdom	6956.00	400.00	750.00	150.00	8695.00	2015-07-12 00:00:00.000
2	Alfa Romeo	Giulia	Convertible Dreams	United Kingdom	20000.00	1360.00	750.00	150.00	25000.00	2017-11-01 00:00:00.000
3	Alfa Romeo	Giulia	Glitz	Germany	4800.00	500.00	750.00	150.00	6000.00	2016-02-17 00:00:00.000
4	Alfa Romeo	Giulia	Jason B. Wight	United States	10000.00	500.00	750.00	150.00	12500.00	2016-07-06 00:00:00.000
5	Alfa Romeo	Giulia	M. Pierre Dubois	France	2040.00	500.00	750.00	150.00	2550.00	2016-01-07 00:00:00.000
6	Alfa Romeo	Giulia	Silver HubCaps	United Kingdom	14000.00	1360.00	750.00	150.00	17500.00	2016-04-30 00:00:00.000
7	Alfa Romeo	Giulia	Stefan Van Helsing	Belgium	8400.00	500.00	750.00	150.00	10500.00	2017-11-06 00:00:00.000
8	Alfa Romeo	Giulietta	Prestissimo!	Italy	5200.00	500.00	750.00	150.00	6500.00	2017-05-16 00:00:00.000
9	Alfa Romeo	Giulietta	Screamin' Wheels	United States	17200.00	500.00	500.00	150.00	21500.00	2017-02-09 00:00:00.000
10	Alfa Romeo	Spider	King Leer Cars	United Kingdom	4520.00	500.00	750.00	150.00	5650.00	2017-06-22 00:00:00.000
11	Alfa Romeo	Spider	Mme Anne Duport	France	9200.00	500.00	750.00	150.00	11500.00	2017-11-12 00:00:00.000
12	Alfa Romeo	Spider	Stefan Van Helsing	Belgium	10000.00	500.00	750.00	150.00	12500.00	2017-07-01 00:00:00.000
13	Alfa Romeo	Spider	Wonderland Wheels	United Kingdom	10000.00	500.00	750.00	150.00	12500.00	2016-04-30 00:00:00.000
14	Aston Martin	DB2	Glitz	Germany	36000.00	500.00	750.00	550.00	45000.00	2017-05-24 00:00:00.000
15	Aston Martin	DB2	Ronaldo Bianco	Italy	49200.00	1360.00	750.00	550.00	61500.00	2017-05-10 00:00:00.000

FIGURE 5-1. JOINING DATA FROM MULTIPLE IDENTICALLY STRUCTURED QUERIES USING THE UNION OPERATOR

How It Works

SQL lets you read data from multiple tables at once if—and only if—the structure of the queries is identical. You carry out this operation by writing a SELECT query for each table and then by amalgamating the queries using the UNION operator.

Clearly using UNION to merge the data from several tables is only useful if you have a database that contains identically structured tables. Because this is often the case for data analysis and reporting (where the original, relational data is kept separate) or when dealing with data sent from outside suppliers, you could find this technique useful in practice.

In this example, you joined the three tables sequentially (or "vertically") rather than "horizontally," as you have done in many queries so far in this book. Put another way, you have added the contents of one table to the contents of another. Figure 5-2 illustrates conceptually what you have done.

FIGURE 5-2. COMPILING A DATASET FROM MULTIPLE IDENTICAL TABLES

Tricks and Traps

Although simple enough, the UNION operator does require you to remember that

- You can use aliases to rename the columns in a UNION query just as you can in an SQL query; however, you only need to add aliases to the *first query* in the series—that is, the query for 2015 sales in this example. The other queries use the aliases that you applied to the topmost query. After all, a column can only have one name, so the name is taken from the topmost query.

- In a UNION query, it is vital that you select the columns from each of the separate queries in the same order.

- If the underlying tables are not identical, you can replace the name of any columns that are missing from a table with NULL in the SELECT statement. For instance, if the table Sales2016 does not contain a TransportInCost field, you can write the following SQL so that the query over the three tables will still work:

```
SELECT  MakeName, ModelName, CustomerName, CountryName, Cost,
RepairsCost, PartsCost, NULL, SalePrice, SaleDate
```

2. Isolate Identical Data in Multiple Tables Using the INTERSECT Operator

The sales director needs to compare elements that are similar across separate time periods. Her exact requirement is to find all the makes bought this year that were also bought the previous year. The following query does exactly this, using the separate tables of yearly sales that you saw in the previous section:

```
SELECT      MK.MakeName

FROM        Data.Make AS MK

INNER JOIN Data.Model AS MD ON MK.MakeID = MD.MakeID

INNER JOIN Data.Stock AS ST ON ST.ModelID = MD.ModelID

WHERE       YEAR(DateBought) = 2015


INTERSECT

SELECT      MK.MakeName

FROM        Data.Make AS MK

INNER JOIN Data.Model AS MD ON MK.MakeID = MD.MakeID

INNER JOIN Data.Stock AS ST ON ST.ModelID = MD.ModelID

WHERE       YEAR(DateBought) = 2016
```

Running this query gives the results that you can see in Figure 5-3.

	MakeName
1	Alfa Romeo
2	Aston Martin
3	Bentley
4	Ferrari
5	Jaguar
6	Porsche
7	Triumph

FIGURE 5-3. USING THE INTERSECT OPERATOR

How It Works

In this query you actually have two separate queries:

The first	Joins the Stock, Make, and Model tables and adds only the MakeName field to the SELECT clause. This query then filters the results so that *only vehicles bought in 2015* are returned.
The second	Duplicates the first query, but it sets the year to *2016*.

Combining these two queries with the INTERSECT operator runs both queries and then identifies which results are common to both. Only these shared results are finally output.

A Venn diagram (see Figure 5-4) can help you better understand how an INTERSECT query works.

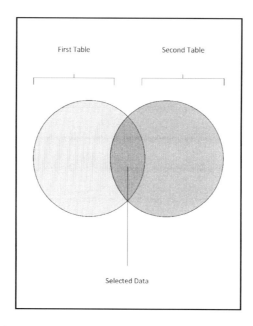

FIGURE 5-4. HOW AN INTERSECT QUERY WORKS

Tricks and Traps

As you might imagine, there are several key points to note with an operator as powerful as INTERSECT:

- The two queries in this example are not, technically, subqueries, since they are both on the same "level." Consequently, they do not have to be placed inside parentheses. However, they are completely separate datasets—just like subqueries.

- You can see that an INTERSECT query automatically removes any duplicates in the final result. If you run each query separately, you see that many examples of each make are sold in either of the two years (this is shown in Figure 5-5); however, the final result removes all duplicates from the output.

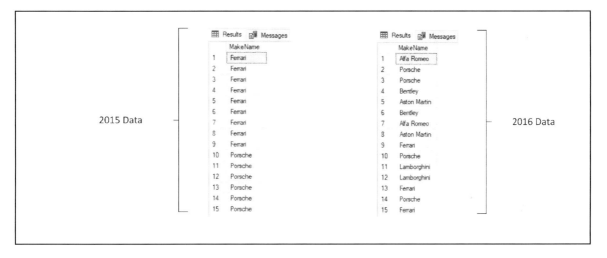

FIGURE 5-5. DUPLICATE DATA BEFORE IT IS REMOVED USING THE INTERSECT OPERATOR

- An INTERSECT query *must have the same fields in the same order in the SELECT clause.* If this is not the case, it does not return the correct result— or, indeed (in most cases), any result at all. In all other respects queries can be completely different, as long as they return the datasets that you want to compare.

- You are not limited to just two queries in an INTERSECT query. You can add multiple queries—all linked with the INTERSECT keyword—if you need to.

- You do not have to select *all* the fields that are in each table to isolate data; however, any fields that you *do* select must be identical in all the source tables if the record is to be returned.

3. Isolating Nonidentical Records Using the EXCEPT Operator

Sometimes it is not overlap of data that interests you but the data that is *not* shared between two datasets. A practical example of this is when the CEO requests a list of all the vehicle models sold this year but not in the previous year. The following SQL shows you how to isolate this kind of result:

```
SELECT      MK.MakeName + ' ' + MD.ModelName AS MakeModel

FROM        Data.Make AS MK

INNER JOIN Data.Model AS MD ON MK.MakeID = MD.MakeID

INNER JOIN Data.Stock AS ST ON ST.ModelID = MD.ModelID

INNER JOIN Data.SalesDetails SD ON ST.StockCode = SD.StockID

INNER JOIN Data.Sales AS SA ON SA.SalesID = SD.SalesID

WHERE       YEAR(SaleDate) = 2015

EXCEPT

SELECT      MK.MakeName + ' ' + MD.ModelName

FROM        Data.Make AS MK

INNER JOIN Data.Model AS MD ON MK.MakeID = MD.MakeID

INNER JOIN Data.Stock AS ST ON ST.ModelID = MD.ModelID

INNER JOIN Data.SalesDetails SD ON ST.StockCode = SD.StockID

INNER JOIN Data.Sales AS SA ON SA.SalesID = SD.SalesID

WHERE       YEAR(SaleDate) = 2016
```

Running this query gives the results that you can see in Figure 5-6.

FIGURE 5-6. USING THE EXCEPT OPERATOR TO ISOLATE DATA

How It Works

This query is similar in certain respects to the queries that you saw in the two previous examples. Once again, you have multiple queries that output identical field sets in the same order. This time, however, the EXCEPT operator is used to link the datasets returned by the individual queries.

This operator finds all the elements (the make and model of vehicles sold in a specific year) and then compares these rows with the make and model of vehicles sold the following year. Any models of car that are present in *both datasets* are *left out of the final result*. This way you can see which cars were sold in 2015 but not in 2016.

Figure 5-7 shows you, conceptually, how this approach works.

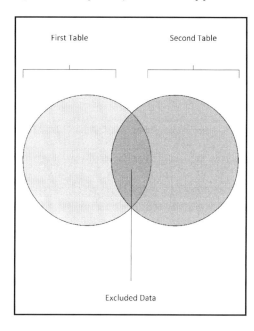

FIGURE 5-7. EXCLUDING THE SHARED ITEMS FROM TWO SETS OF DATA

Tricks and Traps

We have only one comment to make here:

- The two queries used in this example are, once again, completely separate. Indeed, they have to be different for the query to work properly. Consequently, each query has its own WHERE clause, and this is what allows you to specify completely different datasets, even if the two queries are otherwise identical.

4. Joining Multiple Identical Tables in a Subquery

The CEO has gone back to the sales data that you joined together in the first section of this chapter and is now requesting that you produce a simple list of makes and models from all three tables that were sold to German clients.

After a little thought, you adapt the query that you used previously to satisfy her request. The SQL looks like this:

```
SELECT   MakeName, ModelName
FROM
(
    SELECT   MakeName, ModelName, CustomerName, CountryName, Cost
    ,RepairsCost, PartsCost, TransportInCost, SalePrice, SaleDate
    FROM     DataTransfer.Sales2015

    UNION

    SELECT   MakeName, ModelName, CustomerName, CountryName, Cost
    ,RepairsCost, PartsCost, TransportInCost, SalePrice, SaleDate
    FROM     DataTransfer.Sales2016

    UNION

    SELECT   MakeName, ModelName, CustomerName, CountryName, Cost
    ,RepairsCost, PartsCost, TransportInCost, SalePrice, SaleDate
    FROM     DataTransfer.Sales2017
) SQ
WHERE    CountryName = 'Germany'
```

Running this code produces the output that you can see in Figure 5-8.

	MakeName	ModelName
1	Alfa Romeo	Giulia
2	Aston Martin	DB2
3	Aston Martin	DB9
4	Aston Martin	Rapide
5	Austin	Lichfield
6	Bentley	Flying Spur
7	Ferrari	360
8	Lamborghini	Diabolo
9	Lamborghini	Jarama
10	Porsche	924
11	Porsche	944

FIGURE 5-8. USING A DERIVED QUERY WITH TABLES JOINED USING THE UNION OPERATOR

How It Works

The ability of SQL to deliver the output from multiple identical tables is certainly useful in many occasions; however, you need a way to make the resulting data easy to filter. Moreover, undoubtedly you will have times when you want to select only some of the columns that each table contains.

This is a perfect opportunity for wrapping the UNION query inside an outer query and treating the UNION query as a derived table. This simple technique allows you to select only the fields that you require, then filter the data using a single WHERE clause, and even group the data if you so choose.

Tricks and Traps

We have only a couple of comments to make here:

- It is perfectly possible to apply the same SELECT and WHERE clauses to each query that is used in a UNION query. However, this can be both more laborious and more error-prone than making the UNION query into a derived table.

- Extending a query to include a derived table is a great example of code reuse, where just a small tweak can make SQL that you created previously even more applicable, so remember to save your code snippets in case they turn out to be important at a later date.

Conclusion

Despite being brief, this chapter helped you to extend your knowledge of the way that data analysis in SQL Server depends on using datasets correctly. You saw how to filter separate datasets individually in order to effect comparisons over time as well as combine multiple tables to create a single result set.

Finally, you saw how to extract overlapping data from two tables. Then you discovered how to do the opposite and return data that is present in one table but not in another.

Core Knowledge Learned in This Chapter

The concepts that you have seen in this chapter are

Concept	Description
UNION	*This operator lets you pull data from multiple tables or views that are identical in structure.*
INTERSECT	*This operator returns a subset of data that is common to two tables or views.*
EXCEPT	*This operator returns a subset of data that is present in one table or view, but not in another.*

Chapter 6:
Using SQL for More Advanced Calculations

In the first part of this book you saw how to perform elementary math on the data in a SQL Server database. Although SQL is not a language that is designed to carry out advanced mathematical calculations, it can go much further than the simple addition, subtraction, division, and multiplication that you have seen previously. However, these more advanced calculations also require you to understand more completely how SQL handles numbers.

Additional Calculation Techniques

The aim of this chapter is to extend your skills when it comes to performing essential math with SQL Server. This does not mean that you will be following a math course in SQL. Instead we take a more real-world approach and show you how SQL Server deals with numbers internally. Initially this means showing you how to ensure that SQL accepts data as being numeric. This may be necessary because what appears to be a number to us humans may not be interpreted as a numeric value by SQL. Making sure that numbers are correctly handled will help you to write robust SQL that can handle potentially unpleasant surprises and deliver the results that you expect to see. After you learn this, you begin learning to use SQL to write more complex formulas to analyze your data.

In this chapter you will learn how to

- Ensure that you are using the appropriate data types in certain types of calculation.
- Understand numeric data types.
- Remove currency symbols from source data so that you can calculate columns that are not "pure" numbers.
- Handle divide-by-zero errors.

- Use calculated columns several times in a SQL snippet—without having to copy the calculation.

- Test for errors in SQL calculations—and deal with them—so that your queries do not fail, but perform the appropriate calculation where this is feasible.

This chapter is for you, then, if you want to extend the results of your analysis with some more complex calculation techniques. It gives you the confidence to deliver sound and accurate metrics to enhance your analysis with SQL.

1. Calculating the Percentage Represented by Each Record in a Dataset

All businesses like repeat customers, so it is perfectly understandable that the CEO of Prestige Cars wants to know what percentage of individual sales can be attributed to each client. The following SQL does this for you:

```
SELECT        CustomerName

              , FORMAT (

                      CAST(COUNT(CustomerName) AS NUMERIC)

                      / (SELECT CAST(COUNT(*) AS NUMERIC)

                         FROM Data.Sales)

                      , '0.00 %')

              AS PercentageSalesPerCustomer

FROM          Data.Sales SA

INNER JOIN    Data.Customer CU

              ON CU.CustomerID = SA.CustomerID

GROUP BY      CustomerName

ORDER BY      CustomerName
```

Running this query gives the results that you can see in Figure 6-1. If you scroll down the list, you will see all the customers and the percentage of individual sales for each one. Moreover, if you add up all the percentage sales per customer, you will find that the total is 100 percent.

	CustomerName	PercentageSalesPerCustomer
1	Alex McWhirter	0.31 %
2	Alexei Tolstoi	2.47 %
3	Alicia Almodovar	2.16 %
4	Andrea Tarbuck	0.62 %
5	Andy Cheshire	0.62 %
6	Antonio Maura	1.85 %
7	Autos Sportivos	0.31 %
8	Beltway Prestige Driving	0.62 %
9	Birmingham Executive Prestige Vehicles	1.85 %
10	Bling Bling S.A.	0.31 %
11	Bling Motors	0.93 %
12	Boris Spry	0.62 %
13	Bravissima!	0.62 %
14	Capots Reluisants S.A.	1.85 %
15	Casseroles Chromes	1.23 %

FIGURE 6-1. CONVERTING INTEGERS TO THE NUMERIC DATA TYPE WITH THE CAST() FUNCTION

How It Works

Given the SQL experience that you have acquired by now, we imagine that this query is not too hard to understand. Indeed, you might even be wondering exactly what is so "advanced" about it. Take a closer look; this query should draw your attention to an apparently minor point that we first looked at briefly in *Volume I*.

After joining the Sales and Customer tables, you group on the CustomerName field to see a record for each customer. Then you select

First:	The customer name.
Second:	The number of records for each customer. This is done using the COUNT() function.
Then:	You create a subquery to calculate the total number of records in the joined table set.
Finally:	You divide the number of sales (or records representing an individual sale) by the total number of sales to give the percentage of individual sales per customer. To make the result more instantly comprehensible, this is formatted as a percentage.

So far, so good, you are probably thinking. Yet this query performs one extra step over and above the basic counts and math. It also forces the results of each calculation to be output as a NUMERIC data type. This is done using the CAST() function, which specifies that the data is converted to a NUMERIC data type.

Here is the reason for this: when SQL uses the COUNT() function, it returns the figures for both the sales per customer and the overall sales as *integers*—or whole numbers if you prefer. This is logical in that a total number of records is never anything other than a whole number (fractions of records simply do not exist). However, this means that when SQL Server divides the sales per customer by the overall sales, it *also returns an integer*. This is because using an integer data type in a calculation forces all other numeric data to be treated as integers—no matter what the precise data type is that has been defined in the database. Given that the result of this calculation is always less than 1, the output simply cannot be displayed accurately, even if the calculation is performed correctly. In this case, as the resulting percentage is less than 1, a 0 is returned. So if you do not use the CAST() function, and instead use a query like this,

```
COUNT(CustomerName) / (SELECT COUNT(*) FROM Data.Sales)
```

SQL Server gives the results that you can see in Figure 6-2.

	CustomerName	PercentageSalesPerCustomer
1	Alex McWhirter	0.00 %
2	Alexei Tolstoi	0.00 %
3	Alicia Almodovar	0.00 %
4	Andrea Tarbuck	0.00 %
5	Andy Cheshire	0.00 %

FIGURE 6-2. DIVIDING BY INTEGERS

We are sure that you will agree that this result is extremely disconcerting. The upshot is that, when calculating ratios, you *must* cast any field or function that uses integers to a data type that accepts decimals. By far the easiest way to do this is to cast the result as NUMERIC. This automatically applies up to 19 decimals, which should suffice for most ratios.

Tricks and Traps

Here are a couple of points to remember when calculating percentages:

- You can, of course, be more precise in the choice of data type and the number of decimals that you want to use. To specify 4 decimals and a maximum of 6 figures before the decimal point, you would write

```
CAST(COUNT(*) AS NUMERIC(10,4))
```

This conversion says, "Allow 10 characters in all. Because there are 4 decimals, deduce that I want 6 in the mantissa."

- You can multiply the result of the division in the calculation by 100 if you wish; however, this does not alter the fact that the figures are integers. Consequently, the result still does not display any decimals.

2.   Replacing Multiple Subqueries

The sales director wants to see a list of all vehicles sold in 2017, with the percentage of sales each sale represents for the year as well as the variation to the average sales figure. You know that this will require adding a couple of subqueries—and then you remember that SQL allows you to use a single subquery in cases like these! After a few minutes, you produce the code that follows:

```
SELECT       MakeName, ModelName, SalePrice

             ,(SalePrice / CRX.TotalSales) * 100 AS PercentOfSales

             ,SalePrice - CRX.AverageSales AS DifferenceToAverage

FROM         Data.SalesByCountry

CROSS JOIN   (SELECT SUM(SalePrice) AS TotalSales

                     ,AVG(SalePrice) AS AverageSales

             FROM    Data.SalesByCountry

             WHERE   YEAR(SaleDate) = 2017) AS CRX

WHERE        YEAR(SaleDate) = 2017
```

Running this code produces the output that is shown in Figure 6-3.

	MakeName	ModelName	SalePrice	PercentOfSales	DifferenceToAverage
1	Aston Martin	DB6	45000.00	0.5719315080245168	-34475.505050
2	Porsche	911	49500.00	0.6291246588269685	-29975.505050
3	Aston Martin	DB6	225000.00	2.8596575401225840	145524.494950
4	Triumph	TR6	12500.00	0.1588698633401436	-66975.505050
5	Porsche	Boxster	22500.00	0.2859657540122584	-56975.505050
6	Aston Martin	Virage	125000.00	1.5886986334014355	45524.494950
7	Rolls Royce	Silver Shadow	85000.00	1.0803150707129762	5524.494950
8	Peugeot	203	1250.00	0.0158869863340144	-78225.505050
9	Mercedes	280SL	22500.00	0.2859657540122584	-56975.505050
10	Ferrari	355	125950.00	1.6007727430152865	46474.494950
11	Triumph	TR7	8850.00	0.1124798632448216	-70625.505050
12	Triumph	TR5	9950.00	0.1264604112187543	-69525.505050
13	Aston Martin	Vanquish	56500.00	0.7180917822974489	-22975.505050
14	Aston Martin	Rapide	55000.00	0.6990273986966316	-24475.505050
15	Aston Martin	Vanquish	56950.00	0.7238110973776940	-22525.505050

FIGURE 6-3. REPLACING MULTIPLE SUBQUERIES BY A CROSS JOIN

How It Works

Some calculations require multiple subqueries. This, potentially, means writing very similar subqueries several times. You might need one subquery to return a total, another to get an average, yet another to find a standard deviation, and so on. Fortunately, you can apply a workaround to make the SQL both more comprehensible and easier to maintain.

The trick is to write a subquery that calculates all the aggregate values that you need in a single query and then uses the CROSS JOIN operator to apply the output from the subquery for every single record returned from the main query.

The overall query works like this:

First: It begins with a subquery (once again it is the subquery that contains the heart of the solution). The subquery quite simply calculates the total sales and average sales for 2017. It uses the SalesByCountry view as the source of this data.

Then:	The main query extracts the make name, model name, and sale price from the same data source (the SalesByCountry view) for the same year (2017 as well). The next step: Is to join the main query to the subquery using the CROSS JOIN function. This ensures that every record can use the output from the subquery in the main query and that the join does not filter the data in any way.
Finally:	The SELECT clause of the main query is extended to use the output from the cross-joined subquery. In this example, we are dividing the sale price of each vehicle sold by the total sales for the year to calculate the percentage of total sales that this figure represents. As a final flourish, we subtract the average selling price from the sale price of each car to find out how much each sale differs from the average sale price for the year.

If you want to verify that the calculations are accurate, you can always select the SQL for the subquery and run it. You will see the output that is shown in Figure 6-4.

FIGURE 6-4. THE OUTPUT FROM THE SUBQUERY

Tricks and Traps

Using CROSS JOIN can simplify certain calculations. Nonetheless, you need to be aware that

- The subquery is a perfectly standard subquery. This means that it is completely independent of the main query, so any filters that you apply to restrict the output from the subquery may have to be applied to the main query as well—assuming that you want to use them both to examine similar ranges of data.

- CROSS JOIN does not require an ON clause because it is not attempting to link the tables or queries in any way. Indeed, it specifically wants to use all the fields from both tables and/or queries together.

- Since the subquery is aliased, you need to use the subquery alias when referring to the fields that are output from the subquery in the calculations in the main query's SELECT clause.

3. Reusing Calculated Values in Queries

If you are analyzing profit margins, then you need to control your costs. That, at least, is the mantra of the finance director. He wants to see cars with indirect costs (that is, the total of the repair, parts, and transport costs) over a certain threshold—£10,000.00 in this case. This you can do using the following SQL:

```
SELECT       MakeName

             ,Cost AS PurchaseCost

             ,TotalOtherCosts

             ,Cost + TotalOtherCosts AS VehicleCost
FROM         Data.SalesByCountry
CROSS APPLY

    (

    SELECT RepairsCost + PartsCost + TransportInCost

        AS TotalOtherCosts

    ) SQ
WHERE        TotalOtherCosts > 10000
```

Running this query gives the results that you can see in Figure 6-5.

	MakeName	PurchaseCost	TotalOtherCosts	VehicleCost
1	Lamborghini	176400.00	10600.00	187000.00
2	Ferrari	164000.00	11950.00	175950.00
3	Lamborghini	135600.00	12700.00	148300.00
4	Ferrari	100760.00	13400.00	114160.00
5	Ferrari	316000.00	13400.00	329400.00
6	Aston Martin	180000.00	10600.00	190600.00
7	Rolls Royce	111600.00	13400.00	125000.00
8	Bugatti	176400.00	13400.00	189800.00
9	Ferrari	204000.00	12700.00	216700.00
10	McLaren	236000.00	14350.00	250350.00
11	Rolls Royce	132000.00	14350.00	146350.00
12	Ferrari	124000.00	11950.00	135950.00
13	Bugatti	284000.00	18700.00	302700.00
14	Bugatti	284000.00	13400.00	297400.00
15	Lamborghini	116000.00	12700.00	128700.00

FIGURE 6-5. USING CROSS APPLY TO REUSE A CALCULATED ELEMENT

How It Works

This query uses the data in the SalesByCountry view to save you from having to join multiple tables again. Then it displays several metrics for each car purchased.

However, it is the way that the query is designed that really interests us. This is because it reuses a calculated metric several times, while only defining it once. The metric is the total for the repair cost, the parts cost, and the transport cost. Instead of having to add the three fields three times in three separate locations (twice in the SELECT clause and once in the WHERE clause), you define a calculated metric only *once* but reuse it as many times as you want.

You do this by using the CROSS APPLY clause in SQL. The clause works like this:

First:	After the FROM clause in the query, you use a CROSS APPLY similar to the way you use a JOIN.
Then:	You create a subquery—in parentheses, of course—that defines the calculated field TotalOtherCosts. In this example, it is the sum of the repair cost, the parts cost, and the transport cost.
Finally:	You use this calculated field in the query just like a "normal" field.

The outcome is that the query uses the result of the CROSS APPLY in every record that is produced. This saves you from having to duplicate the SQL that defines the calculated field several times.

Tricks and Traps

CROSS APPLY is an extremely powerful operator; however, if you use it, you should be mindful of the following points:

- Using CROSS APPLY like this is particularly useful when the calculated field is used in the WHERE clause. This is because you only have to make any changes once—in the CROSS APPLY clause—for them to affect the filter and the data that is displayed. This means you have less risk of making mistakes and forgetting to change the code in several places.

- The CROSS APPLY clause is pretty much an extension of the main query rather than a completely independent subquery. Consequently, it does not have its own FROM clause but uses the table(s) in the core query. Nonetheless, it must have an alias for the code to work.

- Queries that use CROSS APPLY can sometimes run fairly slowly. Be careful when using CROSS APPLY to handle large datasets.

4. Remove Decimals in Calculations

If you are trading high-value products, you might not need to show pennies (or cents or centimes) in your results. Indeed, the financial director wants a list of vehicles sold that shows core costs without pennies to avoid rounding errors. An easy way to deliver on this requirement is shown in the following SQL:

```
SELECT      MakeName

            ,ModelName

            ,CAST(Cost AS INT) AS Cost

            ,CAST(RepairsCost AS INT) AS RepairsCost

            ,CAST(PartsCost AS INT) AS PartsCost

            ,CAST(SalePrice AS INT) AS SalePrice

FROM        Data.SalesByCountry
```

Running this query gives the results that you can see in Figure 6-6.

	MakeName	ModelName	Cost	RepairsCost	PartsCost	SalePrice
1	Ferrari	Testarossa	52000	2175	1500	65000
2	Ferrari	355	176000	5500	2200	220000
3	Porsche	911	15600	660	0	19500
4	Porsche	924	9200	500	750	11500
5	Porsche	944	15960	1360	500	19950
6	Aston Martin	DB4	23600	500	750	29500
7	Aston Martin	DB5	39600	2500	1500	49500
8	Aston Martin	DB6	60800	3250	750	76000
9	Porsche	911	15680	890	500	19600
10	Aston Martin	DB5	29200	1950	500	36500
11	Porsche	944	6800	250	225	8500
12	Aston Martin	DB6	36000	1250	750	45000
13	Bentley	Flying Spur	64400	500	750	80500
14	Ferrari	355	135600	5500	2200	169500
15	Porsche	944	7160	500	750	8950

FIGURE 6-6. USING THE CAST() FUNCTION FOR A SPECIFIC NUMERIC DATA TYPE CONVERSION

How It Works

You have seen the CAST() function a few times in previous chapters and in *Volume I*, but we have never really explained how useful it can be when dealing with numbers. In this example, you take the SalesByCountry view (to avoid having to join seven tables) and selected five key fields. However, in this view, the fields that contain numeric values are all either in the Money or the Numeric data types. Since both of these data types allow decimals, the fastest way to remove any decimals and present only whole number is to convert these fields to integers.

This is done by applying the CAST() function to the numeric fields and specifying that each is converted as an INT. The result is that the values are now integers—and the decimals have disappeared.

In this exercise, you have effectively done something similar to what you did in Section 2 when you calculated percentages. Previously you wrote SQL to include decimals. This time, you removed any decimals from the calculation. Both techniques use the same function—CAST().

5. Numeric Data Types

In Chapter 10 of Volume I you saw how to find out the data type of a field. In the last couple of sections, you have seen how to convert numeric data types to other numeric data types as and when required.

As a result, now is probably a good moment to explain all the various ways that SQL Server can store and manipulate numbers. In other words, it is time to look at all the numeric data types that SQL Server offers. Each has its uses and limitations, and they are given in Table 6-1.

TABLE 6-1. NUMERIC DATA TYPES

Data Type	Range	Comments
Bit	0 or 1	Essentially used for true or false (also called Boolean) values
Tinyint	0 to 255	An integer value without any decimals
SmallInt	−32,768 to +32,767	An integer value without any decimals
Int	−2,147,483,648 to +2,147,483,647	An integer value without any decimals
Bigint		An integer value without any decimals
SmallMoney	−214,748.3648 to +214,748.3647	Four decimals are set
Money		Four decimals are set
Numeric	−10^38 (then subtract one) to +10^38 (then subtract one)	You must specify the precision and scale (total allowable numbers and numbers after the decimal)
Decimal	−10^38(then subtract one) to +10^38 (then subtract one)	You must specify the precision and scale (total allowable numbers and numbers after the decimal)
Float	−1.79E+308 to −2.23E−308, 0 and 2.23E−308 to 1.79E+308	Potentially huge numbers—but not stored precisely

Data Type	Range	Comments
Real	*−3.40E +38 to −1.18E − 38, 0 and 1.18E −38 to 3.40E +38*	*Potentially huge numbers— but not stored precisely*

You may be wondering why there are so many numeric data types—especially for integers. The reasons are largely a question of the space that data can take up on disk and in memory. Put simply, if a field uses a data type that can contain the maximum value that will ever be stored in that field, it will take up less space. It will also make fetching data from disk into memory faster.

This means that database designers nearly always try and use appropriate numeric data types so that databases run faster and cost less to maintain. It is as simple as that.

Originally this was because disk storage and main memory were extremely expensive. Now, despite ever-lower hardware costs, the exponential growth of data means that it is still important to choose appropriate numeric data types when designing and building databases.

Tricks and Traps

Handling numeric data types can require a little practice. So here are a few essential points to help you:

- When casting numeric data to an integer data type, you must *always* use an integer type that can hold the largest value that you are converting to an integer. So, for example, if the field that you want to cast contains values in the millions, you cannot use the SmallInt data type since it only goes up to 32,767. This data type physically cannot store a larger value. Indeed, if you try a data type conversion on a field that contains values that are simply too large for the destination data type to hold, then SQL Server refuses to display any output and only shows an error message.

- When casting numbers (or texts that can be converted to numbers, as you discover in the following section) to the Numeric or Decimal data types, you should specify the total allowable numbers (including decimals) as well as the number of decimal places.

So, for instance, the following code

```
CAST(COST AS NUMERIC(10,2))
```

converts the contents of the Cost field to the numeric data type. It allows a maximum value of 99999999.99—ten figures in all, and two decimal places.

- You should only convert to the Float or Real data type if your calculations do not require total accuracy. These data types can handle extremely large values, but they do not necessarily restitute the number that they contain completely accurately, so we do not advise you to use them for business or financial calculations. Remember that these data types were specifically designed for scientific data analysis where precision is less important.

- The CAST() function is very powerful, but it can be rather picky about the data that it converts. If a field that you are trying to convert using CAST() contains a text or a number that cannot be converted (whatever the reason) then the *whole query fails to work*.

6. Handling Source Data Where Figures Are Stored as Text

The sales director has been using a spreadsheet to juggle some data and has then had it loaded into SQL Server by the Prestige Cars IT department. You now have to query that data. However, all the figures have been saved as strings of text—and not always cleanly. This can make handling the data trickier than it needs to be. The following SQL helps you work around this kind of issue by converting texts to numbers wherever possible:

```
SELECT      CountryName

            ,MakeName

            ,TRY_CAST(Cost AS NUMERIC(20,4)) AS Cost

            ,TRY_CAST(SalePrice AS NUMERIC(20,4)) AS SalePrice
FROM        SourceData.SalesText
```

Running this query gives the results that you can see in Figure 6-7.

FIGURE 6-7. USING THE TRY_CAST() FUNCTION TO CONVERT TEXT TO NUMERIC VALUES

How It Works

This example uses a table of data that is new to you. This is the SalesText table that we are introducing to make the point that not all the data that you will have to deal with will be perfect. In this example, the original data in the table SalesText really looks like the output shown in Figure 6-8.

FIGURE 6-8. INVALID NUMERIC DATA THAT CANNOT BE CONVERTED "AS IS" TO A NUMERIC VALUE

As you can see, the Cost field contains spaces as well as currency units. These make it impossible for SQL Server to convert the underlying values to numbers.

Nonetheless, SQL Server can help you deal with situations like this. In these cases, you can use the TRY_CAST() function to convert strings that are composed of numbers into numeric values where this is technically possible. Unlike the CAST() function, the TRY_CAST() function does *not* cause the entire query to fail if a string cannot be successfully converted to a number. Instead it returns a *NULL* in the place of the unusable source data.

To prove this point, try executing the following code snippet where TRY_CAST() has been replaced by CAST():

```
SELECT          CountryName

                ,MakeName

                ,CAST(Cost AS NUMERIC(20,4)) AS Cost

                ,CAST(SalePrice AS NUMERIC(20,4)) AS SalePrice

FROM            SourceData.SalesText
```

All that happens is that you see an error message saying

```
Msg 8114, Level 16, State 5, Line 1

Error converting data type varchar to numeric.
```

As you can see, using TRY_CAST() is an extremely practical way of dealing with imperfect data.

Tricks and Traps

We have only one comment to make here:

- Converting invalid source data is a vast subject and one that is outside the scope of a book such as this one. TRY_CAST() merely helps your query to function; it does not solve the underlying bad data problem. When faced with complex data that causes SQL to choke, you are probably best advised to have the data converted by IT professionals.

7. Converting Formatted Source Data into Useable Numbers

After you complained that the data that you were given was not usable, the sales director had the IT department process his spreadsheet so that SQL Server can read it. Unfortunately, it left the currency symbols in the numeric fields. If you want to glance back at Figure 6-7, you will see the original data. The good news is that SQL Server can handle this without any real difficulty, as you can see from the following code snippet:

```
SELECT      MakeName

            ,ModelName

            ,PARSE(VehicleCost AS money USING 'EN-GB') AS VehicleCost

FROM        SourceData.SalesInPounds
```

Running this query gives the results that you can see in Figure 6-9.

FIGURE 6-9. USING THE PARSE() FUNCTION

How It Works

Although not strictly a calculation, making numeric data usable by SQL Server is often a prerequisite to performing math on the data. This is where the PARSE() function can prove invaluable. It can remove formatting from numbers and convert them to valid numeric values.

The PARSE() function requires you to enter (or *pass in*, as the geeks say) three elements:

First:	The field that you want to strip the formatting from.
Second:	The AS keyword followed by the numeric data type that you want to convert the values to.
Third:	The USING keyword and the cultural specification that lets the PARSE() function accurately guess how to handle the formatting elements. In this example, the culture specification is 'EN-GB'. This means that the formatting is in the British English numeric style. Consequently, the decimal point is a period, the thousands separator is a comma, and the currency symbol is the UK pounds sign "£."

To give you a better idea of what this function has done, take a look at the source data in Figure 6-10.

FIGURE 6-10. FORMATTED DATA THAT CAN BE CONVERTED BY THE PARSE() FUNCTION

As you can see, the result of using the PARSE() function is that the currency symbol is stripped out and any decimal or thousands separator is recognized. Finally, only the number is left.

Tricks and Traps

PARSE() is a powerful function, but it does require you to be aware of the following points:

- The PARSE() function only works if the field that you want to convert is *text* (or a string, if you prefer).

- Sometimes the source data cannot be converted to a number despite SQL Server's best efforts. If this happens, you can rewrite the PARSE() function like this:

```
TRY_PARSE(VehicleCost AS money USING 'EN-GB')
```

This prevents the entire query from failing with an annoying error message. Instead, any source values that cannot be parsed appear as NULLs in the output. Source values that can be converted *will* be output in the required numeric data type.

- There are many, many culture specifications that PARSE() recognizes as defining the type of numeric formatting. These are simply too voluminous to list here. We suggest that you search online for the reference that matches the data format that you have to use.

8.   Avoiding Divide-by-Zero Errors

The people in the Finance department really love their ratios. This time they want to see what the multiple of the cost of parts is when compared to the cost of each vehicle in stock. Happy to oblige, as ever, you use the following SQL:

```
SELECT      MD.ModelName
            ,ST.Cost
            ,CASE
                WHEN PartsCost != 0 THEN ST.Cost / ST.PartsCost
                ELSE 0
            END AS PartsCostMultiple
FROM        Data.Stock ST
            INNER JOIN Data.Model MD
            ON ST.ModelID = MD.ModelID
```

Running this query gives the results that you can see in Figure 6-11.

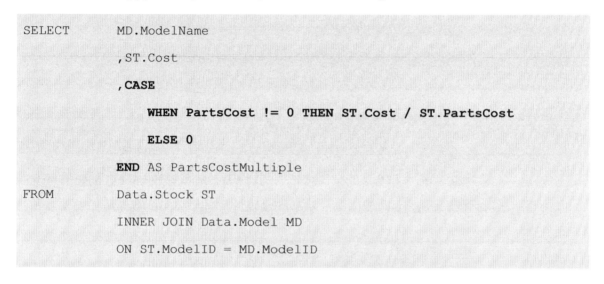

	ModelName	Cost	PartsCostMultiple
1	Testarossa	52000.00	34.6666
2	355	176000.00	80.00
3	911	15600.00	0.00
4	924	9200.00	12.2666
5	944	15960.00	31.92
6	Testarossa	176000.00	55.873
7	DB4	23600.00	31.4666
8	DB5	39600.00	26.40
9	DB6	60800.00	81.0666
10	Testarossa	172000.00	1146.6666
11	911	15680.00	31.36
12	DB5	29200.00	58.40
13	944	6800.00	30.2222
14	DB6	36000.00	48.00
15	Flying Spur	64400.00	85.8666

FIGURE 6-11. USING CASE STATEMENTS TO HANDLE DIVIDE-BY-ZERO ERRORS

How It Works

At its heart, this query is straightforward. It joins the Stock and Make tables so that you can access the Make name and vehicle cost elements. Then it divides the Cost field by the PartsCost field.

However, at least one record has a zero as the parts cost. This, unfortunately, is a problem for SQL Server, as it prevents any data from being returned and instead causes the following error message to appear:

```
Divide by zero error encountered
```

This is, to put it mildly, a pain. However, it can be handled using a CASE statement. What this does is

First:	Test the contents of the PartsCost field. If the field contains anything other than a zero, it divides the Cost field by the PartsCost field.
Otherwise:	It returns a zero and does not calculate anything, because this would be a division by zero, which is what we are trying to avoid.

Take a look at the third record in Figure 6-10; this shows zero for the parts cost multiple. This is the record that has a zero in the PartsCost field—or it is one of them, at least. In any case, the calculation now works perfectly, and you can hand your results to the people in Finance.

Tricks and Traps

You can apply many techniques to avoid divide-by-zero errors. You may also want to note that

- You can also use the IIF() function to handle divide-by-zero errors. For this particular example, the code is

```
IIF(PartsCost != 0,  ST.Cost / ST.PartsCost, 0 ) AS PartsCostMultiple
```

9. Finding the Remainder in a Division Using the Modulo Function

The marketing director's latest idea has left you speechless. She wants you to generate a list of clients who will receive a letter saying that they have won a special customer discount on their next purchase of a classic sports car. She insists that this process must be completely random and must produce a list of around one third of the client base.

Once you have recovered from your bemusement at all things concerning marketing wizardry, you write the following code:

```
SELECT      CustomerID

FROM

      (

      SELECT       CustomerID

                   ,CustomerID % 3 AS ModuloOutput

                   ,CASE

                         WHEN CustomerID % 3 = 1 THEN 'Winner'

                               ELSE NULL

                         END AS LuckyWinner

      FROM         Data.Customer

      ) Rnd

WHERE       LuckyWinner IS NOT NULL
```

Running this query gives the results that you can see in Figure 6-12.

FIGURE 6-12. USING THE MODULO FUNCTION TO RETURN THE REMAINDER IN A CALCULATION

How It Works

As befits a language that can carry out basic math, SQL can calculate the remainder after dividing one number by another. This is called a *modulo* operation, and SQL Server calls the function that carries out this calculation the modulo operator.

What happens is

First: A field is defined that contains a numeric value. In this example, it is the CustomerID field.

Then: The modulo operator (%) is added after the field name.

Finally: The value that you are dividing the field by is added.

So, the key part of this code is

```
CustomerID % 3
```

However, as merely finding the remainder is of little practical interest, a small amount of logic is added to the calculation. What this logic does is to say, "if the remainder is 1, then flag the record." The logical selection is then used as a subquery so that only winning records are returned in the final output.

To make this clearer, take a look at Figure 6-13 where you can see the output from the subquery. This illustrates how the modulo function displays the remainder of a calculation and also shows the output from the CASE statement for every record.

	CustomerID	ModuloOutput	LuckyWinner
1	0001	1	Winner
2	0002	2	NULL
3	0003	0	NULL
4	0004	1	Winner
5	0005	2	NULL
6	0006	0	NULL
7	0007	1	Winner
8	0008	2	NULL
9	0009	0	NULL
10	0010	1	Winner

FIGURE 6-13. THE MODULO FUNCTION APPLIED TO ALL RECORDS

Tricks and Traps

A couple of interesting aspects to this example are

- The figure that is used by a modulo operator does not have to be a number, provided that the text value can be converted internally by SQL Server to a number.

- You do not have to display the modulo output in a calculation. We did it here to make the use of this operator clearer.

10. Creating Financial Calculations

"Money is expensive" is one of the finance director's recurring mantras. It would appear that he has devoted countless hours to developing spreadsheets that count the cost of unsold stock in the showroom. Now, unfortunately, he wants you to adapt his basic compound interest calculation to SQL so that your reports can show how much "dead metal" (to use the term he uses to describe unsold stock) actually costs the company.

To help you in your work he has added that

- You are to use a standard compound interest calculation.
- The interest is to be compounded monthly.
- The rate that he wants to apply is 0.75 percent per month.
- You are only to calculate interest when a vehicle is in stock for over two months.

As a further hint, he has kindly emailed you the exact calculation that he wants you to apply. This is the one in Figure 6-14.

$$CI = K * \left(1 + \frac{P}{100} \right)^{t}$$

FIGURE 6-14. A COMPOUND INTEREST CALCULATION

In this formula

- CI is the compound interest (including the original capital value)
- K is the initial value
- P is the interest rate
- t is the number of periods

After some thought, you come up with the following SQL that shows not only the interest charge, but also the number of months in stock as well as the cost price and the total cost including interest.

```
SELECT

 InitialCost

,MonthsSincePurchase

,(InitialCost * POWER(1 + (0.75 / 100), MonthsSincePurchase))

- InitialCost AS InterestCharge

,InitialCost * POWER(1 + (0.75 / 100), MonthsSincePurchase)

 AS TotalWithInterest

FROM

(

    SELECT

     DATEDIFF(mm, DateBought, SL.SaleDate) AS MonthsSincePurchase

    ,(Cost + PartsCost + RepairsCost) AS InitialCost


    FROM        Data.Stock SK
    INNER JOIN  Data.SalesDetails SD

                ON SK.StockCode = SD.StockID
    INNER JOIN  Data.Sales SL

                ON SL.SalesID = SD.SalesID
    WHERE       DATEDIFF(mm, DateBought, SL.SaleDate) > 2
) SRC
```

Running this code snippet gives the result that you can see in Figure 6-15.

	InitialCost	Months Since Purchase	InterestCharge	TotalWithInterest
1	38000.00	23	7125.266000	45125.266000
2	7930.00	9	551.618730	8481.618730
3	130550.00	12	12246.503850	142796.503850
4	45075.00	29	10906.211775	55981.211775
5	40600.00	16	5155.875200	45755.875200
6	188650.00	8	11620.651350	200270.651350
7	11250.00	4	341.313750	11591.313750
8	153600.00	16	19505.971200	173105.971200
9	1725.00	11	147.770400	1872.770400
10	6522.00	11	558.700608	7080.700608
11	9210.00	5	350.597070	9560.597070

FIGURE 6-15. CALCULATING COMPOUND INTEREST

How It Works

Creating complex calculations in SQL is a vast subject. Indeed, entire books and papers have been written on this subject. So, although we want to show you the basics of using SQL to handle intricate financial mathematics, we are not delving too profoundly into this subject.

Given that this challenge could be complex, we have started by breaking it down into two parts:

An inner query   That calculates the total cost of a vehicle by adding up the purchase cost, cost of spares, and any repair costs. This query then also determines the number of months between the purchase date and the sale date.

This query uses the Stock, SalesDetails, and Sales tables to source the required information. Once the joins are in place, it adds a WHERE clause to restrict the output to vehicles where the time between purchase and sale is more than two months.

An outer query   That displays the two fields isolated by the inner query (InitialCost and MonthsSincePurchase). The outer query then uses these two fields as core elements in calculating the compound interest.

What is both interesting and new in this query is the compound interest calculation, so now you need to look at this in more detail.

Essentially you have applied a two-step process to calculating compound interest:

First:	Take the arithmetical formula and adapt it so that it can be read on a single line.
Second:	Convert the single-line formula to SQL.

Converting the formula from Figure 6-14 to a single line gives you the following:

$$CI = K * (1 + P/100)t$$

The SQL that delivers the compound interest (CI) takes the initial value (K) to be the purchase cost, cost of spares, and any repair costs. It then "hard-codes" the interest rate as 0.75 and divides by 100 to express it as a percentage. Finally it uses the POWER() function to apply the number of periods (t) as the exponent for the formula. The number of periods is, in fact, the number of months between purchase and sale.

The POWER() function takes two parameters:

First:	The base value you wish to raise to the power of the exponent (one plus the percentage interest rate in this example)
Second:	The exponent to apply (the number of months in this example)

As a final tweak, this calculation is applied a second time. Only on this occasion, the initial cost is subtracted from the compound interest to leave the actual interest amount. This way you can see the total cost as well as the interest.

This is, of course, only a simple example. Financial calculations can get much more complicated than this one. However, it is a starting point on which you can build to develop much more complex analyses if you need to.

Tricks and Traps

There is one idea that you can take away from this example:

- It is possible to write a query like this one without actually using a subquery; however, we feel that the improved simplification and increased clarity that a subquery brings to both the analysis and the coding make a subquery worth any extra effort.

11. Using a Tally Table to Produce a Sequential List of Numbers

The CFO has come with a request for you. He wants to be able to calculate the straight-line depreciation for any vehicle in stock. After a few minutes' thought, you come up with the following code:

```
SELECT              RowNo AS PeriodNumber

                    ,Cost

                    ,Cost / 5 AS StraightLineDepreciation

                    ,Cost - ((Cost / 5) * RowNo) AS RemainingValue


FROM                Data.Stock

CROSS APPLY

(

SELECT 1 AS RowNo

UNION ALL

SELECT 2

UNION ALL

SELECT 3

UNION ALL

SELECT 4

UNION ALL

SELECT 5

) Tally

WHERE               StockCode =

                          'A2C3B95E-3005-4840-8CE3-A7BC5F9CFB5F'
```

Running this piece of code gives the result that you can see in Figure 6-16.

	PeriodNumber	Cost	StraightLineDepreciation	RemainingValue
1	1	176000.00	35200.00	140800.00
2	2	176000.00	35200.00	105600.00
3	3	176000.00	35200.00	70400.00
4	4	176000.00	35200.00	35200.00
5	5	176000.00	35200.00	0.00

FIGURE 6-16. USING A TALLY TABLE TO CALCULATE STRAIGHT-LINE DEPRECIATION

How It Works

Producing a depreciation table requires a sequence of time periods against which the series of amortization amounts can be calculated. However, SQL Server is not a spreadsheet where you can just enter a series of numbers to represent the time periods. You need another solution. The answer is a concept called a *tally table*. This is a recordset (it can be a table but does not have to be) that contains a series of numbers, generally starting from 1, that increment regularly and have no gaps in the series. This suite of numbers can then be used to create sets of records.

In the case of a depreciation table, the first thing that you need is a recordset that contains the number of records corresponding to the number of years over which the vehicle will be amortized. In this example, we presume that this is a five-year period, so a recordset containing five rows is created using a set of UNION queries. You can see this in the CROSS APPLY clause of the SQL. Running the code inside the CROSS APPLY clause produces the result that you can see in Figure 6-17.

	RowNo
1	1
2	2
3	3
4	4
5	5

FIGURE 6-17. THE OUTPUT FROM A TALLY TABLE

Once you have the tally table, you can calculate the depreciation and the residual value of a specific car. Calculating the depreciation each year is as simple as dividing the cost of the vehicle by the number of years. Calculating the residual value means subtracting the accumulated depreciation each year from the cost. So, to work out the accumulated amortization amount, you multiply the depreciation amount by the number of years. This number is provided by the tally table; in effect, it takes the single record for the car cost and makes it into a table of five records by using a CROSS APPLY clause to multiply the number of records in the SELECT clause (one) by the number of records in the CROSS APPLY clause (all five of them). As a final, and necessary, flourish, the row number of the tally table is used as the multiplier to calculate the accumulated depreciation.

Tricks and Traps

We have only a few comments here:

- If you need to include a salvage cost in the calculation for the depreciation, you can subtract the salvage cost from the cost of the vehicle every time the Cost field is used.

- You will discover other ways to create a tally table in a later chapter.

- You can use tally tables in many situations to resolve otherwise seemingly impossible SQL issues. Although they may not be something that you use daily, they can be a valuable resource in certain circumstances.

12. Generating Completely Random Sample Output from a Dataset

The CEO wants to call up a handful of clients at random and ask them about the service that they have received from Prestige Cars. She asks you to produce a totally random list of sales with the relevant customers. It takes you just a few seconds to produce the following piece of SQL to satisfy her request.

```
SELECT      TOP 5 PERCENT *

FROM        Data.SalesByCountry

ORDER BY    NEWID()
```

Running this code delivers the results that you can see in Figure 6-18.

	CountryName	MakeName	ModelName	Cost	RepairsCost	PartsCost	TransportInCost	Color	SalePrice	LineItemDiscount	InvoiceNumber	SaleDate	CustomerName	SalesDetailsID
1	Germany	Porsche	924	9200.00	500.00	750.00	150.00	British Racing Green	11500.00	NULL	EURDE004	2015-02-16 08:00:00.000	WunderKar	4
2	United Kingdom	Porsche	924	13200.00	500.00	750.00	150.00	British Racing Green	16500.00	NULL	GBPGB068	2016-08-13 00:00:00.000	Peter McLuckie	74
3	United States	Porsche	911	14000.00	2000.00	500.00	150.00	British Racing Green	17500.00	NULL	USDUS041	2016-04-30 00:00:00.000	Jason B. Wight	44
4	France	Rolls Royce	Silver Seraph	79950.00	1490.00	750.00	750.00	Blue	99950.00	NULL	EURFR172	2017-07-01 18:26:00.000	Mme Anne Duport	188
5	United States	Aston Martin	DB6	90872.00	500.00	225.00	750.00	Night Blue	113590.00	NULL	USDUS284	2018-08-01 00:00:00.000	Jayden Jones	307
6	Germany	Ferrari	360	79600.00	500.00	750.00	750.00	Black	99500.00	500.00	EURDE043	2016-04-30 00:00:00.000	Glitz	46
7	France	Jaguar	XK120	47200.00	2000.00	750.00	550.00	Blue	59000.00	4500.00	EURFR311	2018-10-31 00:00:00.000	Casseroles Chromes	337
8	France	Ferrari	F50	248000.00	9250.00	7900.00	1950.00	Silver	310000.00	NULL	EURFR235	2018-03-15 00:00:00.000	Capots Reluisants S.A.	257
9	United Kingdom	Delorean	DMC 12	79600.00	1490.00	750.00	750.00	Night Blue	99500.00	NULL	GBPGB157	2017-05-22 11:18:00.000	Pierre Blanc	170
10	United Kingdom	Aston Martin	Vanquish	44000.00	500.00	150.00	550.00	Silver	55000.00	NULL	GBPGB088	2016-09-11 00:00:00.000	Magic Motors	95
11	United Kingdom	Jaguar	XK150	18392.00	390.00	150.00	150.00	Night Blue	22990.00	NULL	GBPGB017	2015-07-15 00:00:00.000	Alexei Tolstoi	18
12	United Kingdom	Aston Martin	DB2	50000.00	500.00	750.00	550.00	British Racing Green	62500.00	1250.00	GBPGB207	2018-01-02 00:00:00.000	Silver HubCaps	226
13	France	Delahaye	135	20400.00	1360.00	750.00	150.00	Dark Purple	25500.00	NULL	EURFR300	2018-09-15 00:00:00.000	Khader El Ghannam	324
14	United Kingdom	Aston Martin	DB4	45560.00	500.00	1500.00	550.00	Pink	56950.00	NULL	GBPGB210	2018-01-02 00:00:00.000	Clubbing Cars	229
15	France	Jaguar	XK120	15680.00	1360.00	150.00	150.00	Night Blue	19600.00	1250.00	EURFR091	2016-09-16 00:00:00.000	La Bagnole de Luxe	98
16	United Kingdom	Porsche	924	7160.00	360.00	750.00	150.00	Black	8950.00	950.00	GBPGB021	2015-09-15 10:00:00.000	Posh Vehicles Ltd	23
17	United Kingdom	Austin	Cambridge	18000.00	1360.00	750.00	150.00	Black	22500.00	NULL	GBPGB225	2018-02-13 00:00:00.000	Impress.TheNeighbours.Com	245
18	United States	Mercedes	250SL	18080.00	1360.00	500.00	150.00	Black	22600.00	500.00	USDUS179	2017-08-04 11:29:00.000	Screamin' Wheels	195

FIGURE 6-18. GENERATING RANDOM OUTPUT FROM A TABLE USING NEWID()

How It Works

T-SQL has a function—NEWID()—that adds a 32-character unique alphanumeric identifier to a record. This string is guaranteed to be unique by SQL Server. Not only that,
but its structure is completely random; that is, there is no sequence or order to the way
that it is generated.

This query uses NEWID() to randomize data selection like this:

First:	You write a simple SELECT query to return data from the SalesByCountry view.
Then:	You add a NEWID() field to the output from a query to produce a completely random identifier. The NEWID() field does not have to be in the SELECT clause to be added to the dataset. Adding it to the ORDER BY clause still adds the field, but without it being visible; so by sorting the data using this field, you have a recordset in a random sort order.
Finally:	You add a TOP *n* PERCENT clause to the SELECT clause to output only the first few percent (5 percent in this example) of the recordset.

The final result is a random subset of data from a database.

Tricks and Traps

We have one comment to make about this technique:

- If you want to see what one of these unique identifier fields looks like, you can run code like the following snippet:

```
SELECT      NEWID()

FROM        Data.SalesByCountry
```

This gives the kind of result that you can see in Figure 6-19.

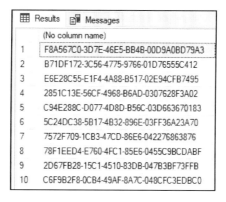

FIGURE 6-19. GENERATING UNIQUE IDENTIFIERS USING NEWID()

Conclusion

This chapter explained some of the techniques that you may need to use when carrying out more advanced calculations in SQL. These include handling data type conversions, managing divide-by-zero errors, and avoiding other circumstances where SQL can, potentially, prevent some calculations from working properly. You also learned more about numeric data types and how to convert numbers to numeric values when they are stored as text. Finally, you saw a few examples of how you can use SQL to carry out more complex calculations.

Core Knowledge Learned in This Chapter

The keywords that you have seen in this chapter are

Concept	Description
CAST()	*The CAST() function is used to convert data types—where this is possible. It can convert a numeric data type to a different numeric data type or convert a string that is, in effect, a number, to a numeric data type.*
TRY_CAST()	*The TRY_CAST() function is also used to convert data types; however, it is less likely to cause an entire query to fail if a single value cannot be converted. Instead, it outputs a NULL in place of a value that cannot be converted.*
PARSE()	*The PARSE() function converts text (strings) that contains formatted numbers to numeric values without the formatting.*
TRY_PARSE()	*The TRY_PARSE() function also converts text (strings) that contains formatted numbers to numeric values without the formatting; however, it is less likely to cause an entire query to fail if a single value cannot be converted. Instead it outputs a NULL in place of a value that cannot be converted.*
CROSS JOIN	*Applies all the records returned by one query to another query without filtering the data.*
CROSS APPLY	*The CROSS APPLY operator carries out an operation on each row of the query using the elements defined in the CROSS APPLY subquery.*
% (modulo)	*The % function—called the modulo function—returns the remainder after dividing one value by another.*
POWER()	*POWER() is a math function used to raise one value to the power of another.*
NEWID()	*This function adds a 32-character unique alphanumeric identifier to a record.*

Please note that you can also use the CAST(), TRY_CAST(), PARSE(), and TRY_PARSE() functions to convert (or attempt to convert) values to dates. Please see Chapter 9 for examples of using them with dates.

Chapter 7:
Segmenting and Classifying Data

Selecting and filtering information can certainly help you reach a deep insight into your data, yet there are times when you really need to prioritize and classify lists of data in order to analyze the elements that really matter. In this chapter, you see how applying a few analytical functions can help you deliver real insight from your data. This can help both you and your organization stay one step ahead of the competition.

Ranking and Segmenting Data

SQL Server offers a useful set of functions that can help you when it comes to segmenting datasets. Specifically, it can

- Rank data according to a given criterion
- Break down recordsets into multiple segments
- Isolate the top or bottom elements in multiple data segments
- Determine median values

Analyzing data in this way is a first step on the path to in-depth statistical analysis. We do not—rest assured—expect you to be an expert in statistics in order to use the SQL functions that you meet in this chapter. However, we hope that, as you learn how to slice and dice data in this chapter, you come to appreciate the power of SQL in data analysis.

1. Organizing Data by Rank

Turning data into information is what analysis is all about. In order to tailor your offering for your clients you need to see how customer sales compare. In fact, the sales director wants a list that shows sales per customer for 2018 with an indicator of their relative rank. The following SQL can help you deliver this:

```
SELECT      CustomerName

            ,MakeName + ', ' + ModelName AS MakeAndModel

            ,SalePrice

            ,RANK() OVER (ORDER BY SalePrice DESC)

                    AS SalesImportance

FROM        Data.SAlesByCountry

WHERE       YEAR(SaleDate) = 2018
```

Running this query gives the results that you can see in Figure 7-1. A figure that indicates the relative position of each sale shows the rank for each record.

	CustomerName	MakeAndModel	SalePrice	SalesImportance
1	La Bagnole de Luxe	Bugatti, 57C	365000.00	1
2	Andrea Tarbuck	Bugatti, 57C	355000.00	2
3	Bling Bling S.A.	Bugatti, 57C	345000.00	3
4	Capots Reluisants S.A.	Ferrari, F50	310000.00	4
5	Laurent Saint Yves	Ferrari, F40	269500.00	5
6	Kieran O'Harris	Lamborghini, Diabolo	255000.00	6
7	Smooth Rocking Chrome	Ferrari, Dino	195000.00	7
8	Stephany Rousso	Ferrari, F50	195000.00	7
9	Capots Reluisants S.A.	Bentley, Brooklands	189500.00	9
10	Sondra Horowitz	Rolls Royce, Phantom	182500.00	10
11	King Leer Cars	Ferrari, Mondial	155000.00	11
12	Antonio Maura	Lamborghini, 400GT	145000.00	12
13	Andy Cheshire	Ferrari, Daytona	145000.00	12
14	Smooth Rocking Chrome	Ferrari, 360	135000.00	14
15	El Sport	Ferrari, 360	128500.00	15

FIGURE 7-1. THE RANK() FUNCTION

How It Works

This query starts by joining all the tables that are required to let you display the CustomerName, Make, Model, and SalePrice fields, only it does this using the SalesByCountry view to save you from having to join all the tables. Then, once a WHERE clause has been added to filter on a specific year for sales, these fields are added to the SELECT clause. Then, as a final touch, the customers are clearly ranked by order of importance using a new function—RANK().

As its name implies, RANK() indicates where a row stands in a list of elements. The RANK() function also sorts the records so that you can see clearly what the relative importance of each row is.

However, the RANK() function needs to know how to classify the data that it will convert into an ordered hierarchy, so to set up a ranked dataset, you need the following elements at a minimum:

RANK()	This function tells SQL Server that you want to classify a dataset.
OVER	This keyword is compulsory and follows the RANK() keyword.
ORDER BY	This statement is added inside parentheses after the OVER keyword and you then add the field that will be used to "grade" the results.

In this example, the vehicle sale price is used as the basis for grading and sorting the output. The final result is a list of customers ordered and ranked by the value of purchases each has made relative to the others.

Tricks and Traps

The RANK() function can be a really powerful addition to your SQL toolkit; however, you need to be aware of the following points when using it:

- The RANK() function is one of a group of SQL functions that are known as the *windowing functions*. You will see these in both this chapter and the next.

- The ORDER BY clause in a windowing function works just like a standard SQL ORDER BY clause. You can use multiple fields separated by a comma, or add the ASC (for ascending) or DESC (for descending) keywords to tell SQL Server how to sort your data.

- It is not strictly necessary to add an alias for the column that displays the result of the RANK() function, but it helps make the output clearer.

- Adding a RANK() function sorts the output data automatically.

2. Creating Multiple Groups of Rankings

Classifying product sales can be essential for an accurate understanding of which products sell best. At least that is what the CEO said when she requested a report showing sales for 2017 ranked in order of importance by make. The following short piece of SQL shows you how to look at the relative sales value of each model for each make of car:

```
SELECT          MakeName + ', ' + ModelName AS MakeAndModel

                ,SD.SalePrice

                ,RANK() OVER (PARTITION BY MakeName

                            ORDER BY SD.SalePrice DESC) AS SalesImportance
FROM            Data.Make AS MK

INNER JOIN      Data.Model AS MD ON MK.MakeID = MD.MakeID

INNER JOIN      Data.Stock AS ST ON ST.ModelID = MD.ModelID

INNER JOIN      Data.SalesDetails SD ON ST.StockCode = SD.StockID

INNER JOIN      Data.Sales AS SA ON SA.SalesID = SD.SalesID

WHERE           YEAR(SA.SaleDate) = 2017

ORDER BY        MakeName
```

Running this query gives the results that you can see in Figure 7-2.

	MakeAndModel	SalePrice	SalesImportance
1	Alfa Romeo, Giulia	25000.00	1
2	Alfa Romeo, Giulietta	21500.00	2
3	Alfa Romeo, Spider	12500.00	3
4	Alfa Romeo, Spider	11500.00	4
5	Alfa Romeo, Giulia	10500.00	5
6	Alfa Romeo, Giulietta	6500.00	6
7	Alfa Romeo, Spider	5650.00	7
8	Aston Martin, DB6	225000.00	1
9	Aston Martin, Virage	125000.00	2
10	Aston Martin, DB9	99500.00	3
11	Aston Martin, Rapide	99500.00	3
12	Aston Martin, Rapide	86500.00	5
13	Aston Martin, DB9	77500.00	6
14	Aston Martin, Vantage	66500.00	7
15	Aston Martin, DB2	61500.00	8

FIGURE 7-2. APPLYING THE PARTITION BY CLAUSE TO A RANK() FUNCTION

How It Works

The core of this code snippet is the set of tables that allows you to access the Make-Name, ModelName, SalePrice, and SaleDate fields. Once you have created the required dataset, you can then assemble a query that lists the fields that you need.

With the core elements of the query in place, you can add a RANK() function. As was the case in the previous example, you need the RANK() keyword, the OVER clause, and an ORDER BY statement with the field that you are using to sort the data.

This time you want to classify the output in a subtler way. Specifically, you want to grade each model of car, not compared to all the sales for the year, but relative to all models of the same make rather than relative to all sales for the year.

This is done—quite simply—by adding the PARTITION BY clause and a field name inside the parentheses that follow the OVER keyword. In this way, you are, in effect, telling SQL that you want to break the data down into subgroups by make of car. The PARTITION BY clause is, in effect, creating subgroups by make of vehicle. The ORDER BY clause then grades the records for each subgroup on the SalePrice field.

Tricks and Traps

When partitioning—or grouping datasets, if you prefer to think of it like that—you need to remain aware of a couple of key points:

- SQL Server can handle situations where there is a tie that occurs when data is ranked. What it does is give any tied rows the same ranking, and then it makes the next-lowest record two or more places lower. Figure 7-3 shows you an example of this from further down the list.

	MakeAndModel	SalePrice	SalesImportance
13	Aston Martin, DB9	77500.00	6
14	Aston Martin, Vantage	66500.00	7
15	Aston Martin, DB2	61500.00	8
16	Aston Martin, Vanquish	56950.00	9
17	Aston Martin, Vanquish	56500.00	10
18	Aston Martin, DB9	56500.00	10
19	Aston Martin, DB9	56500.00	10
20	Aston Martin, Rapide	55000.00	13
21	Aston Martin, DB2	49500.00	14

FIGURE 7-3. THE EFFECT OF TIED RECORDS WHEN USING THE RANK() FUNCTION

- Most, if not all, of the time, you are likely to find yourself ranking data on a numeric field. You will nearly always partition data using a text field. This is not, however, inevitable, merely likely. You can just as easily partition on a numeric field and order on an alphabetical field.

3. Creating Multiple Ranked Groups and Subgroups

The finance director has realized that he does not yet know how to grade customers on a scale of profitability per sale, so he has requested an immediate report that shows the profit per vehicle sold ranked in order of importance by make per customer. After a little thought, you come to the conclusion that what he wants is a list of customers in which you can see which makes of vehicle each client bought and where the data is ranked by customer and make. The following SQL query uses a windowing function and a CTE (Common Table Expression) to deliver this essential piece of analysis:

```sql
;
WITH

AllSalesProfit_CTE (CustomerName, MakeName, ModelName, SalePrice,
ProfitPerModel)

AS

(

SELECT      CustomerName, MakeName, ModelName

            ,SalePrice

            ,((SalePrice -

                (Cost + ISNULL(RepairsCost,0)

                + PartsCost + TransportInCost))

                / SalePrice) * 100

FROM        Data.SalesByCountry

)


SELECT      CustomerName, MakeName, ModelName, ProfitPerModel, SalePrice

            ,RANK() OVER

                        (PARTITION BY CustomerName, MakeName

                        ORDER BY ProfitPerModel DESC) AS SalesImportance

FROM        AllSalesProfit_CTE

ORDER BY    CustomerName, MakeName, SalesImportance
```

Running this query gives the results that you can see in Figure 7-4.

	CustomerName	MakeName	ModelName	ProfitPerModel	SalePrice	SalesImportance
1	Alex McWhirter	Jaguar	XJ12	9.523809523809524	17850.00	1
2	Alexei Tolstoi	Aston Martin	Virage	15.682926829268293	102500.00	1
3	Alexei Tolstoi	Aston Martin	DB6	14.618705035971223	69500.00	2
4	Alexei Tolstoi	Ferrari	355	14.170731707317073	205000.00	1
5	Alexei Tolstoi	Jaguar	XK150	16.998695084819487	22990.00	1
6	Alexei Tolstoi	Jaguar	XJS	13.097345132743363	22600.00	2
7	Alexei Tolstoi	Jaguar	E-Type	11.645569620253165	39500.00	3
8	Alexei Tolstoi	Jaguar	XJS	5.929648241206030	9950.00	4
9	Alexei Tolstoi	Porsche	911	15.059847660500544	45950.00	1
10	Alexei Tolstoi	Triumph	GT6	-20.000000000000000	3500.00	1
11	Alicia Almodovar	Alfa Romeo	Giulietta	-4.604569420035149	5690.00	1
12	Alicia Almodovar	Aston Martin	DB6	16.082698585418934	45950.00	1
13	Alicia Almodovar	Ferrari	Testarossa	18.140000000000000	250000.00	1
14	Alicia Almodovar	Porsche	959	16.075949367088608	39500.00	1
15	Alicia Almodovar	Porsche	928	12.789968652037618	15950.00	2

FIGURE 7-4. COMBINING A CTE WITH A RANK() FUNCTION TO CREATE MULTIPLE RANKED GROUPS AND SUBGROUPS

How It Works

This piece of code is in two parts:

First: A CTE that calculates the net profit for every car sold.

Finally: A query that uses the data from the CTE to classify the output.

A CTE can help you define the core data that is required by the overall query. Although not absolutely necessary, it can help isolate the core data that you then use to categorize and hierarchize data. This example uses a CTE to define the core data that is required. Once the essential data has been isolated using the SalesByCountry view, the relevant fields (Customer, Make, Model, and Profit) are output and a RANK() function is added to the final query that delivers the categorized output based on the recordset defined by the CTE.

If you think back to Chapter 3, you will remember that a CTE can be executed separately from the rest of the query. So if you select the SQL that is contained inside the CTE and execute it, you obtain the output that you can see in Figure 7-5 (remember that the final column is aliased in the CTE header).

FIGURE 7-5. CTE OUTPUT TO BE USED IN A RANKING QUERY

This dataset calculates sales figures and profit per sale, so it can be used in the final query to group and rank the records by customer and make.

A couple of aspects of this query make it a little subtler than the previous two that you have seen.

First:	The output is ranked by customer *and* make. As you can see, the PARTITION BY clause (rather like an ORDER BY clause) can specify multiple fields. All the fields that you use in the PARTITION BY clause must be comma-separated.
Second:	You can override the sort order that is provided by the RANK() function by adding a standard ORDER BY clause in the final query. In this example, the ORDER BY clause is applied to guarantee that the final output is both clear and comprehensible.

Tricks and Traps

We have a couple of remarks to make about using CTEs when ranking datasets:

- You could just as easily use a derived table instead of a CTE. The two techniques are essentially interchangeable, and the approach that you choose is largely a matter of personal preference.

- If the query inside the CTE does *not* have column names, then you *must add names to the output fields inside the parentheses* at the top of the CTE.

4.   **Filtering Data by Ranked Items**

Buyer psychology is a peculiar thing. To better understand Prestige Cars' clients, the sales director has decided that she wants to find the bestselling make for each color of vehicle sold. The following short SQL snippet gives you this information:

```
SELECT      Color, MakeName

FROM

            (

            SELECT       DISTINCT MakeName, Color

                         ,RANK() OVER (PARTITION BY MakeName

                                       ORDER BY SalePrice DESC) AS
ColorRank

            FROM        Data.Make AS MK

            INNER JOIN  Data.Model AS MD

                        ON MK.MakeID = MD.MakeID

            INNER JOIN  Data.Stock AS ST

                        ON ST.ModelID = MD.ModelID

            INNER JOIN  Data.SalesDetails SD

                        ON ST.StockCode = SD.StockID

            ) SQ

WHERE       ColorRank = 1

ORDER BY MakeName
```

Running this query gives the results that you can see in Figure 7-6.

FIGURE 7-6. FILTERING ON THE RESULTS OF A RANK() FUNCTION IN A SUBQUERY

How It Works

This query works by breaking down the problem into its two constituent parts, the better to answer the question that is asked.

First:	A derived table joins all the required tables to produce a list of sales that displays only the make, color, sale price, and the hierarchy of each color sold per make using the RANK() function. The OVER clause specifies that the data is partitioned (grouped, if you prefer) by make of car and the value used to rank the data is the selling price.
Finally:	The outer query returns the make, color, and sale price of each car if —and only if—it is ranked *first* for each make. The outer query does this by applying a WHERE clause to the output from the derived table so that only records where the rank equals 1 are allowed through to the final data set.

To make this clearer, Figure 7-7 shows a few of the records from the data that is returned by the derived table to the outer query.

	MakeName	Color	ColorRank
16	Alfa Romeo	Green	5
17	Alfa Romeo	Night Blue	4
18	Alfa Romeo	Night Blue	9
19	Alfa Romeo	Night Blue	19
20	Alfa Romeo	Red	14
21	Aston Martin	Black	1
22	Aston Martin	Black	5
23	Aston Martin	Black	6
24	Aston Martin	Black	9
25	Aston Martin	Black	24
26	Aston Martin	Black	26
27	Aston Martin	Black	28

FIGURE 7-7. GROUPING AND CLASSIFYING DATA USING THE RANK() FUNCTION

This output shows you that the derived table has, effectively, classified sales by color for each make. Then the outer query effectively discards most of the data that the derived table has returned so that only the top-ranked records for each make are displayed.

Tricks and Traps

There are a couple of points worth noting at this juncture:

- Remember that you *have to add an alias* to all columns that are used in a derived table. This is required by SQL itself and not just because you are using the output of the RANK() function to filter data. If you forget to add an alias to a column, you get an error message.

- You could have just as easily used a CTE instead of a derived table to perform the initial ranking of the data. It is entirely up to you which you prefer to use.

5. Classifying Data by Strict Order of Rank

Segmenting data in order to deliver real insight is what SQL is all about. Management now wants you to push the envelope and perform a more complex analysis of the Prestige Cars' sales data by finding the ten highest-selling sales values but only when these cars belong to the category of the five bestselling colors by quantity sold. The SQL that does this is slightly longer than some of the code snippets that you have seen so far; however, it is definitely worth a closer look:

```
SELECT      Color, MakeAndModel, SalesImportance
FROM
(
SELECT      ST.Color, MakeName + ', ' + ModelName AS MakeAndModel
            ,SD.SalePrice
            ,DENSE_RANK() OVER (ORDER BY SD.SalePrice DESC)
                AS SalesImportance
FROM        Data.Make AS MK
INNER JOIN  Data.Model AS MD ON MK.MakeID = MD.MakeID
INNER JOIN  Data.Stock AS ST ON ST.ModelID = MD.ModelID
INNER JOIN  Data.SalesDetails SD ON ST.StockCode = SD.StockID
INNER JOIN
            (
            SELECT TOP (5)  Color, COUNT(*) AS NumberOfSales
            FROM            Data.Stock AS ST
            INNER JOIN      Data.SalesDetails SD
                            ON ST.StockCode = SD.StockID
            GROUP BY        Color
            ORDER BY        NumberOfSales
            ) CL
            ON CL.Color = ST.Color
```

```
) RK

WHERE        SalesImportance <= 10

ORDER BY     SalesImportance
```

Running this query gives the results that you can see in Figure 7-8.

	Color	MakeAndModel	SalesImportance
1	Green	Lamborghini, Jarama	1
2	Dark Purple	Ferrari, F40	2
3	Green	Ferrari, F50	3
4	Green	Ferrari, Testarossa	3
5	Green	Rolls Royce, Phantom	4
6	Dark Purple	Rolls Royce, Wraith	5
7	Night Blue	Ferrari, Testarossa	5
8	Green	Aston Martin, Vantage	6
9	Green	Aston Martin, Virage	6
10	Dark Purple	Ferrari, Dino	7
11	Green	Rolls Royce, Phantom	8
12	Night Blue	Aston Martin, DB6	9
13	Pink	Aston Martin, Virage	10

FIGURE 7-8. USING THE DENSE_RANK() FUNCTION TO CLASSIFY ITEMS

How It Works

Sometimes an analytical request can seem more complicated than it really is. However, if you break the problem down into its component parts, then it can prove to be easier than you think. This query is case in point. Let's look more closely at what is required and then see how SQL can provide the information that you want to extract from the data.

Top five by color	First you need to isolate the five bestselling colors by quantity. This has to be done first, as it restricts the data only to those vehicles whose color is one of the five bestselling colors.
Top ten bestselling	Then you need to find the bestselling cars that make up the ten best sales by value *if* the vehicle color is one of the five bestselling colors.

Getting this query right requires a nested derived table inside a derived table. Let's begin at the lowest level of the query—the inner derived table that deduces the five bestselling colors by quantity.

The inner derived table finds the five bestselling colors by joining the Stock and SalesDetails tables and then by counting the number of sales per color. Then it selects only the top five records, giving you the list of the five bestselling colors. If you select the query that makes up the inner derived table (the one that is aliased as CL), you see something like the data in Figure 7-9.

	Color	NumberOfSales
1	Pink	11
2	Canary Yellow	15
3	Dark Purple	16
4	Green	24
5	Night Blue	32

FIGURE 7-9. USING A DERIVED TABLE TO FILTER A SUBSET OF ELEMENTS THAT ARE PASSED UP TO AN OUTER QUERY

Once you have the list of colors that make up the five bestselling colors, you can build the "core" query that returns the make and model of car sold along with its color, the sale price, and the ranking of the sale relative to the selling prices of all vehicles sold. The inner derived table is used in the outer derived table's JOIN clause to filter the colors so that only the five returned by the inner query are used in the outer query. If you select this query (which includes the inner derived table, aliased as RK), you see something like the data in Figure 7-10.

	Color	MakeAndModel	SalesImportance
1	Green	Lamborghini, Jarama	1
2	Dark Purple	Ferrari, F40	2
3	Green	Ferrari, F50	3
4	Green	Ferrari, Testarossa	3
5	Green	Rolls Royce, Phantom	4
6	Dark Purple	Rolls Royce, Wraith	5
7	Night Blue	Ferrari, Testarossa	5
8	Green	Aston Martin, Vantage	6
9	Green	Aston Martin, Virage	6
10	Dark Purple	Ferrari, Dino	7
11	Green	Rolls Royce, Phantom	8
12	Night Blue	Aston Martin, DB6	9
13	Pink	Aston Martin, Virage	10

FIGURE 7-10. A DERIVED TABLE THAT FILTERS DATA BASED ON AN INNER DERIVED TABLE

Once you have a list of all the sales of cars in a ranked dataset, it is easy to add the final step. This consists of using this list as the data source for the outermost query where you select only those cars whose rank is 10 or less. This is done in the WHERE clause that says, "WHERE SalesImportance <= 10". An ORDER BY clause is added as a final tweak to present that data in an order that visually enhances the result by sorting the output in sequence.

Notice that this SQL uses the DENSE_RANK() function rather than the RANK() function. The two are virtually identical but have one vital difference. You saw in previous examples that the RANK() function skips numbers if there is a tie. The DENSE_RANK() function does not do this and continues the numbering sequentially. This way, you are sure to get the top ten sales values—even if there are duplicate values for some sales. This is why the final output shows thirteen records when you only asked for the top ten. There are only ten distinct top-selling prices, but these represent thirteen different sales since there can always be more than one sale at the same price.

Tricks and Traps

A query as complex as this one inevitably means that there will be a few key points to take away:

- This query could also be solved by nesting the inner derived table inside a CTE and then using the output from the CTE for the final query. Once again, how you solve it is simply a question of personal preference.

- The inner derived table can be used by the outer derived table either in a JOIN with the outer query (as is the case here) or in a WHERE clause. Either of these approaches gives the same result.

- You might be tempted to use a TOP 10 clause in the outer derived table to get the top ten sales. However, this might not give you exactly the top ten values. This is because TOP n merely returns a specified number of rows. In the case of this query, it is perfectly possible that the top ten values could represent eleven or more sales. Only showing the TOP 10 would not exactly answer the question since it might not display a full ten *values*, just ten *records*.

6.   Segment Data into Deciles

While we are still exploring the area of data classification, suppose that the sales director wants to group sales into *deciles*— that is "*buckets*" of equal size where each group
of data contains one tenth of the records in the total dataset. The following SQL does
this for you:

```
SELECT       ST.Color, MakeName + ', ' + ModelName AS MakeAndModel

             ,SD.SalePrice

             ,NTILE(10) OVER (ORDER BY SD.SalePrice DESC) AS SalesDecile

FROM         Data.Make AS MK

INNER JOIN   Data.Model AS MD ON MK.MakeID = MD.MakeID

INNER JOIN   Data.Stock AS ST ON ST.ModelID = MD.ModelID

INNER JOIN   Data.SalesDetails SD ON ST.StockCode = SD.StockID

ORDER BY     SalesDecile, Color, MakeAndModel
```

Running this query gives the results that you can see in Figure 7-11. You have to
scroll down the result to see how the SalesDecile field changes every 35 records or so.

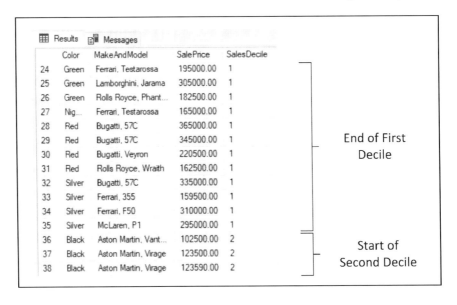

Figure 7-11. Using the NTILE() function to group data into segments

How It Works

You can see from the output that this query has added a field that indicates the decile (or segment, or bucket, if you prefer) that each record belongs to. You can then use this segmentation to pursue your analysis.

This query delivers an easy solution to a potentially complex question—all thanks to the NTILE() function. What this windowing function does is segment the dataset into as many separate subgroups as you have specified when you apply the function. Whatever the number of records in the dataset, the NTILE() function subdivides them into the number of groups that you specify as a parameter of the function.

This query is, at its heart, a simple SELECT query where you joined the necessary tables and selected the required fields. Then you added a final field using the NTILE() function.

Just like the RANK() and DENSE_RANK() functions, the NTILE() function requires you to add the OVER keyword and an ORDER BY clause inside parentheses—in addition to a value that is used for classifying the data. The NTILE() function requires one further element—the number of "buckets" that you want to appear in the output. This is defined by adding a number inside the parentheses just after the NTILE() function. The number that you add is the number of groups into which the dataset will be divided.

Tricks and Traps

We have only one comment to make here:

- NTILE() can also contain a PARTITION BY clause to add a further level of segmentation should you need it. It works exactly as it does for the RANK() function as you saw previously in Section 4.

7. Plot Values for a Percentile

SQL can be particularly useful when it comes to teasing out meaning from statistics. At least, that is what the sales director seems to believe, since she has come to you with this request: provide her with a dataset that contains the total cost for vehicles for each cost percentile and the corresponding repair cost. She wants to use this to create a chart that displays any potential correlation between the cost of a car and its repair cost.

```sql
;
WITH PercentileList_CTE

AS

(

SELECT     RepairsCost

           ,Cost

           ,NTILE(100) OVER (ORDER BY Cost DESC) AS Percentile

FROM       Data.Stock

)


SELECT     Percentile

           ,SUM(Cost) AS TotalCostPerPercentile

           ,SUM(RepairsCost) AS RepairsCostPerPercentile

               ,SUM(RepairsCost) / SUM(Cost) AS RepairCostRatio

FROM       PercentileList_CTE

GROUP BY   Percentile

ORDER BY   RepairCostRatio DESC
```

Execute this code snippet and you obtain the results that you can see in Figure 7-12.

	Percentile	TotalCostPerPercentile	RepairsCostPerPercentile	RepairCostRatio
1	100	1520.00	1000.00	0.6578
2	99	2312.00	1500.00	0.6487
3	98	2840.00	1500.00	0.5281
4	97	3080.00	1500.00	0.487
5	96	3748.00	1500.00	0.4002
6	95	6720.00	2000.00	0.2976
7	94	7480.00	2000.00	0.2673
8	93	8036.00	2000.00	0.2488
9	92	11320.00	2000.00	0.1766
10	91	13640.00	2000.00	0.1466
11	90	17600.00	2000.00	0.1136
12	89	18160.00	2000.00	0.1101
13	88	19560.00	2000.00	0.1022
14	72	42592.00	4190.00	0.0983
15	87	20912.00	2000.00	0.0956

FIGURE 7-12. PURCHASE COST VERSUS REPAIRS COST PER PERCENTILE

How It Works

This piece of SQL is essentially in two stages:

A CTE That attributes each sale to a percentile of sales. It also gives the repair cost for each sale. This CTE uses the NTILE() function and specifies that the function is to distribute the results over 100 groups, in effect segmenting the sales into percentiles.

A query That aggregates the output from the CTE to obtain the total for each percentile.

The CTE produces the output that you can see in Figure 7-13.

	RepairsCost	Cost	Percentile
1	2000.00	340000.00	1
2	9250.00	316000.00	1
3	3950.00	292000.00	1
4	9250.00	284000.00	1
5	9250.00	284000.00	2
6	5500.00	276000.00	2
7	2000.00	268000.00	2
8	9250.00	248000.00	2
9	3950.00	244000.00	3
10	5500.00	236000.00	3

FIGURE 7-13. ATTRIBUTING EACH SALE TO A PERCENTILE

Once you have the percentile that each sale belongs to, it is simple to aggregate the output so that you are grouping the result on each percentile and using the SUM() function to return the total for sales and repair costs per percentile.

Tricks and Traps

It is well worth noting that

- Although SQL Server cannot generate charts, it can isolate the data that you can then copy and paste into a spreadsheet. Alternatively, you can connect many applications directly to a SQL Server database. Indeed, you can use SQL Server Management Studio (SSMS) to hone your queries and then copy the query into the application that you are using to display and/or analyze the data.

- If all you want is the output from a query for a spreadsheet, then simply click inside the output in SSMS and right-click. Select Copy with Headers from the context menu. You can then paste the entire table into a spreadsheet.

- Be careful when copying large result sets from SSMS into other applications. It is easy to forget that they can run to millions of records and prove too much for either the destination workstation or the capacity of the spreadsheet.

8. Extract Data from a Specific Quintile

Prestige Cars caters to a wide range of clients, and the sales director does not want to forget about the 90 percent that are outside the top 10 percent of customers. She wants you to take a closer look at the second quintile of customers—those making up the second 20 percent of sales. Her exact request is this: "Find the sales details for the top three selling makes in the second 20 percent of sales." Here is the SQL to do this:

```
;
WITH Top20PercentSales_CTE
AS
(
SELECT       SalesDetailsID, MakeName, ModelName, SD.SalePrice
             ,NTILE(5) OVER (ORDER BY SalePrice DESC) AS SalesQuintile
FROM         Data.Make AS MK
INNER JOIN   Data.Model AS MD ON MK.MakeID = MD.MakeID
INNER JOIN   Data.Stock AS ST ON ST.ModelID = MD.ModelID
INNER JOIN   Data.SalesDetails SD ON ST.StockCode = SD.StockID
)

SELECT       MakeName, ModelName, SalePrice
FROM         Top20PercentSales_CTE CTE
WHERE        MakeName IN (
                         SELECT   TOP 3 MakeName
                         FROM     Top20PercentSales_CTE
                         WHERE    SalesQuintile = 2
                         GROUP BY MakeName
                         ORDER BY SUM(SalePrice) DESC
                         )
ORDER BY   SalePrice DESC
```

Running this query gives the results that you can see in Figure 7-14.

	MakeName	ModelName	SalePrice
1	Aston Martin	DB6	225000.00
2	Bentley	Brooklands	189500.00
3	Rolls Royce	Phantom	182500.00
4	Rolls Royce	Wraith	165000.00
5	Rolls Royce	Wraith	162500.00
6	Rolls Royce	Silver Seraph	139500.00
7	Rolls Royce	Silver Shadow	135000.00
8	Aston Martin	Virage	125500.00
9	Aston Martin	Virage	125000.00
10	Aston Martin	Vantage	125000.00
11	Aston Martin	Virage	123590.00
12	Aston Martin	Virage	123500.00
13	Rolls Royce	Silver Seraph	120000.00
14	Rolls Royce	Phantom	119600.00
15	Aston Martin	DB6	113590.00

FIGURE 7-14. USING THE NTILE() FUNCTION TO ISOLATE A SEGMENT OF DATA

How It Works

The ability to segment and classify your customers can make or break a business. This query shows you how to isolate a segment of sales data to produce exactly this kind of really useful information. The SQL in this example uses a CTE as the core of the query. The CTE uses the NTILE() function to list makes, models, and sale prices for all cars sold. Then it calculates the quintile for each sale.

Once the quintile has been defined, the subsequent query carries out two operations:

First: It uses a subquery to isolate the top three makes belonging to the second quintile.

Then: Once these makes have been found, the outer query outputs all sales for these makes from the CTE.

Tricks and Traps

Segmenting data can be a challenge—but an interesting one. Be sure to remember the following essential points when you have to deal with this kind of query:

- What is interesting here is that the CTE is used twice. The key technique is first to define the quintile, and then to select a specific quintile from the dataset. However, because the CTE also joins the tables required to list the make, model, and sale price, it can be *reused in the main query* so you don't have to rewrite all the SQL that is needed to produce this specific output.

- You can, of course, isolate deciles, percentiles—indeed any segment of data. All you have to do is enter the appropriate figure inside the parentheses that are part of the NTILE() function. For a *decile*, you would have entered the following SQL in the preceding example:

```
NTILE(10)  OVER  (ORDER BY SalePrice DESC) AS SalesDecile
```

9.   Display Median Values

The CEO has a solid background in statistics and has just asked for a report that shows the difference between the median discount and the actual discount for all sales per customer. SQL can also isolate a median value from a dataset—as this piece of SQL shows:

```
SELECT      DISTINCT  CU.CustomerName

            ,TotalSalePrice

            ,TotalSalePrice - PERCENTILE_CONT(0.5)

            WITHIN GROUP(ORDER BY TotalSalePrice)

                        OVER(PARTITION BY CustomerName)

                AS SaleToMedianDelta

FROM        Data.Sales AS SA

INNER JOIN Data.Customer CU ON SA.CustomerID = CU.CustomerID
```

Running this query gives the results that you can see in Figure 7-15.

	CustomerName	TotalSalePrice	SaleToMedianDelta
1	Alex McWhirter	17850.00	0
2	Alexei Tolstoi	3500.00	-44200
3	Alexei Tolstoi	22600.00	-25100
4	Alexei Tolstoi	22990.00	-24710
5	Alexei Tolstoi	45950.00	-1750
6	Alexei Tolstoi	49450.00	1750
7	Alexei Tolstoi	69500.00	21800
8	Alexei Tolstoi	102500.00	54800
9	Alexei Tolstoi	205000.00	157300
10	Alicia Almodovar	5690.00	-10260
11	Alicia Almodovar	12500.00	-3450
12	Alicia Almodovar	15950.00	0
13	Alicia Almodovar	39500.00	23550
14	Alicia Almodovar	45950.00	30000
15	Alicia Almodovar	250000.00	234050

FIGURE 7-15. DISPLAYING MEDIAN VALUES WITH THE PERCENTILE_CONT() FUNCTION

How It Works

There are times when you need to get a purely statistical answer from your data. Finding a median (rather than an average) value and comparing this to sales prices is one example of this. However, SQL does not have a median function in the same way that it has an AVG() function. Nonetheless, you can calculate a median using the built-in PERCENTILE_CONT() function. Finding a median value requires you to use the following SQL elements:

PERCENTILE_CONT(0.5)	The PERCENTILE_CONT() function finds a percentile in a dataset. Because you are looking for the median value, you need to indicate this by entering 0.5 inside the parentheses.
WITHIN GROUP	This lets you specify the numeric field that you want to extract the median value from. You also have to include the ORDER BY clause.
OVER (PARTITION BY)	As with the other windowing functions that you have seen in this chapter, PERCENTILE_CONT() allows you to segment the dataset into subgroups so that you can find the median value for each of the fields (or combinations of fields) that you specify after the PARTITION BY clause.

In this example, the query joins the Sales and Customer tables since they contain the fields that you need. Once the CustomerName and SalePrice fields have been selected, you add the clause required to extract the median value per customer and then subtract this from the sale price for each vehicle sold. In this case, this means specifying the Sale-Price field for the WITHIN GROUP argument and partitioning by the CustomerName in the OVER clause.

Conclusion

This chapter introduced you to some of the ways that you can use SQL to segment and classify data. You saw how to deliver hierarchies of data that can also segment the output according to the criteria that you specify. You also saw how to subset data into deciles and quintiles that you can extract for further analysis.

Core Knowledge Learned in This Chapter

The keywords that you have seen in this chapter are

Concept	Description
RANK()	*The RANK() function hierarchizes data according to the criterion that you define.*
OVER	*The OVER keyword is used by the RANK() function to introduce the ranking criteria*
PARTITION BY	*The PARTITION BY keyword is used by the RANK() function to separate the data into multiple hierarchies.*
DENSE_RANK()	*The DENSE_RANK() function hierarchizes data without any gaps in the ranking.*
NTILE()	*The NTILE() function distributes the rows in an ordered partition into a specified number of groups.*
PERCENTILE_CONT()	*The PERCENTILE_CONT() function is used (among other things) to calculate a median value.*
WITHIN GROUP	*The WITHIN GROUP keyword is used by the PERCENTILE_CONT() function to return a median value.*

Chapter 8:
Rolling Analysis

Few metrics exist in isolation. Most of the time, you not only want to compare these metrics with other figures, but you also want to see how they evolve over time. This lets you discern trends, track growth, and establish a solid factual base that you can use to make predictions.

Running Totals, Running Averages, Running Counts, and Comparative Values

SQL Server provides a range of functions that can help you show how data evolves over time—or, indeed, over any sequence or progression. These functions are both simple and easy to use. They help you deliver a range of running calculations, including

- Running totals
- Running averages
- Running counts

Fortunately, SQL Server does not require you to learn any new functions in order to deliver this kind of rolling analysis. It simply extends the use of a handful of functions that you know already, such as SUM(), AVG(), and COUNT(). Once you have mastered these extensions, you are also able to use this new approach with a few new functions to isolate

- Comparative values across a range of records
- The first or last element in a series
- The relative standing of a record in a recordset

Indeed, the great thing about these calculations is that they all work in a very similar way. The upshot is that once you have mastered the basics of how these functions work, you can apply them to your queries to give your analysis a new power and depth.

This set of functions goes under the name of *windowing functions*, because they group datasets into "windows" of data behind the scenes. They also allow you to specify what elements are calculated and exactly how they are grouped. This means that you can ask SQL Server to restart the running total at specific breakpoints. Consequently, you can restart a running calculation with every new year, month, or day if you want—and, in so doing, you can track how metrics evolve over time.

1. Adding a Running Total

The sales director does not always want complex analyses; sometimes she wants fairly simple lists as well. This time he has requested a list of sales for 2017 that includes running totals of both sales to date and average sales. Fortunately, windowing functions make this not too difficult, as the following code snippet displays:

```
SELECT      InvoiceNumber

            ,FORMAT(SaleDate, 'd', 'en-gb') AS DateOfSale

            ,SD.SalePrice

            ,SUM(SD.SalePrice)

            OVER (ORDER BY SaleDate ASC) AS AccumulatedSales

            ,AVG(SD.SalePrice)

            OVER (ORDER BY SaleDate ASC) AS AverageSalesValueToDate

FROM        Data.SalesDetails SD

INNER JOIN  Data.Sales AS SA ON SA.SalesID = SD.SalesID

WHERE       YEAR(SaleDate) = 2017

ORDER BY    SaleDate
```

Running this query gives the results that you can see in Figure 8-1.

	InvoiceNumber	DateOfSale	SalePrice	AccumulatedSales	AverageSalesValueToDate
1	EURFR110	01/01/2017	22500.00	22500.00	22500.000000
2	GBPGB111	05/01/2017	125000.00	147500.00	73750.000000
3	GBPGB112	10/01/2017	85000.00	232500.00	77500.000000
4	GBPCH114	11/01/2017	22500.00	255000.00	63750.000000
5	GBPGB115	12/01/2017	125950.00	380950.00	76190.000000
6	GBPCH116	13/01/2017	8850.00	389800.00	64966.666666
7	GBPGB117	14/01/2017	9950.00	399750.00	57107.142857
8	EURFR113	21/01/2017	1250.00	401000.00	50125.000000
9	EURFR118	30/01/2017	56500.00	457500.00	50833.333333
10	GBPGB119	31/01/2017	55000.00	569450.00	51768.181818
11	GBPGB120	31/01/2017	56950.00	569450.00	51768.181818
12	EURFR121	07/02/2017	365000.00	934450.00	77870.833333
13	EURFR122	08/02/2017	395000.00	1329450.00	102265.384615
14	USDUS123	09/02/2017	21500.00	1350950.00	96496.428571
15	GBPGB124	10/02/2017	6500.00	1357450.00	90496.666666

FIGURE 8-1. GENERATING RUNNING TOTALS WITH THE OVER CLAUSE

How It Works

A classic analytical requirement is to see how values change over time. This short piece of SQL shows not only how to list sales values, but also how the running total and average sale price change with each new sale.

The core of this query is a list of sales dates and values taken from the Sales and SalesDetails tables. The data is filtered to limit the result to sales for a given year. Finally, to give this initial list some coherence, it is sorted by sales date.

Then two windowing functions are added to enhance the output and to turbocharge the level of information that the query delivers. They do this by extending the use of two functions that you have come to know well: SUM() and AVG().

Each of these functions is extended with an OVER clause that causes the function to be applied to the field that you are calculating from the beginning of the dataset up to and including the current record. This way, both the SUM() function and the AVG() function perform their tasks (adding up the total sales and averaging the sale price, respectively) for each record, up to and including the current record, while the AVG() function also calculates the average sale price for each record up to and including the current record. The final result is a mixture of the detailed sales information for each sale and the overall data up to that date. Essentially, the OVER clause ensures that the functions are only applied to a part of the dataset, and not to the entire set, as has been the case up until now.

As you analyze how data evolves over time, it is important to ensure that the OVER function orders the data using a field, or fields, that sequence the records over time. In this example, we are using the SaleDate field so that the OVER function essentially says, "from the start of the filtered dataset up to the current record where the dataset is ordered by sale date."

Since this is a new use of the SUM() and AVG() functions, you may find that looking at an image makes it easier for you to grasp the concepts that are being applied. Figure 8-2 shows how windowing functions work more graphically.

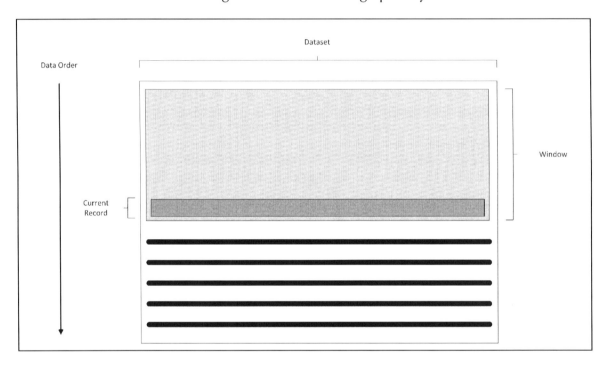

FIGURE 8-2. WINDOWING FUNCTIONS USED TO CREATE RUNNING TOTALS DESCRIBED CONCEPTUALLY

Tricks and Traps

Windowing functions are extremely powerful; however, they do require you to remain aware of a few key points if you are to use them correctly:

- Because you are listing the individual records for each sale, it helps if you display some piece of information (such as the invoice number in this example) that lets the reader see what makes each record unique.

- In this example, we formatted the date purely for presentation purposes. You can, of course, leave the date data in its raw state when you output the query results.

- When using several running totals in a single query, it is important to make sure that they use the same ORDER BY clause in the OVER operator or you could get results that are not what you are looking for.

- A running total, just like any other aggregation, needs an alias if you want a column title to be displayed in the output.

2. Using Windowing Functions in an Aggregated Query

Because Prestige Cars is perfectly capable of buying several cars on the same day, the CFO wants a report that displays the purchase cost per day with the cumulative cost for the year 2016. This is exactly what the following SQL code achieves:

```
SELECT       DateBought

            ,SUM(Cost) AS PurchaseCost

            ,SUM(SUM(Cost))

                OVER (ORDER BY DateBought ASC) AS CostForTheYear

FROM        Data.Stock

WHERE       YEAR(DateBought) = 2016

GROUP BY    DateBought

ORDER BY    DateBought
```

Running this query gives the results that you can see in Figure 8-3.

	DateBought	PurchaseCost	CostForTheYear
1	2016-01-02	35760.00	35760.00
2	2016-01-10	45560.00	81320.00
3	2016-01-31	44800.00	126120.00
4	2016-02-01	52712.00	178832.00
5	2016-02-10	4800.00	183632.00
6	2016-02-11	38280.00	221912.00
7	2016-02-27	125560.00	347472.00
8	2016-03-15	31600.00	379072.00
9	2016-03-19	2920.00	381992.00
10	2016-04-17	176400.00	558392.00
11	2016-04-26	82360.00	640752.00
12	2016-04-29	14000.00	654752.00
13	2016-05-02	93600.00	748352.00
14	2016-05-11	10000.00	758352.00
15	2016-05-25	7960.00	766312.00

FIGURE 8-3. USING WINDOWING FUNCTIONS IN AN AGGREGATED QUERY

How It Works

Sometimes you might need to see an aggregated value, such as the cost of goods bought per day, alongside the running total over time of these same costs. You do this by grouping data from the Stock table on the DateBought field and by displaying this field alongside the SUM() of the Cost field. To avoid getting drowned in data, make sure the output is restricted to only purchases for 2016.

After this, ask SQL Server to provide a running total using a SUM()...OVER windowing function. However, because this function is a grouped query (or an *aggregated query*, if you prefer), it needs to be aggregated as well. You have to make the SUM(Cost) function into an aggregate function by writing it as *SUM(SUM(Cost))*.

Tricks and Traps

We have only one point that really needs your attention here, but it is a very important one. This example is based on a simple technique that you must bear in mind when aggregating data using windowing functions:

- It may seem peculiar, and even counterintuitive, to wrap a SUM() function inside another SUM() function. But if you write this query as

```
SUM(Cost)) OVER (ORDER BY DateBought ASC)
```

then the query fails. Remember, if you are grouping data in a query, you must *also* group data used in running totals.

3. Grouping Running Totals

You can use running totals to get an idea of how your key metrics evolve. Sometimes, however, you want to reset a grouping element so that you can start over when some key piece of data changes—like beginning a new year, for instance. So, when the sales director requests a list that shows all sales to date with a running count of sales per year, you are relieved that you can use a windowing function to answer her query. The following SQL snippet shows you how to reset a counter or a running total:

```
SELECT      FORMAT(SaleDate, 'd', 'en-gb') AS DateOfSale

            ,CU.CustomerName, CU.Town

            ,SD.SalePrice

            ,COUNT(SD.SalesDetailsID)

            OVER (PARTITION BY YEAR(SaleDate)

                ORDER BY SalesDetailsID ASC)

                    AS AnnualNumberOfSalesToDate
FROM        Data.SalesDetails SD

INNER JOIN  Data.Sales AS SA ON SA.SalesID = SD.SalesID

INNER JOIN  Data.Customer CU ON SA.CustomerID = CU.CustomerID

ORDER BY    SaleDate
```

Running this query gives the results that you can see in Figure 8-4.

FIGURE 8-4. GROUPED RUNNING TOTALS USING OVER AND PARTITION BY

How It Works

This query begins by joining the Customer, Sales, and SalesDetails tables so that you can return sales and customer information—such as the date of sale, customer name, and sale price—for each sale. No filter is applied because you want to see all sales since Prestige Cars began trading. The query is sorted by date to ensure that the data appear in a clear and comprehensible way.

You can now add the running counter of sales over time. You build it like this:

First:	Work out the number of sales by adding a COUNT() function.
Second:	Extended this function to make it a windowing function by adding an OVER clause.
Third:	Order the resulting counter by a *unique field combination*— the SaleDate field and the SalesDetailsID field—so there is no aggregation of the data and each individual record displays.
Finally:	Add a PARTITION BY clause so that the counter *restarts* when the field specified after the PARTITION BY clause (the year) *changes*.

The end result is a list of all sales over time where you can see not only the accumulated sales as the year progresses, but also the total sales for the year at year end.

Once again, a visual representation may help you understand this better. Figure 8-5 shows you how a PARTITION BY clause works with a windowing function.

FIGURE 8-5. A PARTITION BY CLAUSE WITH A WINDOWING FUNCTION

Tricks and Traps

When you add a PARTITION BY clause to a windowing function, you need to remember the following key points:

- It is important to use the appropriate fields in the ORDER BY clause of the OVER function to achieve your desired output. If you use the wrong fields, it probably will not return the result that you expect. In practice, this means you need to select a field that contains the finest level of granularity of the data that is meaningful. In this example, each individual sale is what matters, so you use the SalesDetailsID field in both the COUNT() function and the ORDER BY clause because it contains a unique value for each record. This ensures that all records are output individually and not aggregated in any way.

- If you use the SaleDate field instead of the SalesDetailsID field in this query, SQL Server counts the days with sales throughout the year. Since there may well be days with multiple sales—or no sales at all—the resulting recordset will not give the same results.

- Generally, you want to make sure that you are repeating the field(s) that you are using to sort the data in the query (that is, the field or fields that you are using in the main ORDER BY clause) in the OVER clause. This ensures that the output is visually coherent with the actual data analysis.

4. Applying Windowing Functions to a Subquery

The CEO is obsessed with analyzing key metrics over time. Her latest request is that you obtain the total sales for each date and then add the running total of sales by value for each year. The following code snippet shows how to do this:

```
SELECT      FORMAT(SaleDate, 'd', 'en-us') AS DateOfSale

            ,DailyCount AS NumberOfSales

            ,SUM(DailyCount) OVER

                    (PARTITION BY YEAR(SaleDate) ORDER BY SaleDate ASC)

                    AS AnnualNumberOfSalesToDate

            ,SUM(DailySalePrice) OVER

                    (PARTITION BY YEAR(SaleDate) ORDER BY SaleDate ASC)

                    AS AnnualSalePriceToDate

FROM        (

            SELECT      SaleDate

                        ,COUNT(SD.SalesDetailsID) AS DailyCount

                        ,SUM(SD.SalePrice) AS DailySalePrice

            FROM        Data.SalesDetails SD

            INNER JOIN  Data.Sales AS SA

                        ON SA.SalesID = SD.SalesID

            GROUP BY    SaleDate

            ) DT

ORDER BY    SaleDate
```

Running this query gives the results that you can see in Figure 8-6.

	DateOfSale	NumberOfSales	AnnualNumberOfSalesToDate	AnnualSalePriceToDate
1	1/2/2015	1	1	65000.00
2	1/2/2015	1	2	84950.00
3	1/25/2015	1	3	304950.00
4	2/3/2015	1	4	324450.00
5	2/16/2015	1	5	335950.00
6	3/14/2015	1	6	365450.00
7	3/24/2015	1	7	414950.00
22	10/30/20...	2	26	1328525.00
23	11/10/20...	1	27	1351475.00
24	12/1/2015	1	28	1420975.00
25	1/1/2016	4	4	349500.00
26	1/7/2016	2	6	381550.00
27	1/9/2016	1	7	394200.00
28	1/22/2016	1	8	451150.00
29	2/16/2016	1	9	490650.00
30	2/17/2016	2	11	562540.00
31	2/22/2016	1	12	618540.00
32	2/28/2016	1	13	622190.00

FIGURE 8-6. USING WINDOWING FUNCTIONS AND A SUBQUERY

How It Works

Possibly the easiest way to achieve the objectives that you have set yourself in this query is to break the task into two parts:

First: Create a derived table that counts the number and value of sales per day for each individual date.

Second: Create an outer query that returns the sales per day in addition to the running total of sales revenue from the derived table.

In this example, the subquery is an aggregate query that groups the result by date and provides a COUNT() of sales and a SUM() of sales value. We did not apply any filters so that all sales from the start of trading are included. To get a clearer idea of what is included, take a look at Figure 8-7, which shows the output from the subquery.

FIGURE 8-7. SUBQUERY OUTPUT

The outer query can then take the three fields that are generated by the inner query (sale date, daily sales count, and daily sales value) and use them as follows:

SaleDate — Is displayed in the output "as is" and is also used to sort the query results.

DailyCount — Is also output "as is" to display the number of sales for each day that there are sales.

DailyCount — Is reused in a windowing function to provide the running total of sales to date. We achieve the running total by applying the COUNT() function over the sale date. In this example, this aggregate value is also partitioned by year using the PARTITION BY clause so that the count restarts with each new year.

DailySalePrice — Is reused (and output as AnnualNumberOf SalesToDate) in a separate windowing function that is also ordered by sale date and partitioned by the year. This allows you to show the cumulative sales to date for each year.

Using a subquery to perform the initial aggregation is an effective way of preparing the initial data that you then use to provide the running totals. It also allows you to test the initial data simply by selecting and executing the inner query; this way you can check each part of the process as you build the query.

5. Adding Unique IDs on the Fly Using ROW_NUMBER()

None of the sales staff like using the complex identifiers that appear in the billing system. They have asked you to create your own numbering system to identify sales. The following SQL shows how to add this kind of distinguishing feature without changing the source data:

```
SELECT        FORMAT(SA.SaleDate, 'd', 'en-gb') AS DateOfSale

              ,SD.SalePrice, CU.CustomerName, CU.Town, MK.MakeName

              ,COUNT(SD.SalesDetailsID)

                OVER (PARTITION BY YEAR(SaleDate) ORDER BY SaleDate ASC)

                AS AnnualNumberOfSalesToDate

              ,ROW_NUMBER() OVER (ORDER BY SaleDate ASC) AS SalesCounter
FROM          Data.Make AS MK
INNER JOIN    Data.Model AS MD ON MK.MakeID = MD.MakeID
INNER JOIN    Data.Stock AS ST ON ST.ModelID = MD.ModelID
INNER JOIN    Data.SalesDetails SD ON ST.StockCode = SD.StockID
INNER JOIN    Data.Sales AS SA ON SA.SalesID = SD.SalesID
INNER JOIN    Data.Customer CU ON SA.CustomerID = CU.CustomerID
ORDER BY      SaleDate
```

Running this query gives the results that you can see in Figure 8-8.

	DateOfSale	SalePrice	CustomerName	Town	MakeName	AnnualNumberOfSalesToDate	SalesCounter
1	02/01/2015	65000.00	Magic Motors	Birmingham	Ferrari	1	1
2	02/01/2015	19950.00	Casseroles Chromes	Lyon	Porsche	2	2
3	25/01/2015	220000.00	Snazzy Roadsters	Birmingham	Ferrari	3	3
4	03/02/2015	19500.00	Birmingham Executive Prestige Vehicles	Birmingham	Porsche	4	4
5	16/02/2015	11500.00	WunderKar	Berlin	Porsche	5	5
6	14/03/2015	29500.00	Magic Motors	Birmingham	Aston Martin	6	6
7	24/03/2015	49500.00	Birmingham Executive Prestige Vehicles	Birmingham	Aston Martin	7	7
8	30/03/2015	76000.00	Eat My Exhaust Ltd	Liverpool	Aston Martin	8	8
339	05/12/2018	59500.00	Jason B. Wight	Washington	Aston Martin	119	339
340	05/12/2018	123500.00	Ronaldo Bianco	Milan	Aston Martin	119	340
341	08/12/2018	99500.00	Andrea Tarbuck	Birmingham	Aston Martin	122	341
342	08/12/2018	54500.00	Boris Spry	Birmingham	Aston Martin	122	342
343	08/12/2018	1590.00	Boris Spry	Birmingham	Trabant	122	343
344	16/12/2018	11500.00	Antonio Maura	Madrid	Triumph	123	344
345	17/12/2018	17950.00	Screamin' Wheels	Los Angeles	Alfa Romeo	124	345
346	31/12/2018	5500.00	Laurent Saint Yves	Marseille	Citroen	127	346
347	31/12/2018	950.00	Mrs. Ivana Telford	Liverpool	Reliant	127	347
348	31/12/2018	145000.00	Andy Cheshire	Stoke	Ferrari	127	348

FIGURE 8-8. USING THE ROW_NUMBER() WINDOWING FUNCTION TO ADD UNIQUE IDS TO A RECORDSET

How It Works

Source data does not always come with all the elements that you need. At times, you may require a way of numbering records to identify each row individually. The ROW_NUMBER() function lets you do just this, and it has no effect on the underlying data.

This query starts by joining all the tables that are necessary, which allows you to display the fields that you want to output (SaleDate, SalePrice, CustomerName, Town, and MakeName). Then it adds these fields—with any necessary formatting and aliases—to the SELECT clause.

Then two windowing functions are added:

COUNT()   To display the number of sales per day per year. This function is partitioned by year (so that the counter restarts each time the year changes) and ordered by date.

ROW_NUMBER()   To show an individual and progressively incrementing number to identify each record that is output.

The special feature in this query is the use of the ROW_NUMBER() windowing function. This function lets you add a series of numbers to an output dataset. The series starts at 1 and increases by one for each record in the dataset.

The ROW_NUMBER() also requires you to add an OVER clause containing an ORDER BY statement. To ensure that these virtual IDs are numbered sequentially in a comprehensible manner, the ROW_NUMBER() function is ordered by the sale date. Since we want a continuous range of numbers defined for all the source data, we choose not to add a PARTITION BY clause to the windowing function. The result is a series of numbers that are consecutively incremented in the query output, even if there is no numbering in the source data.

Tricks and Traps

There is one important point to remember when you are applying the ROW_NUMBER() function:

- ROW_NUMBER() is not the same as COUNT()—despite the superficial similarities. If you look at the output for this query for April 30, 2015, you see two records for this date. The COUNT() windowing function shows a total of 12 sales to date for this day—and this is the same for either of the day's sales (as it should be). The ROW_NUMBER() function attributes a different number to each record, even if the ORDER BY clause for the function is the SaleDate field.

  So the ROW_NUMBER() function *always* differentiates the records that are returned. This can mean applying the numbering sequence arbitrarily to certain rows. You can see this in the two sales for April 30, 2015.

  OF course, if you really want to specify a completely comprehensive numbering system, you can extend the sort order that is applied by the ROW_NUMBER() function. So, you could, for instance, tweak the SQL to read

```
ROW_NUMBER() OVER (ORDER BY SaleDate, Make, Model ASC) AS SalesCounter
```

6. Displaying Records for Missing Data

The CEO has just had another idea; you can tell by the smile on her face as she walks over to your desk. Hiding your trepidation, you listen as she tells you that she needs a weekly calendar of sales for 2016. She makes it clear that she wants to see a list of all the weeks in the year, whether there were any sales in that week or not.

After a little effort, you produce the following SQL to deliver the sales report that she was hoping for:

```
;
WITH Tally_CTE
AS
(
SELECT      TOP 52 ROW_NUMBER() OVER (ORDER BY StockCode) AS Num
FROM        Data.Stock
)


SELECT          Num, SalesForTheWeek
FROM            Tally_CTE CTE
LEFT OUTER JOIN
                (
                SELECT          SUM(TotalSalePrice) AS SalesForTheWeek
                                ,DatePart(wk, SaleDate) AS WeekNo
                FROM            Data.Sales
                WHERE           YEAR(SaleDate) = 2016
                GROUP BY        DatePart(wk, SaleDate)
                ) SLS
                ON CTE.Num = SLS.WeekNo
```

Running this SQL produces output like that shown in Figure 8-9.

FIGURE 8-9. DISPLAYING MISSING DATA USING A SEQUENCE LIST

How It Works

Delivering data when the data exists is rarely an issue; however, you may need to apply slightly different querying techniques if you need to show "missing" data. By this, we mean that SQL does not naturally create complete lists of dates, or date elements such as weeks, where there is no corresponding data in a database.

To understand this problem more clearly, run the SQL from the preceding snippet that returns the total sales per week for 2016, which is contained in the derived table with the alias SLS. The output from the derived table looks like that shown in Figure 8-10.

FIGURE 8-10. THE SOURCE DATA WITH MISSING VALUES

Although the figures are accurate, the data contains holes since there are no sales for certain weeks. Since these holes could be precisely the data that you want to focus on, it is important to return a full list of weeks—whether they contain data or not.

Forcing SQL Server to return a complete sequence (whether it is dates, weeks, or any other series of information) requires you to extend the SQL with a list that contains an unbroken and consecutive list of all the elements that you need to view. You can then use this list as the basis for a query that adds the aggregated output that you require.

A sequence like this is often called a *tally table* or a *numbers list*. What you have done in this SQL is

First:	Created a CTE (Common Table Expression) that contains a numbers list.
Second:	Joined the CTE to a query (the derived subquery in this example) that calculates the sales per week.

Let's begin by looking at the numbers table. Although we call this a table, it is really a dataset generated by a CTE. If you run the code inside the CTE named Tally_CTE, you see the output in Figure 8-11.

FIGURE 8-11. A SEQUENCE LIST OR TALLY TABLE

As you can see, this CTE simply returns a sequence of numbers. You obtain this sequence by

First:	Choosing a table that contains more records than you need in the numbers table (the CTE output). This can be any table in the database.

| *Then:* | Selecting the first *n* records from this table that correspond to the number of items in the sequence that you require. In this example, there are 52 weeks in the year, so you use TOP 52 to limit the number of elements in the tally table. |
| *Finally:* | Since you are *not interested in the actual data* that the source table (Stock) contains, but only in the number of records, you define a ROW_NUMBER() function (ordered by any field in the table) to provide a sequence of numbers. |

The CTE at the start of the SQL serves *only to provide a sequential list* that provides a row for each week in the year.

Once you have the tally table set up, join this to the derived table that returns the actual data for each week of sales. Because you have extracted the week number from the SaleDate field using the DATEPART() function, you can join the week number for each week of sales to the corresponding record in the tally table. Defining the join as a LEFT OUTER join from the tally table (the CTE) to the derived query ensures that every record from the CTE is displayed, whether or not any corresponding data is in the derived query.

The result is the output from Figure 8-9, shown previously, that shows all the weeks in 2016 with the sales figures, even if there are no sales for a specific week.

| Note | If you use a single table as the basis for the tally table, it must contain at least as many records as you need for the sequential list. The next section explains a technique you can use to guarantee enough rows if you are worried that a single source table will not contain enough records. |

7. Displaying a Complete Range of Dates and Relevant Data

You really impressed the CEO with your calendar of weekly sales. The only downside is that she clearly told the sales director to look at increasing sales and avoiding days with no sales, because the sales director has just requested a list of daily sales for a six-month period (from January 1 to June 30, 2017, to be precise).

After a little head-scratching, you come up with the following piece of SQL:

```
;

WITH Tally_CTE

AS

(

SELECT      TOP 10000 ROW_NUMBER() OVER (ORDER BY ST1.StockCode) -1 AS
Num

FROM        Data.Stock ST1

CROSS JOIN Data.Stock ST2

)

,DateRange_CTE

AS

(

SELECT      DATEADD(DD, Num,'20170101') AS DateList FROM Tally_CTE

WHERE       Num <= DATEDIFF(DD, '20170101', '20170630')

)


SELECT          CAST(DateList AS DATE) AS SaleDate, SalesPerDay

FROM            DateRange_CTE CTE

LEFT OUTER JOIN

                (

                SELECT      CAST(SaleDate AS DATE) AS DateOfSale

                            ,SUM(TotalSalePrice) AS SalesPerDay

                FROM        Data.Sales

                GROUP BY    CAST(SaleDate AS DATE)

                ) SLS

                ON CTE.DateList = SLS.DateOfSale
```

Running this code delivers the output that you can see in Figure 8-12.

	SaleDate	SalesPerDay
1	2017-01-01	22500.00
2	2017-01-02	NULL
3	2017-01-03	NULL
4	2017-01-04	NULL
5	2017-01-05	125000.00
6	2017-01-06	NULL
7	2017-01-07	NULL
8	2017-01-08	NULL
9	2017-01-09	NULL
10	2017-01-10	85000.00
11	2017-01-11	22500.00
12	2017-01-12	125950.00
13	2017-01-13	8850.00
14	2017-01-14	9950.00
15	2017-01-15	NULL

FIGURE 8-12. A COMPLETE RANGE OF DATES INCLUDING DATES WITHOUT ANY CORRESPONDING DATA

How It Works

Once again, the source data used in this example does not necessarily contain records for empty values—that is, there is not necessarily a sale every day during the relevant period. Once again, you need to ensure that you have a sequence of a range of dates where there are no missing values.

You accomplish this using two CTEs:

The first CTE   Is a tally table (or a numbers dataset if you prefer) that ensures a large sequence of numbers. This guarantees that you can request a range of dates over several years if necessary.

The second CTE   Uses the tally table to create a sequence of dates between a start date and an end date.

As each of these CTEs carries out a specific task, it is probably easier to look at each of them in turn.

The tally table CTE works like this:

First: It specifies a large incremented list of a range of numbers (10,000 in this case—enough for nearly 30 years of individual days) using the ROW_NUMBER() function. Because the tally table begins at 1 by default, in this example, we tweaked it to start at 0 by subtracting 1 from the output of the function. This way, the DATEADD() and DATEDIFF() functions begin and end with the actual start and end dates the SQL snippet uses (DATEADD() starts the list of dates by adding 0 days to the start date—effectively beginning at the date used in the code).

Second: It uses two tables (or the same table twice with two different aliases) that are joined using the CROSS APPLY operator. This approach multiplies the number of records in the first table by the number of records in the second table producing a large set of records that become the basis for the number sequence.

The DateRange CTE works like this:

First: The DATEADD() function is used to increment a start date (January 1, 2017) with a sequence of days. This CTE is based on the value in the first CTE, which it, in effect, converts to a date by adding the value in the first CTE to the start date.

Second: A WHERE clause filters the upper limit of the date range to June 30, 2017. It does this by using the DATEDIFF() function to calculate the number of days between the start and end dates, which are also specified in the DATEDIFF() function. The number of days becomes the upper threshold for the largest record number from the tally dataset.

If you run the following code snippet just after the two CTEs (in line 15 of the code, on the blank line before the final SELECT clause), you can see the range of continuous calendar dates shown in Figure 8-13.

```
SELECT * FROM DateRange_CTE
```

FIGURE 8-13. A COMPLETE RANGE OF DATES BASED ON A TALLY TABLE

Finally, the second CTE—DateRange_CTE—is joined to the derived query that aggregates daily sales. As was the case in the previous example, it is the range of dates that is the "core" table in the query so that an unbroken range of dates is output. A LEFT OUTER join to the derived table ensures that the derived table and the second CTE join on their respective date fields.

Tricks and Traps

We have a couple of comments worthy of note at this point:

- The cross join to get a large number of records from two tables is called, technically, a *Cartesian join*. This kind of join shows each record from one table joined to each record from the other table. Although this can be dangerous when you are carrying out precise queries, this approach is useful when you need to create a tally table.

- Unless you are sure that the date fields that you are using to join the derived table and the tally dataset are of the DATE data type, it is worth converting the date fields to DATEs. This ensures that the join is successful.

8.   Comparing Data with the Data from a Previous Record

Prestige Car's sales director is keen to track customer spend. She wants you to track sales over time and highlight the difference between previous and current sale values per customer for each sale. The following piece of SQL lets you satisfy his demand:

```
SELECT      CustomerName

            ,SaleDate

            ,TotalSalePrice

            ,TotalSalePrice - LAG(TotalSalePrice,1)

                        OVER (PARTITION BY CustomerName

                        ORDER BY SaleDate)

                              AS DifferenceToPreviousSalePrice

FROM        Data.Sales SA

INNER JOIN Data.Customer CU

            ON SA.CustomerID = CU.CustomerID

ORDER BY    SaleDate
```

Running this query gives the results that you can see in Figure 8-14.

	CustomerName	SaleDate	TotalSalePrice	DifferenceToPreviousSalePrice
1	Magic Motors	2015-01-02 00:00:00.000	65000.00	NULL
2	Casseroles Chromes	2015-01-02 10:33:00.000	19900.00	NULL
3	Snazzy Roadsters	2015-01-25 00:00:00.000	220000.10	NULL
4	Birmingham Executive Prestige Vehicles	2015-02-03 00:00:00.000	19500.00	NULL
5	WunderKar	2015-02-16 00:00:00.000	11500.00	NULL
6	Magic Motors	2015-03-14 00:00:00.000	29500.00	-35500.00
7	Birmingham Executive Prestige Vehicles	2015-03-24 00:00:00.000	49500.20	30000.20
8	Eat My Exhaust Ltd	2015-03-30 00:00:00.000	76000.90	NULL
9	Sondra Horowitz	2015-04-04 00:00:00.000	36500.00	NULL
10	M. Pierre Dubois	2015-04-06 00:00:00.000	19600.00	NULL
11	Wonderland Wheels	2015-04-30 00:00:00.000	89000.00	NULL
12	London Executive Prestige Vehicles	2015-05-10 00:00:00.000	169500.00	NULL
13	M. Pierre Dubois	2015-05-20 00:00:00.000	8950.00	-10650.00
14	Glittering Prize Cars Ltd	2015-05-28 00:00:00.000	195000.00	NULL
15	La Bagnole de Luxe	2015-06-04 16:37:00.000	22950.00	NULL

FIGURE 8-14. COMPARING DATA BETWEEN RECORDS USING THE LAG() FUNCTION

How It Works

Although we have seen how to compare individual pieces of data with groups of data, so far in this book, we have not compared individual records to other records. As a first example of how to look at how a sequence of records varies from record to record, this piece of SQL shows how each sale compares to the previous one for the same customer.

In this piece of code you meet the LAG() function for the first time. This function allows you to look back over a subset of records and return data from a previous record, or records.

The query works like this:

First: A perfectly normal query is constructed that returns a list of individual sales with the sale price and the customer who bought the car using the Sales and Customer tables.

Then: A LAG() function is added that goes back through the recordset until it finds the previous sale for the same customer as the one in the current record. It returns the previous sale price and, for this customer, subtracts this from the current record's sale price to give the difference in the sale price for the vehicle.

Just like the other windowing functions that you have seen, the LAG() function requires a few parameters to work properly. In this example they are

OVER	This operator introduces a windowing function.
PARTITION BY	This operator tells SQL Server how to group the data when searching for a previous record. Since this example has PARTITION BY CustomerName inside the OVER clause, SQL only jumps back to records that have the same customer name as the current record.
ORDER BY	This clause sorts the subset of data (that is grouped by customer) in chronological order, since it is the SaleDate field that provides the sort order.
Field	This indicates the *data to return from the preceding record.* In this example, it is the SalePrice field.
Offset Value	This is the number of records to jump back for this customer. The value is set to 1 in this example because we want the *previous* record for the same customer.

Once all these elements are in place, the LAG() function can "subset" the data into an invisible group based on the customer field. Since this data subset is a list of records over time relative to the current record, the function steps back into the preceding record for the customer and returns the previous sale price. As you can see in the output, there is, by definition, no previous sale for the first sale for each customer. This is why the LAG() function returns a NULL value.

If you can visualize what is happening, it may help you d eal with previous records. Take a look at Figure 8-15; in it, you can see a high-level overview of how the LAG() value works.

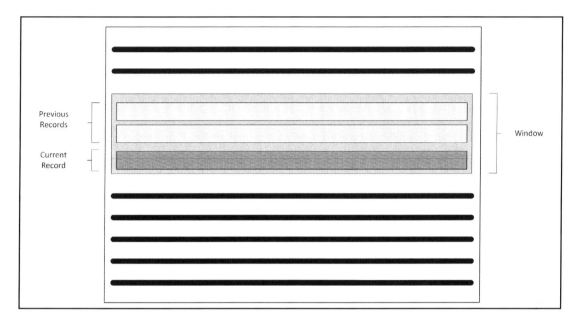

FIGURE 8-15. CONCEPTUAL OVERVIEW OF THE LAG() FUNCTION

Tricks and Traps

The LAG() function is extremely powerful. This inevitably means that you have to master a few subtleties if you want to apply it constructively:

- The field that you place inside the LAG() function does *not* have to appear in the SELECT clause; however, it must be in one of the tables contained in the FROM clause of the query.

- If you do not want to see records where there is no difference with any previous sale (because this was the first sale), you can use nearly all of this query as a derived table and wrap it in an outer query. This query then selects the columns from the derived table and adds a WHERE clause to eliminate the PreviousSalePriceDifference records that contain NULLs. The code looks like this:

```
SELECT *

FROM

(

SELECT     CustomerName
```

```
          ,SaleDate

          ,TotalSalePrice

          ,TotalSalePrice - LAG(TotalSalePrice,1)

                        OVER (PARTITION BY CustomerName

                              ORDER BY SaleDate)

                                    AS PreviousSalePriceDifference
FROM        Data.Sales SA

            INNER JOIN Data.Customer CU

            ON SA.CustomerID = CU.CustomerID

) SQ

WHERE PreviousSalePriceDifference IS NOT NULL

ORDER BY    SaleDate
```

Running this query gives the output that you can see in Figure 8-16.

	CustomerName	SaleDate	TotalSalePrice	PreviousSalePriceDifference
1	Magic Motors	2015-03-14 00:00:00.000	29500.00	-35500.00
2	Birmingham Executive Prestige Vehicles	2015-03-24 00:00:00.000	49500.20	30000.20
3	M. Pierre Dubois	2015-05-20 00:00:00.000	8950.00	-10650.00
4	Peter McLuckie	2015-09-15 00:00:00.000	15600.00	2950.00
5	Alexei Tolstoi	2015-10-30 00:00:00.000	22600.00	-390.00
6	Theo Kowalski	2015-10-30 00:00:00.000	123590.00	118090.00
7	Convertible Dreams	2015-11-10 00:00:00.000	22950.00	14255.00
8	Alexei Tolstoi	2015-12-01 00:00:00.000	69500.00	46900.00
9	Eat My Exhaust Ltd	2016-01-01 00:00:00.000	12500.00	-63500.90
10	Wonderland Wheels	2016-01-01 00:00:00.000	165000.00	76000.00
11	Sondra Horowitz	2016-01-01 00:00:00.000	159500.00	123000.00
12	Posh Vehicles Ltd	2016-01-07 00:00:00.000	29500.00	20550.00
13	M. Pierre Dubois	2016-01-07 00:00:00.000	2550.00	-6400.00
14	SuperSport S.A.R.L.	2016-02-16 00:00:00.000	39500.00	-36000.00
15	Magic Motors	2016-02-28 00:00:00.000	3650.00	-25850.00

FIGURE 8-16. USING A SUBQUERY WITH A LAG() FUNCTION IN A DERIVED TABLE

You cannot simply apply the WHERE clause inside the original query to filter the recordset and remove any records with NULL values for the sale price. This is because windowing functions can *only be used in SELECT or ORDER BY clauses*. Consequently, you have to move the ORDER BY clause from the derived table to the outer query.

- A PARTITION BY function is not required when using the LAG() function. However, without one, the LAG() function returns data from a record that precedes the current record in the overall dataset without attempting to filter the comparative dataset by a specific element—such as the customer.

9. Comparing Data over Time Using the FIRST_VALUE() and LAST_VALUE() Functions

Prestige Cars is continuing its drive to maximize revenue per customer. This time, the sales director wants to find the initial and final sale prices for each car sold to each customer and then compare these prices with the current selling price. You create the following piece of SQL to do this for her:

```
SELECT      CustomerName

            ,SaleDate

            ,TotalSalePrice AS CurrentSale

            ,FIRST_VALUE(TotalSalePrice)

            OVER (PARTITION BY CU.CustomerName

                  ORDER BY SaleDate, SalesID)

                        AS InitialOrder

            ,LAST_VALUE(TotalSalePrice)

            OVER (PARTITION BY CU.CustomerName

                  ORDER BY SaleDate, SalesID

                  ROWS BETWEEN CURRENT ROW AND UNBOUNDED FOLLOWING)

                        AS FinalOrder

FROM        Data.Sales SA
```

```
INNER JOIN Data.Customer CU

    ON SA.CustomerID = CU.CustomerID
```

Running this query gives the results that you can see in Figure 8-17.

	CustomerName	SaleDate	Current Sale	InitialOrder	FinalOrder
1	Alex McWhirter	2018-10-31 00:00:00.000	17850.00	17850.00	17850.00
2	Alexei Tolstoi	2016-09-16 00:00:00.000	45950.00	22990.00	45950.00
3	Alexei Tolstoi	2016-09-04 00:00:00.000	3500.00	22990.00	45950.00
4	Alexei Tolstoi	2016-08-02 00:00:00.000	102500.00	22990.00	45950.00
5	Alexei Tolstoi	2016-07-25 00:00:00.000	205000.00	22990.00	45950.00
6	Alexei Tolstoi	2016-05-30 00:00:00.000	49450.00	22990.00	45950.00
7	Alexei Tolstoi	2015-12-01 00:00:00.000	69500.00	22990.00	45950.00
8	Alexei Tolstoi	2015-10-30 00:00:00.000	22600.00	22990.00	45950.00
9	Alexei Tolstoi	2015-07-15 00:00:00.000	22990.00	22990.00	45950.00
10	Alicia Almodovar	2018-04-15 00:00:00.000	45950.00	12500.00	45950.00
11	Alicia Almodovar	2018-04-02 00:00:00.000	15950.00	12500.00	45950.00
12	Alicia Almodovar	2018-03-05 00:00:00.000	5690.00	12500.00	45950.00
13	Alicia Almodovar	2017-09-20 00:00:00.000	250000.00	12500.00	45950.00
14	Alicia Almodovar	2017-05-10 00:00:00.000	12500.00	12500.00	45950.00
15	Alicia Almodovar	2016-12-31 00:00:00.000	39500.00	12500.00	45950.00

FIGURE 8-17. USING THE FIRST_VALUE() AND LAST_VALUE() FUNCTIONS TO COMPARE SALE PRICES

How It Works

A useful way to analyze how data evolves over time is to see how a record compares to the first or last record for a common element. This query starts by joining the Customer and Sales tables so that it can access customer and sale data. Then it outputs the CustomerName, SaleDate, and TotalSalePrice fields.

Then a new twist is added. Two output fields are added that are based, respectively, on the FIRST_VALUE() and LAST_VALUE() functions. These act like the LAG() function that you saw in the previous example in that for each record, they create an invisible dataset that is grouped on a shared field (CustomerName in this example). However, in this case, it is not a selected preceding record that is selected, but the very first (or very last) record in this virtual subgroup.

FIRST_VALUE() and LAST_VALUE() require the following elements to work correctly:

OVER   This clause starts the windowing function.

| PARTITION BY | This function tells SQL Server how to subset the data when searching for the first record; in this example, this means the first value for the customer of the current record. |

The PARTITION BY function is not strictly necessary, but it is used to compare data that share a common element rather than merely returning the first or last value from the entire dataset.

| ORDER BY | This clause sorts the data subset. |
| Field | This indicates the data to return from the preceding record. In this example, it is the SalePrice field. |

The FIRST_VALUE(), LAST_VALUE(), and LAG() functions can be particularly useful because by using them, you avoid having to create multiple, complex subqueries or derived tables to isolate values from the data. These functions traverse the data for each element that is specified in the PARTITION BY clause (the client in this example) and return the record that you are looking for.

Figure 8-18 illustrates how these functions work.

FIGURE 8-18. THE WAY THAT THE FIRST_VALUE(), LAST_VALUE(), AND LAG() FUNCTIONS OPERATE

10. Displaying Rolling Averages over a Specified Number of Records

This time the sales director thinks he has a real challenge for you. She wants to see how average sale prices evolve over time for each customer in a report that shows the rolling average sale value for the last three sales per customer. Fortunately, SQL makes such reports easy as the following code shows:

```
SELECT      CustomerName

            ,SaleDate

            ,TotalSalePrice

            ,AVG(TotalSalePrice)

            OVER (PARTITION BY CustomerName ORDER BY SaleDate

            ROWS BETWEEN 3 PRECEDING AND CURRENT ROW)

                AS AverageSalePrice

FROM        Data.Sales AS SA

INNER JOIN Data.Customer CU ON SA.CustomerID = CU.CustomerID

ORDER BY    CustomerName, SaleDate
```

Running this query gives the results that you can see in Figure 8-19.

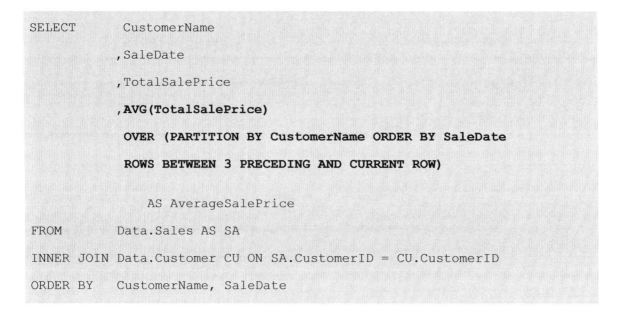

FIGURE 8-19. USING THE ROWS WINDOWING FUNCTION TO DISPLAY A ROLLING AVERAGE

How It Works

A classic analytical metric is the *rolling average*. A rolling average requires you to isolate a certain number of records up to and including a current record and then calculate the average of a value in all the specified records. The ROWS windowing function lets you do exactly this. This approach requires you to specify no fewer than seven different elements as part of the windowing function in order for it to work correctly:

AVG()	Is defined as the aggregation function to apply in the query.
OVER	Indicates that this is a windowing function that is being applied to a set of records.
PARTITION BY	Specifies how records are assembled into a subgroup inside the overall recordset. In this example, the CustomerName field is used so that a rolling average per customer can be calculated.
ORDER BY	Is used inside the OVER operator to define how the records for the subset are sorted. This is essential to define the sequencing for the range of records used for the rolling average.
ROWS BETWEEN	Indicates that this operator applies to a set of records relative to the current record.
PRECEDING	Says how many rows back the function must go to find the starting row for the running average.
AND CURRENT ROW	Tells the windowing function to stop at the current record and include it in the total.

In effect, using all these elements to create the rolling average says, "create virtual groups of records for each customer, order them by date, then calculate the average from three rows before the current row up to and including the current row."

So, in this example, you begin by creating the basic query to show the customer name, sales date, and the selling price for each vehicle sold by Prestige Cars. You then add a final column to the query that calculates the running average using the ROWS function.

Tricks and Traps

A few points are worth remembering when you use the ROWS() windowing function:

- A rolling total can be created in exactly the same way as a rolling average. Just use the SUM() function instead of the AVG() function and you have a rolling total.

- Once again, we prefer to add an ORDER BY clause at the end of the query to guarantee that the output is sorted exactly as we want. This is because the ORDER BY clause inside the OVER function is not guaranteed to sort the final output correctly.

- You may prefer to apply a totally different sort order to the final output. Doing so has no effect on the way the running average is calculated. To make this clearer, try tweaking the sort order code to read

```
ORDER BY    SaleDate, CustomerName
```

This returns a list rather like the one in Figure 8-20.

	CustomerName	SaleDate	TotalSalePrice	AverageSalePrice
1	Magic Motors	2015-01-02 00:00:00.000	65000.00	65000.000000
2	Casseroles Chromes	2015-01-02 10:33:00.000	19900.00	19900.000000
3	Snazzy Roadsters	2015-01-25 00:00:00.000	220000.10	220000.100000
4	Birmingham Executive Prestige Vehicles	2015-02-03 00:00:00.000	19500.00	19500.000000
5	WunderKar	2015-02-16 00:00:00.000	11500.00	11500.000000
6	Magic Motors	2015-03-14 00:00:00.000	29500.00	47250.000000
7	Birmingham Executive Prestige Vehicles	2015-03-24 00:00:00.000	49500.20	34500.100000
8	Eat My Exhaust Ltd	2015-03-30 00:00:00.000	76000.90	76000.900000
9	Sondra Horowitz	2015-04-04 00:00:00.000	36500.00	36500.000000
10	M. Pierre Dubois	2015-04-06 00:00:00.000	19600.00	19600.000000
11	Wonderland Wheels	2015-04-30 00:00:00.000	89000.00	89000.000000

FIGURE 8-20. USING A DIFFERENT SORT ORDER IN THE WINDOW FUNCTION AND THE OVERALL QUERY

As you can see, the output is based on the sale date, not on the customer name. However, the calculation for the running average has *not* changed. It still calculates the average from last three records per customer, up to and including the current record for that customer; however, the output is less intuitively comprehensible and shows no clear pattern, even if it is arithmetically accurate.

- If you want to show a running average or a running total that does not include the current row, you can replace CURRENT ROW with 1 PRECEDING in the SQL. This carries out the calculation up to but not including the current row.

- You can specify any row range relative to the current row for a running total—you can even cover rows that are further down the display list (or at a later date than the current record if you prefer). You do this by replacing CURRENT ROW with 3 FOLLOWING in the SQL. You can specify any number for the range of records that you want to use as a basis for your calculation.

11. Show the First Sale and Last Four Sales per Client

Sales at the company are increasing and senior management is convinced that effective analytics is a key factor of corporate success. The latest request to arrive in your inbox is for a report that shows both the first order and the last four sales for each customer. One way of doing this is shown using the following SQL:

```
SELECT
 CustomerName
,SaleDate
,TotalSalePrice
,FIRST_VALUE(TotalSalePrice) OVER (PARTITION BY CustomerName
                                   ORDER BY SaleDate) AS FirstOrder
,LAG(TotalSalePrice, 3) OVER (PARTITION BY CustomerName
                              ORDER BY SaleDate) AS LastButThreeOrder
,LAG(TotalSalePrice, 2) OVER (PARTITION BY CustomerName
                              ORDER BY SaleDate) AS LastButTwoOrder
,LAG(TotalSalePrice, 1) OVER (PARTITION BY CustomerName
                              ORDER BY SaleDate) AS LastButOneOrder
,LAST_VALUE(TotalSalePrice) OVER (PARTITION BY CustomerName
                                  ORDER BY SaleDate) AS LatestOrder
FROM      Data.Sales AS SA
          INNER JOIN Data.Customer CU ON SA.CustomerID = CU.CustomerID
```

Running this query gives the results that you can see in Figure 8-21.

	CustomerName	SaleDate	TotalSalePrice	FirstOrder	LastButThreeOrder	LastButTwoOrder	LastButOneOrder	LatestOrder
1	Alex McWhirter	2018-10-31 00:00:00.000	17850.00	17850.00	NULL	NULL	NULL	17850.00
2	Alexei Tolstoi	2015-07-15 00:00:00.000	22990.00	22990.00	NULL	NULL	NULL	22990.00
3	Alexei Tolstoi	2015-10-30 00:00:00.000	22600.00	22990.00	NULL	NULL	22990.00	22600.00
4	Alexei Tolstoi	2015-12-01 00:00:00.000	69500.00	22990.00	NULL	22990.00	22600.00	69500.00
5	Alexei Tolstoi	2016-05-30 00:00:00.000	49450.00	22990.00	22990.00	22600.00	69500.00	49450.00
6	Alexei Tolstoi	2016-07-25 00:00:00.000	205000.00	22990.00	22600.00	69500.00	49450.00	205000.00
7	Alexei Tolstoi	2016-08-02 00:00:00.000	102500.00	22990.00	69500.00	49450.00	205000.00	102500.00
8	Alexei Tolstoi	2016-09-04 00:00:00.000	3500.00	22990.00	49450.00	205000.00	102500.00	3500.00
9	Alexei Tolstoi	2016-09-16 00:00:00.000	45950.00	22990.00	205000.00	102500.00	3500.00	45950.00
10	Alicia Almodovar	2016-10-30 00:00:00.000	12500.00	12500.00	NULL	NULL	NULL	12500.00
11	Alicia Almodovar	2016-12-31 00:00:00.000	39500.00	12500.00	NULL	NULL	12500.00	39500.00
12	Alicia Almodovar	2017-05-10 00:00:00.000	12500.00	12500.00	NULL	12500.00	39500.00	12500.00
13	Alicia Almodovar	2017-09-20 00:00:00.000	250000.00	12500.00	12500.00	39500.00	12500.00	250000.00
14	Alicia Almodovar	2018-03-05 00:00:00.000	5690.00	12500.00	39500.00	12500.00	250000.00	5690.00
15	Alicia Almodovar	2018-04-02 00:00:00.000	15950.00	12500.00	12500.00	250000.00	5690.00	15950.00

FIGURE 8-21. USING THE FIRST_VALUE(), LAST_VALUE(), AND LAG() FUNCTIONS OVER TIME

How It Works

In order to compare sales (or other metrics) you need to extract elements from several records and place them on the same row. The idea behind this query is to give the recipient an idea of how much each client is spending and see how sales are evolving over time. The output displays

- The first sale made by a customer
- The most recent sale
- The three sales before the most recent sale

Each sale is a separate record in a SQL database. The SQL used here uses three more windowing functions to extract data from a subset of data. In this case, it is the successive sales per customer. The query selects the customer name and the date for each sale using the Sales and Customer tables. It then uses the following functions to compare the current sale with other sales for the same customer:

FIRST_VALUE — Shows the sale price for the first-ever purchase made by this customer.

LAST_VALUE — Shows the sale price for the latest purchase made by this customer.

LAG — Shows a previous specific sale—it can be the preceding sale or any previous sale.

Because you are once again dealing with windowing functions to output data from multiple records in the same row, these functions also need you to apply the following keywords:

OVER	To indicate to SQL Server that you are using a windowing function.
ORDER BY	To specify how the records are being sorted in a subset.
PARTITION BY	To group records by a criterion so that you can compare values meaningfully.

In this example, you are partitioning by the client name so that you can see the sales per client. The ORDER BY clause in the OVER function uses the SaleDate field so that you can compare sales over time.

The FIRST_VALUE and LAST_VALUE functions do what their names imply. They look at all the sales for a common element (defined in the PARTITION BY clause—in this case the customer) and find the oldest and most recent purchases, respectively. The LAG() function lets you go back in time over a set of sales for a customer and return the item in the list that matches the figure that you used in the LAG() function. This way, if you say LAG(SalePrice,1), you display the previous sale to a customer.

12. Calculating Cumulative Distribution

This time a sales person wants to know the relative standing of each sale by make. In other words, she expects to see a list with a column that shows what percentage of sales were made for less than the current record for each make of car. The following piece of SQL does exactly this:

```
SELECT      MK.MakeName, MD.ModelName, SA.InvoiceNumber, SD.SalePrice

            ,ROUND(CUME_DIST()

            OVER (PARTITION BY MK.MakeName ORDER BY SD.SalePrice),2)

            AS RelativeStanding
FROM        Data.Make AS MK
INNER JOIN  Data.Model AS MD ON MK.MakeID = MD.MakeID
INNER JOIN  Data.Stock AS ST ON ST.ModelID = MD.ModelID
INNER JOIN  Data.SalesDetails SD ON ST.StockCode = SD.StockID
INNER JOIN  Data.Sales AS SA ON SA.SalesID = SD.SalesID
ORDER BY    MK.MakeName, SD.SalePrice, RelativeStanding
```

Running this query gives the results that you can see in Figure 8-22. We have scrolled down the data that is returned to give you a better idea of what the output looks like for a couple of makes of car.

	MakeName	ModelName	InvoiceNumber	SalePrice	RelativeStanding
127	BMW	Isetta	GBPGB182	5500.00	0.33
128	BMW	Alpina	EURFR226	21500.00	0.67
129	BMW	E30	EURFR158	33500.00	1
130	Bugatti	Veyron	EURFR143	220500...	0.17
131	Bugatti	57C	GBPGB142	295000...	0.33
132	Bugatti	57C	GBPGB173	335000...	0.5
133	Bugatti	57C	EURFR282	345000...	0.67
134	Bugatti	57C	GBPGB230	355000...	0.83
135	Bugatti	57C	EURFR221	365000...	1
136	Citroen	Rosalie	GBPGB139	990.00	0.17
137	Citroen	Rosalie	GBPGB252	1350.00	0.33
138	Citroen	Rosalie	GBPCH161	2350.00	0.5
139	Citroen	Rosalie	EURFR322	5500.00	0.67
140	Citroen	Traaction ...	EURFR300	25000.00	0.83

Figure 8-22. Displaying cumulative distribution with the CUME_DIST() function

How It Works

Putting things into perspective is what data analysis can be all about, so it can help if you are able to see the relative position of a value compared to other values. In this windowing function, you used the CUME_DIST() function to see how each sale is situated relative to all other sales for the same make of car. Only this time you do not see a strict ranking, but the percentage of cars sold for a lower price. This means that the best-selling car for a specific make will display 1 (100 percent) with all other cars showing a smaller percentage figure.

This query initially requires that you join all the tables that you need to select the required fields. In this case, the tables are Make, Model, Sales, SalesDetails, and Stock.

Then you can add the CUME_DIST() function to the SELECT clause. As is the case with the other windowing functions that you have seen so far in this chapter, you need to specify an ORDER BY element (the sale price in this example). Then you extend the windowing function with a PARTITION BY clause that uses the make of vehicle to group the records into multiple subsets. This lets you isolate the sale price for each record relative to cars of the same make.

The end result is that for each make of car, you can see which is the most expensive sale and what percentage of cars sells for each sale per make.

Tricks and Traps

Creating a cumulative distribution with the CUME_DIST() function does require some attention to detail. The key points to take away are

- The PARTITION BY clause is *optional* with this function. If you want, you can remove it and instead display the percentage of vehicles that sell for less than the current car for *all sales*, irrespective of make.

- The field that you use in the ORDER BY function of the OVER clause to establish the relative standing must be numeric.

- We have added the ROUND() function to the CUME_DIST() function to prevent the display of the 15 decimal places that otherwise appear by default. You can, of course, leave this function out of the query if you prefer.

- You may prefer to sort a dataset such as this by the sale price in descending order so that you can see the most expensive sale per make first. In any case, the sort order that is applied to the overall query is independent of the ORDER BY clause that is applied to the CUME_DIST() function.

13. Classifying Data Using the PERCENT_RANK() Function

To conclude his analyses of vehicle sales, the sales director not only wants to see vehicle sales for each country by value but also wants to get an idea of the percentile in the sale hierarchy for each vehicle sold. The next piece of SQL delivers exactly what she is looking for:

```
SELECT      CO.CountryName, SA.SaleDate, SA.InvoiceNumber

            , FORMAT(PERCENT_RANK()

            OVER (PARTITION BY CO.CountryName

            ORDER BY SA.TotalSalePrice), '0.00 %') AS PercentageRanking
FROM        Data.Sales AS SA

INNER JOIN Data.Customer CU ON SA.CustomerID = CU.CustomerID

INNER JOIN Data.Country CO ON CU.Country = CO.CountryISO2

ORDER BY    CO.CountryName, SA.TotalSalePrice DESC
```

Running this query gives the results that you can see in Figure 8-23.

	CountryName	SaleDate	InvoiceNumber	PercentageRanking
1	Belgium	2016-08-23 00:00:00.000	EURBE074	100.00 %
2	Belgium	2017-03-12 00:00:00.000	EURBE132	83.33 %
3	Belgium	2017-07-01 00:00:00.000	EURBE171	66.67 %
4	Belgium	2017-11-06 00:00:00.000	EURBE193	50.00 %
5	Belgium	2017-02-12 00:00:00.000	EURBE125	33.33 %
6	Belgium	2018-06-03 00:00:00.000	EURBE264	16.67 %
7	Belgium	2018-01-10 00:00:00.000	EURBE218	0.00 %
8	France	2017-02-08 00:00:00.000	EURFR122	100.00 %
9	France	2017-02-07 00:00:00.000	EURFR121	98.36 %
10	France	2018-01-15 00:00:00.000	EURFR221	96.72 %
11	France	2018-07-31 00:00:00.000	EURFR282	95.08 %
12	France	2018-03-15 00:00:00.000	EURFR235	93.44 %
13	France	2017-05-21 00:00:00.000	EURFR156	91.80 %
14	France	2018-05-15 00:00:00.000	EURFR254	90.16 %
15	France	2017-05-12 00:00:00.000	EURFR151	88.52 %

FIGURE 8-23. USING THE PERCENT_RANK() FUNCTION TO CLASSIFY GROUPS OF DATA

How It Works

One useful analytical technique is to indicate the relative rank of a row inside a group of rows. This query starts when you select the necessary tables (Sales, Customer, and Country). Then you add any fields that you want to display and use the ORDER BY clause so that the data that is returned is more comprehensible.

Finally, you add the PERCENT_RANK() function to the SELECT clause. It requires the OVER clause and an ORDER BY function that takes a numeric value as the field to sort on (SalePrice). In this example (although this is optional), you added a PARTITION BY clause to the windowing function to subset the relative sale position by country.

The end result is an ordered list of sales per country. Starting with the highest-value sale, the list displays each vehicle sale in descending order by value and where each record stands in relation to all the other sales for the country. This "ranking" is expressed as a percentage of the number of records that appear below the current record. This means that the top record shows 100 percent, and the bottom record shows 0 percent.

Tricks and Traps

When using PERCENT_RANK() be sure to note that

- The field that you use in the ORDER BY function of the OVER clause to establish the relative standing must be numeric.

- You do not need to add the field used as the basis for the PERCENT_RANK() function to the SELECT clause; however, adding it can make the output easier to understand.

- You do not need to format the output for the PERCENT_RANK() function as a percentage; however, we feel that it makes the output easier to comprehend.

14. Using the LAG() Function with Alphabetical Data

The marketing director wants a list of all the company's customers in alphabetical order. However, here is the twist—she also wants a phone-book-style presentation with all customers grouped by the first letter of their name.

After a little thought, you come up with the following code.

```
SELECT          CASE

                    WHEN LEFT(CustomerName, 1) =

                        LAG (LEFT(CustomerName, 1))

                            OVER (ORDER BY CustomerName) THEN NULL

                    ELSE LEFT(CustomerName, 1)

                END AS IndexLetter

                ,CustomerName
FROM            Data.SalesByCountry
GROUP BY        CustomerName
ORDER BY        CustomerName
```

Running this code gives the output that you can see in Figure 8-24.

	IndexLetter	CustomerName
1	A	Alex McWhirter
2	NULL	Alexei Tolstoi
3	NULL	Alicia Almodovar
4	NULL	Andrea Tarbuck
5	NULL	Andy Cheshire
6	NULL	Antonio Maura
7	NULL	Autos Sportivos
8	B	Beltway Prestige Driving
9	NULL	Birmingham Executive Prestige Vehicles
10	NULL	Bling Bling S.A.
11	NULL	Bling Motors
12	NULL	Boris Spry
13	NULL	Bravissima!
14	C	Capots Reluisants S.A.
15	NULL	Casseroles Chromes
16	NULL	Clubbing Cars
17	NULL	Convertible Dreams
18	D	Diplomatic Cars
19	E	Eat My Exhaust Ltd

FIGURE 8-24. USING THE LAG() FUNCTION TO PRODUCE AN ALPHABETICAL INDEX

How It Works

It is really quite easy to isolate the first letter of the name of every client. Applying the LEFT() function (and specifying 1 as the number of characters to extract) to the CustomerName field in the SalesByCountry View does this. However, tweaking this function so that it only shows the index letter when a new letter of the alphabet occurs requires a little more effort.

The answer is to use the LAG() function. As you have seen, this function shows the contents of a field in the previous record in the output. What this code snippet does is

First: Apply the LAG() function to the LEFT() function that is applied to the customer name, and specify 1 as the number of rows to go backward. In effect this selects the first letter of the customer name in the previous record. The LAG() function is ordered by the CustomerName field to ensure that the customer records are handled in alphabetical order when it is comparing records.

Then:	A CASE statement compares the first letter of the customer name for the current record with the first letter of the customer name for the previous record. If the two are the same, then nothing (or rather NULL) is output. However, if the two are different (which means that the customer name of the current record begins with a different letter than the customer name of the previous record), then the first letter is output.

The end result is a list of customers with a structure rather like the index of a book.

Conclusion

This chapter allowed you to focus on running totals and relative weighting when analyzing your data. You saw how to create running totals, running averages, and running counts using SQL. You then learned how to segment the output so that the "rolling" result restarted when a specified element changed.

Finally, you saw how to extend these techniques to show the first or last element in a series, how to display the first or last element in a series, and ways to illustrate the relative weighting of a value in a list.

Core Knowledge Learned in This Chapter

The functions that you have seen in this chapter are

Concept	Description
ROW_NUMBER()	*This function adds a system-generated sequential number to each record in the dataset.*
LAG()	*This function lets you reach back over the previous records in a recordset or subgroup of records to calculate metrics over a defined series of rows relative to the current record.*
FIRST_VALUE()	*This function returns the starting value in a field in a recordset or subgroup of records.*
LAST_VALUE()	*This function returns the final value in a field in a recordset or subgroup of records.*
ROWS BETWEEN	*Used with a windowing function, this operator lets you define the range of records used in a running calculation.*
PRECEDING	*Used with a windowing function, this operator also lets you define the range of records used in a running calculation.*
CURRENT ROW	*Used with a windowing function, this operator helps you specify a range of records including the current row.*
CUME_DIST()	*This function returns a cumulative distribution—the relative position of a value compared to other values.*
PERCENT_RANK()	*This function returns a figure indicating what percentage of a subgroup of records can be found with smaller values than a defined column in a recordset or subgroup of records.*

Chapter 9:
Analyzing Data over Time

This chapter is all about enhancing your analytical abilities so that you can compare and contrast data over time. Here, we build on the core techniques that you saw in Volume I and extend your knowledge to make you completely at ease when slicing and dicing data that contains a time element. Of course, when we talk about dealing with time, we mean looking at both date and time elements in SQL Server. Mastering these techniques helps you track the evolution of sales, profits, or any metric over any time period—from years to days to hours and seconds.

Time Analysis

Analyzing data over time has the potential to be a vast subject. This is because no two people's requirements are ever going to be identical. So, to give you an idea of what to expect, the kinds of time analysis that you learn in this chapter include

- Month-to-date, quarter-to-date, and year-to-date calculations
- Comparing metrics with those from previous time periods
- Parallel period calculations—comparing figures for the same month in the previous year
- Comparing values for a current month to date with the same month to date from the previous year
- Displaying timespans as years, months, and days
- Calculating weekdays and weekends
- Displaying time differences in hours and minutes
- Grouping data by time slots

Once you have mastered the essentials of adding a time factor to your SQL queries, you will probably be pleasantly surprised at the new analytical horizons that are available for you to apply in your queries. Admittedly, you need to pay close attention to some of the techniques that are used; however, we are sure that you will find that the investment is well worth the sheer power of the analysis that is now possible when you use SQL to slice and dice data over time.

1. Aggregating Values for the Year to Date

The sales director keeps one eye firmly on the accumulated sales for the year so that she can quickly take any corrective actions that may prove necessary. SQL makes giving her the data that she wants really easy, as the following code shows (for sales in 2017):

```
SELECT      MakeName, SUM(SD.SalePrice) AS CumulativeSalesYTD

FROM        Data.Make AS MK INNER JOIN Data.Model AS MD

            ON MK.MakeID = MD.MakeID

INNER JOIN Data.Stock AS ST ON ST.ModelID = MD.ModelID

INNER JOIN Data.SalesDetails SD ON ST.StockCode = SD.StockID

INNER JOIN Data.Sales AS SA ON SA.SalesID = SD.SalesID

WHERE       SA.SaleDate BETWEEN DATEFROMPARTS(YEAR(GETDATE()),1,1)

            AND CONVERT(CHAR(8), GETDATE(), 112)

GROUP BY    MakeName

ORDER BY    MakeName ASC
```

Figure 9-1 shows the results returned by this query (for a query run in late 2017).

	MakeName	CumulativeSalesYTD
1	Alfa Romeo	71150.00
2	Aston Martin	1341400.00
3	Austin	8750.00
4	BMW	39000.00
5	Bugatti	850500.00
6	Citroen	69230.00
7	Delahaye	29500.00
8	Delorean	99500.00
9	Ferrari	2051900.00
10	Jaguar	109000.00
11	Lagonda	156500.00
12	Lamborghini	785000.00
13	McLaren	295000.00
14	Mercedes	155275.00
15	Noble	129500.00

FIGURE 9-1. CALCULATING AGGREGATE VALUES FOR THE YEAR TO DATE

How It Works

Collating the sales for the year to date is a fairly regular requirement in many organizations. In this sort of query, all the effort goes (once again) into the WHERE clause. This is because what you do in this clause is set a range of dates in a BETWEEN...AND operator in order to specify a precise date range. The timespan is defined by

A lower boundary	The first of January for the current year that you passed into the query as DATEFROMPARTS(YEAR(GETDATE()),1,1). This is another way of saying "January 1, 2017" (assuming you run the query anytime in 2017). If you need to revise the DATEFROMPARTS() function, just flip back to *Volume I*.
An upper boundary	The time that the query was run, defined by the GETDATE() function. Since the GETDATE() function returns both date and time values, you ensure that *only the year, month, and day part of the current date* are used by wrapping GETDATE() in the CONVERT() function that you saw in Chapter 8.

The trick that you are using here is finding the *current year*, since the query needs to be dynamic (that is, you want to be able to run it in any year to get the sales for the year to date). It follows that you do not want to enter a fixed year, so you are using the YEAR function to extract the current year from the GETDATE() function. The GETDATE() function, after all, returns the current date and time for the computer hosting the SQL Server database.

Tricks and Traps

Working with dates can involve using several different SQL functions all at the same time. Be sure to remember that

- The actual results vary depending on the date that you run the query. This example was run in November 2017.

- If you are using a version of SQL Server prior to the 2012 version, you cannot use the DATEFROMPARTS() function. Instead, you can write the following code to return January 1 for the current year:

```
CAST(YEAR(GETDATE()) AS CHAR(4)) + '0101'
```

This code snippet extracts the year part from the current date and converts it to a string of four characters. It then adds 0101 (to represent the month and day, which is January 1) to the year to give the date in the format YYYYMMDD for the current year.

It is worth noting that this technique requires one final tweak to work properly. The potential problem lies in the fact that the YEAR() function returns a number, but you need to tell SQL that the date for January 1 needs to be read as a string (a series of letters if you prefer to think of it like this). The CAST() function simply converts the four numbers for the year to four letters. Once this is done, SQL can join this string (2015 here) to the day and month for January 1 (0101)—giving 20150101 as one of the boundaries for the date range to filter on.

- If you are using the BETWEEN ... AND keywords to set a range, you must *always* place the lower boundary after BETWEEN and the upper boundary after AND. This query would not have worked if you typed it as

```
WHERE       SA.SaleDate BETWEEN CONVERT(CHAR(8), GETDATE(), 112)

            AND DATEFROMPARTS(YEAR(GETDATE()),1,1)
```

- Isolating parts of dates is an essential technique for defining date ranges in SQL. We admit that it can get a little laborious at times separating out the year from the month from the day elements that make up a date—and sometimes even having to convert them, individually, to strings. The upside, however, is that this approach does give you unprecedented control and precision when it comes to setting date ranges.

2.   Aggregating Values for the Month to Date

Since the sales staff has monthly targets to meet, you have been asked to write a query that can show sales for the month to date. SQL can do this, of course, as the following piece of code shows:

```
SELECT      MakeName, SUM(SD.SalePrice) AS CumulativeSalesMTD

FROM        Data.Make AS MK INNER JOIN Data.Model AS MD

            ON MK.MakeID = MD.MakeID

INNER JOIN Data.Stock AS ST ON ST.ModelID = MD.ModelID

INNER JOIN Data.SalesDetails SD ON ST.StockCode = SD.StockID

INNER JOIN Data.Sales AS SA ON SA.SalesID = SD.SalesID
```

```
WHERE       SA.SaleDate

            BETWEEN

            DATEADD(MONTH, DATEDIFF(MONTH, 0, GETDATE()), 0)

            AND GETDATE()

GROUP BY    MakeName

ORDER BY    MakeName ASC
```

This SQL gives the following result for November 2017 as you can see in Figure 9-2. You might see something completely different if you are running this query on a different date.

FIGURE 9-2. AGGREGATE METRICS FOR THE MONTH TO DATE

How It Works

If you (or other staff) have monthly targets to meet, then you are likely to want to track metrics for the month to date. This type of query, like its predecessor, sets a date range. This time the range is from the start of the current month to the current date.

First: You need to find the date that corresponds to the first day of the current month and set this as the lower date threshold for the range of dates. The technique that we are using here is, we admit, a bit of an SQL insider's trick, but it works beautifully and, consequently, is well worth learning. You start by applying the DATEDIFF() function to the current date and specifying "month" and "0" as the two other parameters. Then you wrap this function in the DATEADD() function and specify "month" and "0" as the two other parameters. The result is that SQL Server returns the first day of the current month from this combination of functions.

Second: You define the upper date threshold using the GETDATE() function.

You can run this query at any time without having to adjust date parameters because it always adjusts the WHERE clause to look at the sales for the current month.

Tricks and Traps

There are a couple of key points to take away when aggregating values over time:

- You can also write the beginning of month in other ways if you prefer. One classic way is to use code like the following SQL snippet:

```
CAST(YEAR(GETDATE()) AS CHAR(4))

+ RIGHT('0' + CAST(MONTH(GETDATE()) AS VARCHAR(2)),2) + '01'
```

This approach re-creates a date by isolating the year, month, and day from the current date. The YEAR() function is easy to understand, since it defines the first of the month as a hard-coded figure. The month, however, is slightly more problematic because it has to be entered as two digits for the converted date string to be usable by SQL Server. The months of October, November, and December are not a problem, as they are the months 10, 11, and 12, respectively, and are composed of two digits. The problem arises with the first nine months of the year because these are each only a single digit (1 through 9). In the case of the first nine months, you have to add a leading zero—which you do manually, adding a zero (as a string in single quotes to keep SQL from complaining). This means that the last three months will look like 010, 011, and 012, so you then wrap the month figure (with the leading zero) in the RIGHT() function to force SQL to chop off the leftmost character—*if* there is one. This may seem a little clunky, but it is wonderfully effective, since it leaves the leading zero when it is needed and removes it when it is superfluous. The net result is that you get the month as two digits—from 01 to 12.

- When converting the month from a number to a letter, you use the VARCHAR() function instead of the CHAR() function as you did for the year. This is because the month can be one digit or two, and VARCHAR() accepts a variable number of characters—up to the maximum (two in this example) that you specified.

3.   Returning Aggregate Values for the Quarter to Date

Not content with a one-click solution that displays monthly sales, the sales team has now requested a report showing quarterly sales to date as well. The SQL that follows lets you keep them happy:

```
SELECT       MakeName, SUM(SD.SalePrice) AS CumulativeSalesQTD

FROM         Data.Make AS MK INNER JOIN Data.Model AS MD

             ON MK.MakeID = MD.MakeID

INNER JOIN Data.Stock AS ST ON ST.ModelID = MD.ModelID

INNER JOIN Data.SalesDetails SD ON ST.StockCode = SD.StockID

INNER JOIN Data.Sales AS SA ON SA.SalesID = SD.SalesID

WHERE        SA.SaleDate BETWEEN DATEADD(q, DATEDIFF(q, 0, GETDATE()), 0)

             AND CONVERT(CHAR(8), GETDATE(), 112)

GROUP BY     MakeName

ORDER BY     MakeName ASC
```

Figure 9-3 shows what happens when you run this code snippet on November 3, 2017.

	MakeName	CumulativeSalesQTD
1	Alfa Romeo	25000.00
2	Lamborghini	480000.00
3	Porsche	69000.00
4	Triumph	39500.00

FIGURE 9-3. AGGREGATING A METRIC FOR THE QUARTER TO DATE

How It Works

To end this short period-to-date trilogy of solutions, this example shows how to calculate the sales for the quarter to date.

First, as is the case with just about any query, you join the required tables to ensure that you can access the fields that you need. Then you add the GROUP BY and ORDER BY clauses to make this an aggregated query that displays the output in the correct sort order.

Finally, you need to concentrate on getting the WHERE clause right, since this is the key to achieving the desired result.

First:	Deduce the start of the current quarter using the DATEDIFF() and DATEADD() technique that you applied in the previous section. The only difference is that as you are intent on finding the date for the *first day in the quarter*; you use the q parameter for both these functions to indicate to SQL Server that you are looking at *quarterly* data (and not daily or monthly dates).
Finally:	You set the upper threshold using the GETDATE() function to set the current date and time as the upper limit of the date range.

In this example, we use the CONVERT() function to strip out the time element from the GETDATE() function. This, in effect, sets the upper date threshold to midnight at the *start of the current day*. Consequently, it *excludes all sales on the current day* and only includes sales up until the end of the previous day. When writing queries like this, you need to confirm with the business exactly what they mean by "current day" before you write the query.

Tricks and Traps

There are only a couple of short points to remember at this stage:

- Remember that when you use the BETWEEN ... AND operator, you must place the *lower* threshold after the BETWEEN keyword and the *upper* threshold after the AND keyword.

- You can also use the DATEADD() and DATEDIFF() technique that we explained in the previous section to get the start of the current year if you want. One way to do this is to use the following SQL:

```
SELECT DATEADD(YY, DATEDIFF(YY, 0, GETDATE()), 0)
```

4. Isolating Data for the Previous Month

In his push for increased profits, the CFO always wants to know how this month's purchases compare to last month's figures. As a result, he wants to see purchases by make for the previous calendar month. SQL can help you produce data like this really easily as the following code shows:

```
SELECT      MakeName, SUM(Cost) AS TotalCost

FROM        Data.Make AS MK INNER JOIN Data.Model AS MD

            ON MK.MakeID = MD.MakeID

INNER JOIN Data.Stock AS ST ON ST.ModelID = MD.ModelID

WHERE       DateBought BETWEEN

            CAST(YEAR(DATEADD(m, -1, GETDATE())) AS CHAR(4))

            + RIGHT('0' + CAST(MONTH(DATEADD(m, -1, GETDATE()))

            AS VARCHAR(2)),2) + '01'

            AND EOMONTH(DATEADD(m, -1, GETDATE()))

GROUP BY    MakeName
```

Running this code displays the data that you can see in Figure 9-4 (for November 2017—it will, of course, be different if run on another date).

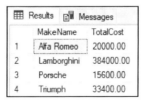

FIGURE 9-4. FILTERING ON DATA FOR THE PREVIOUS MONTH USING THE DATEADD() AND EOMONTH() FUNCTIONS

How It Works

You might be called on at any time to calculate metrics for the preceding month—such as, for instance, when you compile the month end figures at the start of the following month. Once again, in this kind of time-based query you are defining a date range. On this occasion, however, the WHERE clause uses the DATEADD() function to set both the start and end dates for the period to the *first day* and the *last day* of the previous month.

The *first day of the preceding month* is set by assembling the required date as a YYYYMMDD; however, this requires you to assemble the three parts of the date (year, month, and day) separately.

The Year	Is calculated by finding the previous month (which could be December of the previous year) using the DATEADD() function. In this case, you use the m date part type and a −1 to indicate that you want to go back one month. Then you extract the year, using the YEAR() function, and finally, you convert this to a string, as you have done previously.
The Month	Is defined by (once again) finding the previous month using the DATEADD() function with the m date part type and a −1 as the number of months to go back. Then you extract the month, using the MONTH() function, and finally, you convert this to a string, too. Defining the start of the current month requires you to find the current year and then convert this to a string, just as you did in the previous section. Then you have to find the current month.
The Day	Is the easy part. Because it is always the first of the month, all you have to do is to hardcode the value '01'.

The *last day of the preceding month* is easier to calculate, because SQL has a specific function for doing this. The function is EOMONTH(), and it returns the last day of the month for a date. In this example, you want the last day of the previous month, so you use the DATEADD() function with the m date part type and a −1 as the number of months to go back to ask SQL to give you the final day of the previous month.

By using these two date calculations in the BETWEEN...AND clause, you set the entire previous month as the date range. This works no matter how many days are in the month as well going back to previous years.

Tricks and Traps

Isolating dates can seem a little verbose in SQL, but it is not really difficult. Just remember that

- Calculating the first day of the month in this way can seem a little disconcerting at first. However, it is typical of the way that SQL works—nesting functions in functions to break data down into the smallest constituent parts, only to reassemble them in a way that allows you to achieve the desired result.

- You can, of course use either of the other techniques that you saw in previous examples to calculate the first day of the month.

- Another way to specify the beginning of the month is to use the following SQL:

```
SELECT DATEADD(d, 1, EOMONTH(DATEADD(m, -2, GETDATE())))
```

5. Using a Derived Table to Compare Data with Values from a Previous Year

Seasonal variations can often be very revealing, or at least this is what the CFO thinks. He has asked you to provide some analysis of like-for-like sales so he can see the average sales by color for the same month in both the previous year and the current year. The following code lets you keep him happy:

```
SELECT     ST.Color, AVG(SA.TotalSalePrice) AS AverageMonthSales

           ,MAX(AveragePreviousMonthSales) AS
AveragePreviousYearMonthSales

FROM       Data.Make AS MK

INNER JOIN Data.Model AS MD ON MK.MakeID = MD.MakeID

INNER JOIN Data.Stock AS ST ON ST.ModelID = MD.ModelID

INNER JOIN Data.SalesDetails SD ON ST.StockCode = SD.StockID

INNER JOIN Data.Sales AS SA ON SA.SalesID = SD.SalesID

           LEFT OUTER JOIN

               (

                   SELECT     Color, AVG(SA.TotalSalePrice)

                              AS AveragePreviousMonthSales

                   FROM       Data.Make AS MK

                   INNER JOIN Data.Model AS MD

                              ON MK.MakeID = MD.MakeID
```

```
                    INNER JOIN Data.Stock AS ST

                          ON ST.ModelID = MD.ModelID

                    INNER JOIN Data.SalesDetails SD

                          ON ST.StockCode = SD.StockID

                    INNER JOIN Data.Sales AS SA

                          ON SA.SalesID = SD.SalesID

              WHERE       YEAR(SA.SaleDate) = YEAR(GETDATE())- 1

                          AND MONTH(SA.SaleDate) = MONTH(GETDATE())

              GROUP BY    Color

             ) SQ

          ON SQ.Color = ST.Color

WHERE       YEAR(SA.SaleDate) = YEAR(GETDATE())

        AND MONTH(SA.SaleDate) = MONTH(GETDATE())

GROUP BY    St.Color
```

Running this query gives the results that you can see in Figure 9-5—if you run the code in August 2018. For other dates, you get different results.

	Color	Average Month Sales	Average Previous Year Month Sales
1	Black	69683.333333	38800.000000
2	Blue	47250.000000	5500.000000
3	Night Blue	85595.000000	45000.000000
4	Silver	78150.000000	NULL

FIGURE 9-5. DISPLAYING FIGURES FOR A PARALLEL TIME PERIOD USING A DERIVED TABLE

How It Works

This query is in two main parts:

A derived table   That calculates the sales by color for the same month in the previous year.

An outer query   That calculates the sales by color for the current month and year.

Each of these elements uses the same core query. First the Make, Model, Stock, SalesDetails, and Sales tables are joined. Then the Color field is added to the SELECT and GROUP BY clauses to aggregate data by color. Finally, the average sale price is calculated. The only real difference is that the derived table (the inner query) looks at last year's data. This is done by adjusting the GETDATE() function for the year so that it reads

```
YEAR(GETDATE()) - 1
```

Then the two parts of the query are joined. We do this using a LEFT OUTER JOIN to ensure that all the colors for sales this year will be shown. If you use an INNER JOIN instead, then you will not see any colors that sold this year but not last year. Remember that the LEFT OUTER JOIN means "all records from the first dataset, including any that match from the second dataset."

Finally, you added the average sale price for last year's sales to the outer query. However, as this, too, is an aggregate query, you cannot just add the AveragePreviousMonthSales field from the derive table, or SQL Server complains that it is not "contained in either an aggregate function or the GROUP BY clause." To allow the result to be used, you have to wrap it in the MAX() function. Once the result is handled like this, it can appear in the query output. The MAX() function does not alter the result of the AveragePreviousMonthSales field in any way since it is already aggregated and correct. The function merely allows the result to be used in the outer aggregate query.

Using derived tables in subqueries is a standard technique for comparing data over time in SQL. Figure 9-6 explains this concept more visually.

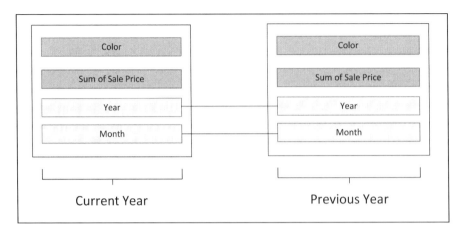

FIGURE 9-6. COMPARING DATA OVER TIME USING A DERIVED TABLE

Tricks and Traps

To extend your SQL knowledge, you might like to note this technique:

- As an alternative way to having the derived table return only the data for the previous year, you can use the DATEADD() function, like this:

```
WHERE       YEAR(SA.SaleDate) = YEAR(DATEADD(yy, GETDATE(), - 1))
```

6.   Finding the Total Amount for Each Weekday

The sales director is on a mission to find out if certain weekdays are better for sales than others. You have prepared the following query for her so she can analyze sales for each day of the week in 2017.

```
;

WITH TallyTable_CTE

AS

(
```

```
SELECT      ROW_NUMBER() OVER (ORDER BY StockCode) - 1 AS ID

FROM        Data.Stock

)

,DateList_CTE

AS

(

SELECT      DATEADD(DD, ID, DATEFROMPARTS(2017, 1, 1))

            AS WeekdayDate

            ,DATENAME(DW, DATEADD(DD, ID, DATEFROMPARTS(2017, 1, 1)))

            AS WeekdayName

FROM        TallyTable_CTE

WHERE       DATEPART(dw, DATEADD(DD, ID, DATEFROMPARTS(2017, 1, 1)))

            BETWEEN 2 AND 6

            AND

            CAST(DATEADD(DD, ID, DATEFROMPARTS(2017, 1, 1)) AS DATE)

            <= '20171231'

)

SELECT       CTE.WeekdayDate

            ,CTE.WeekdayName

            ,SUM(SLS.SalePrice) AS TotalDailySales

FROM        Data.SalesByCountry SLS

INNER JOIN  DateList_CTE CTE

            ON CTE.WeekdayDate = CAST(SLS.SaleDate AS DATE)

GROUP BY     CTE.WeekdayDate

            ,CTE.WeekdayName

ORDER BY     CTE.WeekdayDate
```

If you run this query you see the result shown in Figure 9-7.

	WeekdayDate	WeekdayName	TotalDailySales
1	2017-01-05	Thursday	125000.00
2	2017-01-10	Tuesday	85000.00
3	2017-01-11	Wednesday	22500.00
4	2017-01-12	Thursday	125950.00
5	2017-01-13	Friday	8850.00
6	2017-01-30	Monday	56500.00
7	2017-01-31	Tuesday	111950.00
8	2017-02-07	Tuesday	365000.00
9	2017-02-08	Wednesday	395000.00
10	2017-02-09	Thursday	21500.00
11	2017-02-10	Friday	6500.00
12	2017-02-14	Tuesday	2250.00
13	2017-03-10	Friday	213000.00
14	2017-03-30	Thursday	305000.00
15	2017-03-31	Friday	313940.00

FIGURE 9-7. THE TOTAL SALES FOR WEEKDAYS

How It Works

This query is built in three stages. For the moment, let's take a closer look at the first two parts of the code.

First: A tally table is created to provide a list from 0 to nearly 400. The exact number is irrelevant as long as it is greater than 365—the number of days in the year (or 366 if you are dealing with a leap year). In this example, we are creating a *tally CTE* by creating an initial CTE (Common Table Expression) that uses the Stock table to create a sequential list using the ROW_NUMBER() function. You can base the tally list on any table that contains enough records (or even more than one table if you need a lot of records in the list). If you select the code for the first CTE (named TallyTable_CTE) and run it, you see a list like the one shown in Figure 9-8.

FIGURE 9-8. THE OUTPUT FROM A TALLY TABLE CTE

Second:	A second CTE that uses the tally CTE to generate a sequential list of every date in the year. This is done by using the DATEADD() function, which is applied to every record in the tally table.

What the DATEADD() function does is take January 1, 2017—defined using the DATEFROMPARTS() function—and add to this the number in the ID column of the tally table. This gives a sequence of dates. Indeed, the tally table is deliberately set to start at zero so that the first DATEADD() function in the list of dates returns January 1 (as the function adds zero days to the start date).

This technique is then used a total of four times:

First:	To give the date resulting from the DATEADD() sequence.
Second:	Inside a DATENAME function to return the name of the day of the week.

Third:	Inside the WHERE clause of the second CTE. Specifically the DATEADD() sequence is enclosed in a DATEPART() function to return the number of the day in the week. Because day 0 and day 7 (Sunday and Saturday, respectively) are not weekdays, the WHERE clause excludes these. One way of doing this is to filter so that only day numbers between 2 and 6 (Monday to Friday) pass the conditions set by the WHERE clause.
Finally:	The WHERE clause adds an upper limit to the list that is generated by the two CTEs by setting the date of the last day of 2017.

To get an idea of how these two CTEs work, you can replace the entire final query with a SELECT statement to show the output of the second CTE using the following code.

```
SELECT * FROM DateList_CTE
```

If you run the two CTEs followed by the SELECT statement, you see the output from the second CTE (which uses the date from the first CTE) as shown in Figure 9-9.

	WeekdayDate	WeekdayName
1	2017-01-02	Monday
2	2017-01-03	Tuesday
3	2017-01-04	Wednesday
4	2017-01-05	Thursday
5	2017-01-06	Friday
6	2017-01-09	Monday
7	2017-01-10	Tuesday
8	2017-01-11	Wednesday
9	2017-01-12	Thursday
10	2017-01-13	Friday

FIGURE 9-9. USING A CTE TO ISOLATE THE WEEKDAYS

The output from the second CTE then becomes the basis for the final query, since it displays the dates and weekday names for all the days in the year 2017. The final query joins the CTE output to the SalesByCountry view using the SaleDate field. As a precaution, the SQL applies a CAST() function to the SaleDate field so that any *time* element is removed that would otherwise prevent the tables from joining on the date. Because there could be several sales on a single day—and we want the aggregate value for the sales for each weekday—the final query uses a GROUP BY clause on the date and weekday fields and wraps the sales value in a SUM() function.

Tricks and Traps

Given that this is a fairly complex sequence of SQL, we have a few points to make here:

- If you are looking at a list of weekdays for several years, be sure to create a tally table that contains at least as many records as there are consecutive days in the total number of years.

- You can choose to limit the initial tally table to the exact number of days in the year (or between the two dates if you are using a date range); however, this means calculating the exact number of days and adding this to a WHERE clause in the first CTE.

- This piece of SQL only displays the weekdays where there is a sale. If you want a complete list of dates, including any days where there were *no sales*, you can change the INNER JOIN to a RIGHT OUTER JOIN in the final query. You can see this in the following SQL snippet (since the two CTEs remain the same, we are not showing them again).

```
SELECT              CTE.WeekdayDate

                    ,CTE.WeekdayName

                    ,SUM(SLS.SalePrice) AS TotalDailySales

FROM                Data.SalesByCountry SLS

RIGHT OUTER JOIN    DateList_CTE CTE

                    ON CTE.WeekdayDate = CAST(SLS.SaleDate AS DATE)

GROUP BY            CTE.WeekdayDate

                    ,CTE.WeekdayName

ORDER BY            CTE.WeekdayDate
```

Running this altered query gives the output that you can see in Figure 9-10, where the weekdays without sales are also displayed.

FIGURE 9-10. USING AN OUTER JOIN WITH A TALLY TABLE TO DISPLAY NULL DATE RECORDS

- Because we described the full range of DATEPART() and DATENAME() elements in *Volume I*, we will not repeat them here.

7. Find the Weekend Dates Inside a Date Range

Human resources needs to plan for extra support staff on certain weekends, so they want a simple list of Saturdays and Sundays for the first two weeks of December 2017. The following short piece of SQL delivers this.

```
;
WITH TallyTable_CTE
AS
(
SELECT     ROW_NUMBER() OVER (ORDER BY StockCode) - 1 AS ID
FROM       Data.Stock
)
SELECT     CAST(DATEADD(DD, ID, '20171201') AS DATE) AS WeekdayDate
FROM       TallyTable_CTE
WHERE      ID <= DATEDIFF(DD, '20171201', '20171213')
           AND DATEPART(dw, DATEADD(DD, ID, '20171201')) IN (1,7)
```

Running this piece of code gives the result that you can see in Figure 9-11.

FIGURE 9-11. DISPLAYING WEEKEND DATES

How It Works

Once again, in this example, you use a CTE to produce a sequence of numbers beginning with 0. Then a query uses this list to produce a sequence of dates using the DATEADD() function, as you saw in the previous section. Because the requirement was to start the list on December 1, 2017, this specific date is used as the starting date in the DATEADD() function.

The interesting part of this query resides in the WHERE clause, which does two things:

First: The WHERE clause sets a date range. It does this by ensuring that the number (the ID column from the tally CTE) is less than or equal to the end date for the required range of dates (December 13, 2017). Since the tally table started on December 1, the DATEDIFF() function is used to calculate the number of days between the start date and the end date of the required period.

Second: A DATEPART() function is applied to the DATEADD() function that delivers a range of dates. This function extracts the weekday number from each date. Because we only want to display Saturdays and Sundays, only days numbered 1 and 7 are required. The simplest way to achieve this is to use an IN clause.

Tricks and Traps

We have a couple of points to make here:

- It is perfectly normal that certain dates are repeated at several places in the SQL. This is because the dates are used in several independent functions.

- It is possible to use a DATENAME() function rather than a DATEPART() function in the WHERE clause to filter on Saturday and Sunday to extract only weekends from the list of dates.

8. Count the Number of Weekend Days between Two Dates

As a prelude to delivering some more complex analysis of staff deployment, the HR department wants to know how many weekend days there are in March and April 2018. This requires some clever SQL, as you can see in the following code snippet.

```
;
WITH TallyTable_CTE
AS
(
SELECT      ROW_NUMBER() OVER (ORDER BY StockCode) - 1 AS ID
FROM        Data.Stock
)
,WeekendList_CTE
AS
(
SELECT        CAST(DATEADD(DD, ID, '20180301') AS DATE) AS WeekdayDate
FROM          TallyTable_CTE
WHERE         DATEPART(dw, DATEADD(DD, ID, '20180301')) IN (1,7)
              AND ID <= DATEDIFF(DD, '20180301', '20180430')
)
SELECT      COUNT(*) AS WeekendDays FROM WeekendList_CTE
```

When you run this query, you should see the output that is shown in Figure 9-12.

FIGURE 9-12. COUNTING THE NUMBER OF NON-WEEKDAYS FOR A DATE RANGE

How It Works

What this query does is create a table of all the days between two dates (March 1 and April 30, 2017, in this example). It then deduces the number of the day for each date and excludes Saturdays and Sundays. Finally, it counts the remaining number of records in the list.

The code works like this:

First: A tally CTE is created to provide a sequential list of numbers starting with 0 (zero).

Then: A second CTE uses the tally list as part of a DATEADD() function to create a list of dates. This list begins with 0 to give the starting date —by adding zero days to the lower date threshold that is the third parameter of the DATEADD() function—and then continues adding one day for each record in the tally list. The WHERE clause of the second CTE filters out any weekdays by

- Reusing the same DATEADD() expression and enclosing this in a DATEPART() function that returns the number of the weekday. The filter *only allows days 1 and 7* (Saturdays and Sundays) to appear in the second CTE output.

- Limiting the number of records from the tally list that are used. It does this by creating a DATEDIFF() function that returns the number of days between the lower and upper threshold dates. This number of days is the number of records that the subquery should return. Consequently, the maximum number of records in the tally list is set by filtering on the maximum ID value for the second CTE output.

Finally: A simple SELECT clause using the data from the second CTE counts the number of weekend days between the two dates.

Tricks and Traps

We have a couple of points to make here:

- Once again, you may have to repeat the date thresholds several times in queries like this one. The essential thing is to be careful and consider whether you should be using the lower or upper date thresholds in each case.

- Date tally lists are often fairly short; however, remember that you can make quite large tally lists if you need them by using the same table name two or even three times. This approach gives you code like this:

```
SELECT      ROW_NUMBER() OVER (ORDER BY Y.StockCode) - 1 AS ID

FROM        Data.Stock Y

CROSS JOIN Data.Stock Z
```

9. Aggregate Data for the Last Day of the Month

The sales director is still convinced that some days deliver better sales than others, so now she wants to see the sales for the last day of each month in 2016. SQL can handle this fairly easily, as the following piece of SQL shows:

```
;

WITH TallyTable_CTE

AS

(

SELECT      ROW_NUMBER() OVER (ORDER BY StockCode) AS ID

FROM        Data.Stock

)

,LastDayOfMonth_CTE

AS

(

SELECT          EOMONTH(DATEFROMPARTS(2016, ID, 1)) AS LastDayDate

FROM            TallyTable_CTE

WHERE           ID <= 12

)

SELECT          CTE.LastDayDate
```

```
              ,SUM(SLS.SalePrice) AS TotalDailySales

FROM          Data.SalesByCountry SLS

INNER JOIN    LastDayOfMonth_CTE CTE

              ON CTE.LastDayDate = CAST(SLS.SaleDate AS DATE)

GROUP BY      CTE.LastDayDate

ORDER BY      CTE.LastDayDate
```

If you run this query, you see the output that is shown in Figure 9-13.

FIGURE 9-13. SHOWING AGGREGATE DATA FOR THE LAST DAY OF THE MONTH

How It Works

This query is composed of three fundamental elements.

A tally CTE	That delivers a list of incremental numbers. This CTE uses the ROW_NUMBER() function to create the list of numbers, starting with 1. The row number field is aliased as ID. The table that the set of numbers is based on is completely irrelevant, as it only serves as a basis for the records that are created, and none of the actual data in the underlying table is required.
A second CTE	That uses the tally CTE as the source for its data. This second CTE extracts 12 records from the tally CTE (because there are 12 months in the year). It does this by applying a WHERE clause to the ID field of the tally CTE that sets the maximum ID to 12. Then the second CTE creates a list of the 12 months of a year (2016 in this case) by applying the DATEFROMPARTS() function to the tally list. Since the tally list ID field is defined as being the second parameter of the DATEFROMPARTS() function (the month in other words), the second CTE generates a list of the 12 months in the year. The last day of each month is then extracted from the month date using the EOMONTH() function.

A query That uses the second CTE as its data source. This query joins to the SalesByCountry view on the SaleDate field so that any sales that occurred on the last day of any month are returned. Once again a CAST() function is applied to ensure that the fields used to join the two tables are only using date elements for the join and that any time elements of the data are not used.

This sequence of datasets is probably easier to understand if you display the output from the second CTE. You can do this by placing the following piece of code under the second CTE and deleting the final query.

```
SELECT * FROM LastDayOfMonth_CTE
```

Figure 9-14 shows you the output from the second of two CTEs.

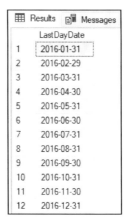

FIGURE 9-14. DISPLAYING THE LAST DAY OF THE MONTH

10. Aggregate Data for the Last Friday of the Month

The HR director has indicated that she is going to want you to calculate sales commissions for payment on the last Friday of every month. However, before you actually carry out the math, she wants a list of the last Friday for every month of 2017. You can deliver this using the following piece of SQL:

```
;
WITH TallyTable_CTE
AS
(
SELECT      ROW_NUMBER() OVER (ORDER BY StockCode) AS ID
FROM        Data.Stock
)
,LastDayOfMonth_CTE
AS
(
SELECT      EOMONTH(DATEFROMPARTS(2017, ID, 1)) AS MonthEndDate
            ,DATEPART(DW, EOMONTH(DATEFROMPARTS(2017, ID, 1)))
            AS MonthEndDay
FROM        TallyTable_CTE
WHERE       ID <= 12
)
SELECT      MonthEndDate
                ,DATEADD(dd
                    ,CASE
                        WHEN MonthEndDay >= 6 THEN 6
                                                - MonthEndDay
                        ELSE (6 - MonthEndDay) - 7
                    END
                ,MonthEndDate) AS LastFridayOfMonth
FROM        LastDayOfMonth_CTE
```

Running this code snippet produces the output that is shown in Figure 9-15.

	MonthEndDate	LastFridayOfMonth
1	2017-01-31	2017-01-27
2	2017-02-28	2017-02-24
3	2017-03-31	2017-03-31
4	2017-04-30	2017-04-28
5	2017-05-31	2017-05-26
6	2017-06-30	2017-06-30
7	2017-07-31	2017-07-28
8	2017-08-31	2017-08-25
9	2017-09-30	2017-09-29
10	2017-10-31	2017-10-27
11	2017-11-30	2017-11-24
12	2017-12-31	2017-12-29

FIGURE 9-15. DISPLAYING THE LAST FRIDAYS OF 2017

How It Works

This query (much like the last one) is based on

- A tally CTE to provide a sequence of numbers
- A second CTE that uses the tally list to produce a series of dates composed of the last day of the month
- A final query that takes the data from the second CTE and delivers the required result

Because the first two elements (the tally list and the CTE of month-end dates) are the same as those used in the previous section, we do not explain them again here.

The output query is a little different, however. It takes the date for the last day of the month and subtracts the required number of days necessary to discover the previous Friday (which is day 6) using a DATEADD() function. This function subtracts a specified number of days from the month-end date.

This requires first testing whether the last day is a Friday or Saturday. If it is (and this is the first part of the CASE statement), then the number of days to subtract is calculated to go back one or two days. If the last day is Sunday through Thursday, then a slightly different calculation is used.

This sequence of datasets is also probably easier to understand if you display the output from the second CTE. You can do this by placing the following piece of code under the second CTE and deleting the final query.

```
SELECT * FROM LastDayOfMonth_CTE
```

Adding this line of code after the second CTE and then running the SQL gives the result that you can see in Figure 9-16.

	MonthEndDate	MonthEndDay
1	2017-01-31	3
2	2017-02-28	3
3	2017-03-31	6
4	2017-04-30	1
5	2017-05-31	4
6	2017-06-30	6
7	2017-07-31	2
8	2017-08-31	5
9	2017-09-30	7
10	2017-10-31	3
11	2017-11-30	5
12	2017-12-31	1

FIGURE 9-16. DISPLAYING THE DAY NUMBER OF THE FRIDAY OF THE MONTH

11. Analyzing Timespans as Years, Months, and Days

The CEO of Prestige Cars is adamant. "Idle stock is a waste of resources," she maintains. To make sure no vehicles are waiting too long between being bought and sold, she has asked you to produce a report that shows the exact number of years, months, and days each car remains in stock. This has required some clever SQL, as you can see:

```
SELECT      ST.StockCode

            ,DATEDIFF(dd, ST.DateBought, SA.SaleDate) / 365 AS Years

            ,(DATEDIFF(dd, ST.DateBought, SA.SaleDate) % 365) / 30

                  AS Months

            ,(DATEDIFF(dd, ST.DateBought, SA.SaleDate)  % 365) % 30

                  AS Days

            ,DATEDIFF(dd, ST.DateBought, SA.SaleDate) / 30
```

```
                    AS TotalMonths

            ,DATEDIFF(dd, ST.DateBought, SA.SaleDate) % 365

                    AS DaysInYear

FROM          Data.Stock ST

  INNER JOIN  Data.SalesDetails SD

              ON ST.StockCode = SD.StockID

INNER JOIN    Data.Sales SA

              ON SD.SalesID = SA.SalesID

ORDER BY      DATEDIFF(dd, ST.DateBought, SA.SaleDate) / 365 DESC

             ,DATEDIFF(dd, ST.DateBought, SA.SaleDate) % 365 DESC
```

Running this query gives the results that you can see in Figure 9-17.

	StockCode	Years	Months	Days	TotalMonths	DaysInYear
1	A6FCB276-6311-4B3E-9C99-23F197952F1C	2	4	21	29	141
2	EDCCE461-5DA8-4E2E-8F08-798431841575	1	11	6	23	336
3	2319EA77-F4D9-4E34-9771-C42DCA3E210C	1	4	17	16	137
4	1A210C04-C981-4EA4-83B9-A6E76B5B9BDB	1	4	1	16	121
5	C001858B-0B5D-4648-8F0D-80269964C921	1	0	9	12	9
6	A0098927-0C7D-4CC8-8022-57A24433EF61	0	11	28	11	358
7	9743A284-D059-4EEB-98AB-ACDE88C1E9F5	0	11	21	11	351
8	CE0A56A6-8218-4F4C-A0E2-63F3DC9E4AE6	0	9	10	9	280
9	7F08368D-B6EA-4DFC-A1EC-B1A1B0221F04	0	8	9	8	249
10	43195E1A-46B2-4554-B1A9-C849B1C0B53B	0	5	5	5	155
11	6943ADF3-01A4-4281-B0CE-93384FE60418	0	4	14	4	134
12	266404D4-FBC5-4DC6-BB7C-A2ED7246D6D7	0	0	28	0	28
13	27C180A1-7C39-4E88-B5DE-ACD0C9594F3C	0	0	24	0	24
14	BEC34DF7-3E37-4322-A406-04BB5DF2A0FE	0	0	24	0	24
15	F075AC9E-1124-4194-A05F-683F9D553335	0	0	24	0	24

FIGURE 9-17. USING DATEDIFF() AND ARITHMETIC OPERATORS TO CALCULATE TIME IN YEARS, MONTHS, AND DAYS

How It Works

What this query does is take advantage of the possibilities the modulo function offers to take a timespan that is represented in years and calculate the following metrics:

- The number of elapsed *years*

- The number of elapsed *months* over and above the elapsed years
- The number of elapsed *days* over and above the elapsed years and months
- The total number of elapsed months
- The number of days over and above any elapsed years

Since this query is based on the judicious use of the modulo function—which SQL Server presents as the percent sign (%)—you need to remember that this function divides one number by another and leaves only the remainder. Also, in these calculations, we are making the simplistic assumptions that there are 365 days in the year and 30 days in a month.

To begin with, this query joins the tables that are required to access the purchase and sales dates. That means joining the Stock and Sales tables using the SalesDetails table as a connecting "bridge" table.

At this point, you can create the five calculations that deliver the information that interests you:

Years elapsed	This calculation takes the number of days between the purchase and sale dates and divides by 365 to give the number of whole years elapsed between the two dates.
Months in excess of years	This calculation takes the number of days between the purchase and sale dates and returns the remainder. This figure is then divided by 30 to give the number of complete months that have passed.
Days in excess of months	This calculation takes the number of days between the purchase and sale dates and returns the remainder to produce the number of days over and above any complete years. It then applies a modulo of 30 to this figure and takes the remainder. This is the number of days over and above any complete years and months.
Total months elapsed	This calculation takes the number of days between the purchase and sale dates and divides by 30 to give the total number of months between the two dates.
Total days in excess of years	This calculation takes the number of days between the purchase and sale dates and returns the remainder.

You may not necessarily need all of these individual calculations when you are analyzing your time-related data; however, having them at hand might prove useful one day!

12. Isolate Time Periods from Date and Time Data

The sales team has been vying to sell cars faster and faster, so they want to know which cars have spent the shortest time in stock in 2017. This can sometimes prove to be only a matter of minutes or even seconds, as the following SQL illustrates:

```
SELECT      ST.DateBought

            ,SA.SaleDate

            ,MK.MakeName + '-' + MD.ModelName AS MakeAndModel

            ,(DATEDIFF(second, ST.DateBought, SA.SaleDate) % (24*60*60))

             / 3600    AS Hours

            ,((DATEDIFF(second, ST.DateBought, SA.SaleDate)

               % (24*60*60)) % 3600) / 60    AS Minutes

            ,(((DATEDIFF(second, ST.DateBought, SA.SaleDate)  % 365)

               % (24*60*60)) % 3600) % 60    AS Seconds

FROM        Data.Stock ST

            INNER JOIN Data.Model MD

            ON ST.ModelID = MD.ModelID

INNER JOIN  Data.Make M

            ON MD.MakeID = MK.MakeID

INNER JOIN  Data.SalesDetails SD

            ON ST.StockCode = SD.StockID

INNER JOIN  Data.Sales SA

            ON SD.SalesID = SA.SalesID

WHERE       (DATEDIFF(dd, ST.DateBought, SA.SaleDate) % 365) = 1

            AND YEAR(SA.SaleDate) = 2017
```

Running this query gives the results that you can see in Figure 9-18.

	DateBought	SaleDate	MakeAndModel	Hours	Minutes	Seconds
1	2016-12-31	2017-01-01 11:12:00.000	Porsche-Boxster	11	12	5
2	2017-03-30	2017-03-31 14:09:00.000	Citroen-Rosalie	14	9	40
3	2017-04-30	2017-05-01 17:12:00.000	Rolls Royce-Phantom	17	12	10
4	2017-04-30	2017-05-01 10:12:00.000	Rolls Royce-Wraith	10	12	55
5	2017-05-11	2017-05-12 13:15:00.000	Ferrari-F50	13	15	25
6	2017-05-12	2017-05-13 20:16:00.000	Ferrari-F40	20	16	40
7	2017-05-15	2017-05-16 16:16:00.000	Alfa Romeo-Giulietta	16	16	55
8	2017-05-18	2017-05-19 21:17:00.000	Triumph-GT6	21	17	50
9	2017-05-19	2017-05-20 14:17:00.000	Reliant-Robin	14	17	35
10	2017-05-20	2017-05-21 16:18:00.000	McLaren-P1	16	18	55
11	2017-05-21	2017-05-22 11:18:00.000	Delorean-DMC 12	11	18	0
12	2017-05-22	2017-05-23 09:19:00.000	BMW-E30	9	19	40
13	2017-05-23	2017-05-24 17:19:00.000	Aston Martin-DB2	17	19	5
14	2017-05-25	2017-05-26 10:20:00.000	Aston Martin-DB9	10	20	50
15	2017-05-26	2017-05-27 21:20:00.000	Citroen-Rosalie	21	20	45

FIGURE 9-18. USING DATEDIFF() AND ARITHMETIC OPERATORS TO CALCULATE TIME IN HOURS, MINUTES, AND SECONDS

How It Works

This query begins by joining the tables that are needed to source the Make, Model, DateBought, and SaleDate fields. Then a WHERE clause is added that filters the records so that only vehicles that are sold within one day of being bought are displayed. This is done by using a DATEDIFF() function to calculate a number of days, and then only the remainder is returned once the number of days is divided by 365 using the modulo function. If this value equals 1, then the car was in stock for less than 24 hours.

Three formulas are added to the SELECT clause to return:

- The hours in stock
- The minutes in stock after any hours are subtracted from the total time in stock
- The seconds in stock after any hours and minutes are subtracted from the total time in stock

These three formulas work like this:

Hours	The DATEDIFF() function calculates the number of seconds between the purchase date and the sale date (which is, in fact, midnight since the DateBought field does not contain hours, minutes, or seconds). Then the modulo (%) function is applied to divide this figure by the number of seconds in the day (60 × 60 × 24 or 86,400). This is necessary in case you are calculating the difference over more than one day. The remainder is the number of seconds in the day that are left once any complete days are removed from the timespan. This is then divided by 3,600 (the number of seconds in an hour) to give the number of complete hours difference.
Minutes	Here the DATEDIFF() function also calculates the number of seconds between the purchase date and the sale date. Then the modulo (%) function is applied to divide this figure by the number of seconds in the day (in case you are calculating the difference over more than one day). The remainder is then calculated using % 3600 to return the number of seconds once any full hours are past. Finally, this figure is divided by 60 to give the number of minutes.
Seconds	The DATEDIFF() function also calculates the number of seconds between the purchase date and the sale date. Then the modulo (%) function is applied to divide this figure by the number of seconds in the day in case you are calculating the difference over more than one day. The remainder is then calculated (using % 3600) to return the number of seconds remaining once any complete hours are past. Finally, the remaining number of seconds is calculated by returning the remainder of the final figure using % 60.

Tricks and Traps

We have one additional point to make here:

- You can wrap the whole query in a CTE or a subquery and then order by the time in seconds between the purchase and sale dates (in descending order) if you want to view the fastest sales first.

13. Listing Data by Time of Day

Now the sales director wants to look at exactly when cars are sold to see if there are certain times of the day that are better for sales. You produced a list of vehicles sold in 2017 that includes the exact time the sale was made. The code for this is shown here:

```
SELECT     MakeName, ModelName, SalePrice

           ,FORMAT(SaleDate, 't') AS TimeOfDaySold

FROM       Data.SalesByCountry

WHERE      YEAR(SaleDate) = 2017

ORDER BY   CONVERT(TIME, SaleDate)
```

If you run this code you see the output displayed in Figure 9-19.

	MakeName	ModelName	SalePrice	TimeOfDaySold
1	BMW	E30	33500.00	9:19 AM
2	Jaguar	XK150	29500.00	9:25 AM
3	Triumph	TR5	9950.00	9:58 AM
4	Aston Martin	Rapide	55000.00	9:59 AM
5	Porsche	959	55600.00	10:07 AM
6	Rolls Royce	Wraith	162500.00	10:12 AM
7	Aston Martin	DB4	36500.00	10:20 AM
8	Aston Martin	DB9	77500.00	10:20 AM
9	Peugeot	205	3950.00	10:25 AM
10	Noble	M600	29500.00	10:25 AM
11	Alfa Romeo	Spider	12500.00	10:25 AM
12	Porsche	944	15750.00	10:33 AM
13	Bentley	Arnage	99950.00	10:39 AM
14	Aston Martin	Vanquish	56500.00	10:59 AM
15	Austin	Lichfield	6500.00	11:02 AM

FIGURE 9-19. DISPLAYING RECORDS BY TIME

How It Works

As long as the source data contains a time element, you can display the time of an event (such as a sale) when querying data. Fortunately, the Sales table (which is used in the SalesByCountry view) contains the SaleDate field that contains both a date and a time element. This query simply selects core information—including the SaleDate—from the SalesByCountry view.

Isolating the time part of a field like this (in fact, it is a DATETIME field) is as simple as selecting the SaleDate field and formatting the output from this field. The trick is to use the FORMAT() function. As you may have seen in the first volume of this series, the FORMAT() function requires two parameters:

First:	The field to format
Second:	The format code to apply

In this example, we used the 't' format code. This code displays the output in a shortened time format with the hour, minutes, and AM/PM indicator.

The FORMAT() function lets you apply a series of built-in time formats. These are shown in Table 9-1.

TABLE 9-1. TIME FORMAT CODES

Description	Format Code	Sample Output
Full date/time short time	f	*Tuesday, May 23, 2017 9:19 AM*
Full Date/Time Long Time	F	*Tuesday, May 23, 2017 9:19:00 AM*
General date/time short time	g	*5/23/2017 9:19 AM*
General date/time long time	G	*5/23/2017 9:19:00 AM*
Round-trip date/time	O	*2017-05-23T09:19:00.0000000*
RFC 1123	R	*Tue, 23 May 2017 09:19:00 GMT*
Short time	t	*9:19 AM*
Long time	T	*9:19:00 AM*
Universal sortable date/time	u	*2017-05-23 09:19:00Z*
Universal full date/time	U	*Tuesday, May 23, 2017 8:19:00 AM*

Tricks and Traps

Inevitably, we have a few points to make here:

- You can extract the time element from DATETIME, DATETIME2, and TIME fields.

- The formatted output is converted to text. This means that you should not use it to sort the data or in-time calculations. Use the underlying data field to carry out these operations.

- If you want to extract the time element from a DATETIME or DATETIME2 field, you can use code like this, which removes the date element from the field:

```
CAST(SaleDate AS TIME)
```

Once a DATETIME or DATETIME2 field has been converted to a TIME field in this way, you can use it to sort the data.

14. Aggregating Data by Hourly Bandings

The CEO has been looking at some of the output that you have prepared for the sales director and is convinced that sales staff need to be aware that certain times of the day produce better sales, so she has asked for a list of 2017 sales aggregated by hour bands. The following SQL delivers this.

```
SELECT      CAST(HourOfDay AS VARCHAR(2)) + '-' + CAST(HourOfDay + 1

            AS VARCHAR(2)) AS HourBand

            ,SUM(SalePrice) AS SalesByHourBand

FROM

    (

    SELECT      SalePrice

                ,DATEPART(hh, SaleDate) AS HourOfDay

    FROM        Data.SalesByCountry

    WHERE       YEAR(SaleDate) = 2017
```

```
    ) A

GROUP BY   HourOfDay

ORDER BY   HourOfDay
```

Running this piece of code produces the output that you can see in Figure 9-20.

	HourBand	SalesByHourBand
1	9-10	127950.00
2	10-11	550250.00
3	11-12	617400.00
4	12-13	1193390.00
5	13-14	1052700.00
6	14-15	106905.00
7	15-16	85000.00
8	16-17	829400.00
9	17-18	672900.00
10	18-19	605450.00
11	19-20	668530.00
12	20-21	1117500.00
13	21-22	240700.00

FIGURE 9-20. DISPLAYING DATA GROUPED AND AGGREGATED FOR HOUR BANDS

How It Works

The heart of this piece of SQL is a subquery that isolates the hour when a sale was made. It does this by applying the DATEPART() function to the SaleDate field of the Sales-ByCountry view. This function can extract date elements from a DATE or DATETIME field (as you have seen previously). However, it can also extract time elements from a DATETIME or TIME field. In this specific example, the first parameter of the DATETIME() function is *hh*, which indicates to SQL Server that it is the hour element that you wish to isolate from the time part of the field.

To make this clearer, take a look at Figure 9-21 where you can see the output from the subquery (aliased as A in the SQL code).

FIGURE 9-21. EXTRACTING THE HOUR PART OF A DATETIME FIELD USING THE DATEPART() FUNCTION

Once the subquery has delivered the sale price and the hour of the sale, the outer query can take this information and use it as the basis for the final result.

The outer query simply aggregates the sale price by hour. As a final flourish, it displays the hour band as a range by displaying the hour twice—by simply adding 1 to the hour figure. Since the hour is a number, it has to be converted to text using the CAST() function so that another text element—the hyphen—can be used in the output.

The DATEPART() function can extract more than just hours from a TIME or DATETIME field. The various time elements that it can isolate are shown in Table 9-2.

TABLE 9-2. TIME FORMAT CODES

Description	Format Code
Hour	hh
Minute	mi
Second	ss
Millisecond	ms

Tricks and Traps

We have one idea to add:

- You can wrap the whole query in a CTE or a subquery and then order by the aggregate amount to see most profitable hours of the day if you want to extract even more analysis from the data.

15. Aggregate Data by Quarter of Hour

As a final part of the sales focus, the CEO wants to know which part of the hour is best for sales. You prepare the following piece of code to show sales for 2017 in quarter-hourly tranches.

```
SELECT          QuarterOfHour

                ,SUM(SalePrice) AS SalesByQuarterHourBand

FROM

    (

        SELECT        SalePrice

                ,(DATEPART(mi, SaleDate) / 15) + 1 AS QuarterOfHour

        FROM        Data.SalesByCountry

        WHERE       YEAR(SaleDate) = 2017

    ) A

GROUP BY     QuarterOfHour

ORDER BY     QuarterOfHour
```

Running this code snippet produces the output that you can see in Figure 9-22.

	QuarterOfHour	SalesByQuarterHourBand
1	1	3086360.00
2	2	2649600.00
3	3	1642115.00
4	4	490000.00

FIGURE 9-22. Data grouped in quarter-hour bands

How It Works

This piece of SQL consists of two queries:

An inner query   That looks at every sale date and time for 2017 (using the SalesByCountry view as the source of the data). This subquery extracts the minute at which each sale took place using the DATEPART() function and the mi parameter. Then the number of minutes is divided by 15 to give each quarter of an hour. The 15-minute slot is then incremented by 1, since otherwise it would begin with 0.

An outer query   That aggregates the sales amount from the inner query (aliased as A) and groups the amounts by each quarter of an hour.

Conclusion

This chapter showed you a more advanced set of techniques that you can use to analyze data over time. You have learned how to compare data across different time periods, to analyze how metrics accumulate over time, and to break down timespans into their constituent parts. Using these kinds of advanced time analysis can really help you discover trends in your source data.

Core Knowledge Learned in This Chapter

The keywords that you have seen in this chapter are listed here. We have included those that you may already have seen in *Volume I*.

Concept	Description
EOMONTH()	*This function returns the date for the last day of the month.*
DATEDIFF()	*This function finds the number of days, months, years, and so on between two given dates.*
CAST()	*This function converts a datetime data type to a date.*
YEAR()	*This function isolates the year part of a date.*
MONTH()	*This function isolates the month part of a date.*
DAY()	*This function isolates the day part of a date.*
DATEPART()	*This function returns the quarter, weekday, and so on for a date.*
DATEADD()	*This function adds or subtracts a number of days, months, years, and so on to or from a given data and finds the date in the future or the past.*
DATENAME()	*This function displays the name of part of the date—such as the month or weekday.*

Chapter 10:
Complex Data Output

Often the way data is presented is perceived as more important than the data itself, so you need to know not only how to analyze the data and deliver accurate results, but also how to shape the output so that the essence of your analysis is immediately comprehensible. The techniques covered in this chapter help you present your analysis in various ways that can make the results easier to read and understand.

Presenting Complex Output with SQL

The techniques that you discover in this chapter include

- Pivoting data to create crosstab tables
- Adding multiple separate subtotals to an aggregate query
- Displaying data from multiple records in separate columns in a single query
- Carrying out search and replace operations on the final output
- Assembling concatenated lists of results

These ways of enhancing the output from a query are as practical as they are useful. They can make your results as alluring as they are revelatory. In the real world, you may not use all of these techniques on a daily basis; nonetheless, it is probably best to know that they are available so that you can apply them when the need arises. What is more, these presentation techniques can only enhance your SQL skills. Indeed, you can apply several of the approaches that you see in this chapter to solve many other analytical challenges.

1. Creating a Pivot Table

The finance director has given you a new challenge—deliver a simple, compact table of sales by color for all the years that Prestige Cars has been trading. T-SQL can pivot data in this way, as the following code snippet shows:

```
SELECT      Color, [2015], [2016], [2017], [2018]

FROM

            (

            SELECT      Color, SD.SalePrice, YEAR(SaleDate)

                                                    AS YearOfSale

            FROM        Data.Stock ST

            INNER JOIN  Data.SalesDetails SD

                        ON ST.StockCode = SD.StockID

            INNER JOIN  Data.Sales SA

                        ON SA.SalesID = SD.SalesID

            ) SQ

PIVOT       (

            SUM(SalePrice) FOR YearOfSale

                        IN ([2015], [2016], [2017], [2018])

            ) AS PVT
```

Running this query gives the results that you can see in Figure 10-1.

	Color	2015	2016	2017	2018
1	Black	374490.00	1251410.00	3112550.00	1983695.00
2	Blue	284600.00	423650.00	708420.00	1186400.00
3	British Racing Green	111500.00	663250.00	872340.00	566385.00
4	Canary Yellow	132000.00	287070.00	104750.00	134045.00
5	Dark Purple	NULL	283000.00	219175.00	662640.00
6	Green	216600.00	370750.00	655090.00	599540.00
7	Night Blue	57990.00	405500.00	457500.00	600830.00
8	Pink	NULL	235950.00	54700.00	191600.00
9	Red	154795.00	442500.00	659150.00	932450.00
10	Silver	89000.00	542205.00	1093900.00	926030.00

FIGURE 10-1. CREATING A PIVOT TABLE USING THE PIVOT OPERATOR

How It Works

Sometimes a simple list of data is not what you want. Comparing data in a list can be much harder than when it is presented as a table of intersecting rows and columns, as is the case with a pivot table. This table style of data presentation is also called a *crosstab*.

What matters when using the PIVOT operator is realizing that it is there to display *three* pieces of data in different ways. It needs

Row headers   These are the data elements that appear in the left-hand column of the output table.

Column headers   These are the data elements that appear at the top of each column. It is important to understand that these are *not field names*, but data from the database.

Table data   These are the aggregated numeric values that appear inside the final pivoted output table.

Therefore, the art of making a pivot table involves assembling these three pieces of data so that they can be used correctly to give you the result you are looking for. Here is what is actually done in this example:

Initially: The inner query (which is technically a subquery) is defined to output the data elements that you want to see in the final pivot table. These are color, year of sale, and sale price. This is the core data that is used in the pivot table and it contains fields from the Stock, Sales, and SalesDetails tables.

If you select the SQL for the subquery and execute it, you see something like the output displayed in Figure 10-2. This is a simple list query and it contains hundreds of rows.

	Color	SalePrice	YearOfSale
1	Red	65000.00	2015
2	Blue	220000.00	2015
3	British Racing Green	19500.00	2015
4	British Racing Green	11500.00	2015
5	Red	19950.00	2015
6	Night Blue	29500.00	2015
7	Black	49500.00	2015
8	Canary Yellow	76000.00	2015
9	Blue	19600.00	2015
10	Blue	36500.00	2015
11	Blue	8500.00	2015
12	Night Blue	45000.00	2017
13	British Racing Green	80500.00	2015
14	Black	169500.00	2015
15	Green	8950.00	2015

FIGURE 10-2. THE SUBQUERY THAT PREPARES DATA FOR THE PIVOT OPERATOR

Then:	You apply the PIVOT operator to the subquery. This is, in effect, another subquery. What it does is isolate two of the fields in the subquery for some special treatment—data to aggregate and column specification.
Finally:	A SELECT clause is applied that provides the *row data* for the output table. In this case, it is the *Color* field. Then you add the column headers that were defined as part of the PIVOT operator.

The PIVOT operator needs the following two elements:

Aggregated element:	A numeric field is aggregated so that it can be displayed in the *body* of the final output table. In this example, it is the SalePrice field.
Column definition:	The content—in whole or in part—of another field is individually listed inside parentheses after the FOR clause to provide the *column headers* of the final output table.

A pivot table has to use an aggregation function to handle the values that are displayed in the table. This is because each intersection of a row and a column (several black cars sold in 2015, for instance) can have more than one value. You can use any of the SQL aggregation functions in a pivot table; consequently, you can just as easily use AVG() or COUNT() here to return the average sale price or the number of vehicles. If you are using SUM() or AVG(), then the field that you are aggregating has to be numeric. COUNT() can also be applied to text fields to return the number of values rather than the sum of the values.

Writing pivot table SQL is easier once you understand the process that the code represents. To help conceptualize this technique, take a look at Figure 10-3.

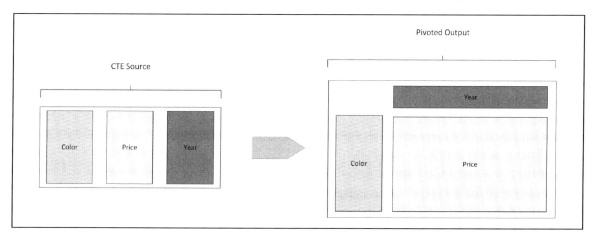

FIGURE 10-3. THE CONCEPT OF THE PIVOT TABLE

Tricks and Traps

Pivot tables require you to pay careful attention to the SQL that you are writing, so be sure to remember the following points when you create your own pivot tables:

- The only tricky part of writing the SQL that creates a pivot table is selecting the data that will constitute the column headers. It helps if you start by isolating this list of individual data elements before you start writing the rest of the code. In this example, you can return the list of years used in the PIVOT operator *and* the SELECT clause with the following SQL snippet:

```
SELECT DISTINCT YEAR(SaleDate) FROM Data.Sales
```

This returns the years (as you can see in Figure 10-4) that you can then copy and paste to create the list of column headers.

FIGURE 10-4. PREPARING THE DATA FOR THE COLUMN TITLES OF THE PIVOT OPERATOR

- The list of data elements to be used as the column headers does not have to be enclosed in square brackets as they are in this example, however, it is good practice to use square brackets—otherwise any spaces or nonalphanumeric data from the dataset stops the pivot query from working.

2. Creating a Pivot Table Displaying Multiple Row Groupings

Fortunately, the finance director was delighted with your first pivot table. Unfortunately, this has created further demands from him for yet more analysis from you. What he would like now is another pivot table, only this time he wants to see the number of colors sold by make *and* model. The following code shows how this can be done:

```
WITH MakeAndModelCostByYear_CTE (MakeName, ModelName, Color, CostPrice)

AS

(

SELECT      MakeName, ModelName, Color, Cost

FROM        Data.Make MK

INNER JOIN  Data.Model MD ON MK.MakeID = MD.MakeID

INNER JOIN  Data.Stock ST ON ST.ModelID = MD.ModelID

)



SELECT      MakeName, ModelName, [Black], [Blue], [British Racing Green]
```

```
           ,[Canary Yellow], [Dark Purple], [Green], [Night Blue]

           ,[Pink], [Red], [Silver]
FROM       MakeAndModelCostByYear_CTE
PIVOT      (

                 COUNT(CostPrice) FOR Color IN

                       (

                       [Black], [Blue], [British Racing Green],

                       [Canary Yellow], [Dark Purple], [Green],

                       [Night Blue], [Pink], [Red], [Silver]

                       )

           ) PVT
ORDER BY   MakeName, ModelName
```

Running this query gives the results that you can see in Figure 10-5.

	MakeName	ModelName	Black	Blue	British Racing Green	Canary Yellow	Dark Purple	Green	Night Blue	Pink	Red	Silver
1	Alfa Romeo	1750	1	1	0	0	0	0	0	0	0	0
2	Alfa Romeo	Giulia	3	0	3	0	0	1	0	0	1	0
3	Alfa Romeo	Giulietta	1	2	0	0	1	0	3	0	0	0
4	Alfa Romeo	Spider	4	1	0	0	0	1	0	0	0	0
5	Aston Martin	DB2	2	1	1	1	0	2	1	0	1	2
6	Aston Martin	DB4	3	0	0	1	0	1	1	1	0	1
7	Aston Martin	DB5	2	2	0	0	0	0	1	0	1	1
8	Aston Martin	DB6	4	0	3	2	0	1	2	0	2	2
9	Aston Martin	DB9	4	1	1	1	1	2	1	0	1	5
10	Aston Martin	Rapide	1	0	0	0	0	0	1	0	1	1
11	Aston Martin	Vanquish	2	0	0	0	1	1	2	0	1	1
12	Aston Martin	Vantage	2	0	1	0	0	1	0	0	0	0
13	Aston Martin	Virage	3	2	0	0	1	1	1	2	2	0
14	Austin	Cambridge	1	0	0	0	0	0	0	0	0	0
15	Austin	Lichfield	0	0	0	0	0	0	1	1	0	0

FIGURE 10-5. A COMPLEX PIVOT OPERATION BASED ON A CTE

How It Works

Pivot tables can be more complex than the simple table that you saw in the previous example. For more detailed output where more than one column of aggregated data is required, a CTE (Common Table Expression) can help you simplify both the SQL and the way that you approach the problem. This query follows the same pivot function principles that you saw previously:

- Identify and select the columns to display.
- Identify the data to pivot as column headers.
- Identify the value to aggregate and display in the table.

This query also begins by defining the source data for the pivot operation. This time, however, a CTE is used to do this. The CTE is based on the Make, Model, and Stock tables. If you select the query used in the CTE, you see a result like that shown in Figure 10-6.

	MakeName	ModelName	Color	Cost
1	Ferrari	Testarossa	Red	52000.00
2	Ferrari	355	Blue	176000.00
3	Porsche	911	British Racing Green	15600.00
4	Porsche	924	British Racing Green	9200.00
5	Porsche	944	Red	15960.00
6	Ferrari	Testarossa	Black	176000.00
7	Aston Martin	DB4	Night Blue	23600.00
8	Aston Martin	DB5	Black	39600.00
9	Aston Martin	DB6	Canary Yellow	60800.00
10	Ferrari	Testarossa	Red	172000.00

FIGURE 10-6. USING A CTE TO RETURN THE DATA USED IN A PIVOT

This CTE isolates the two fields that appear as row headers (MakeName and ModelName) as well as the value field (Cost) and the field that contains the data elements that are to be pivoted as column headers (Color).

The query is then built in four sections:

SELECT   This clause is where the output fields are defined: first the two fields that make up the row headers are specified followed by all the unique data fields from the Color column that become the column headers.

FROM   This clause uses the CTE as the data source.

PIVOT	This clause first specifies the aggregation that is used—COUNT() in this example. Then it states the field that is aggregated—CostPrice. Finally, a FOR expression is used to indicate which field contains the column headers (Color) and to list unique data elements from this field (the list of colors).
ORDER BY	Although optional, this clause guarantees comprehensible results by sorting the output.

All these elements together create the pivot SQL that you saw in boldface at the start of this section.

Tricks and Traps

We have only one point that you really need to remember when pivoting data like this:

- You only need to add square brackets for each field name in the pivot list if the data contains spaces or nonalphanumeric characters. That said, we consider it good practice always to add square brackets.

3.   Unpivoting Data

Data is not always perfectly organized. Suppose that someone in the company comes to you with an already pivoted dataset. Let's imagine that it looks exactly like the pivot table that you can see in Figure 10.1. The challenge this time is to unpivot the data and display multiple records in fewer columns. The code to do this is as follows:

```
SELECT     Color, UPT.SaleValue, UPT.SaleYear

FROM       Data.PivotTable

UNPIVOT    (SaleValue FOR SaleYear IN ([2015], [2016], [2017],[2018]))

           AS UPT
```

Running this short piece of code gives the output that you can see in Figure 10.7.

	Color	SaleValue	SaleYear
1	Black	374490.00	2015
2	Black	1251410.00	2016
3	Black	3112550.00	2017
4	Black	1983695.00	2018
5	Blue	284600.00	2015
6	Blue	423650.00	2016
7	Blue	708420.00	2017
8	Blue	1186400.00	2018
9	British Racing Green	111500.00	2015
10	British Racing Green	663250.00	2016
11	British Racing Green	872340.00	2017
12	British Racing Green	566385.00	2018
13	Canary Yellow	132000.00	2015
14	Canary Yellow	287070.00	2016
15	Canary Yellow	104750.00	2017
16	Canary Yellow	134045.00	2018

FIGURE 10-7. UNPIVOTING DATA USING THE UNPIVOT OPERATOR

How It Works

This piece of SQL takes a source table that contains the following three kinds of element:

First	Color information in the left column.
Then	Years in the other column headers.
Finally	Values from the intersection of these rows and columns across all the remaining rows and columns.

The SQL uses a new operator—the *UNPIVOT* operator—to "unpick" this structure and deliver output where there are only three columns of data. These are Color, Year and the value for each combination of he first two elements.

To help you understand teh challenge more clearly, take a look at Figure 10.8. Here you can see, schematically, how the UNPIVOT operator works.

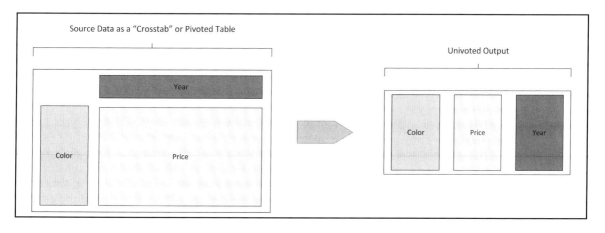

FIGURE 10-8. How pivoted data can be converted to a classis table structure

The UNPIVOT operator carries out the following operations:

- Identify the columns to unpivot and display as a single column.
- Identify the value to aggregate and display in the output.

As the core transformation is handled by the UNPIVOT operator itself, let's look at this first.

First	After the FROM clause that identifies the data source, you enter the UNPIVOT keyword, and a left parenthesis.
Next	You specify a column name that will be used for the values that will be unpivoted from the data in a set of columns that you will enumerate.
Then	You add the FOR keyword, followed by an alias (or column name if you prefer) where the column headers from all unpivoted columns will appear.
Next	You enter the IN operator.
Then	You enter a comma-separated list of all the column names in the source data containing data that you want to unpivot. This must be wrapped inside parentheses.
Finally	You end the unpivot operation with a final right parenthesis, the AS keyword and an alias—UPT in this example.

Adding an alias to the unpivoted data allows you to reference, independently, columns from the data source and column that result from the application of the UNPIVOT operator.

Finally you can add the SELECT clause of the SQL. Here, the Color field has *no alias* as it is pulled directly from the initial source table whereas the SaleValue and SaleYear fields are derived from the fields created by the UNPIVOT operator. So these two fields (SaleValue and SaleYear) *must use the alias that was set for the UNPIVOT operator* (UPT in this example).

Tricks and Traps

Unpivoting data also requires you to pay careful attention to the SQL that you are writing, so be sure to remember the following points when you npivot data:

- The square brackets that enclose the column headers that will be unpivoted—years in this example—are not strictly necessary. However it can be good practive to add them. This means that column names containg spaces or that could be misunderstood by SQL will be handled gracefully.

- If you are unpivoting a table that is, otself, the result of a pivot operation you need to be aware that you will not be outputting the data as it was originally. This is because the values have already been aggregated by the PIVOT operator. Consequently you will only be siing aggregated data when you unpivot the result of a pivot operation.

4. Adding Totals to Aggregate Queries

Although pleased with the lists of data that you can now deliver at the drop of a hat, the finance director wants one more thing. He prefers a more spreadsheet-like output that includes the subtotals in some cases; this will save him extra work in a spreadsheet. The following SQL snippet delivers exactly what he is looking for—a list of sales by color and make including the grand total:

```
SELECT      MakeName, Color, SUM(Cost) AS Cost

FROM        Data.Make MK

INNER JOIN  Data.Model MD ON MK.MakeID = MD.MakeID

INNER JOIN  Data.Stock ST ON ST.ModelID = MD.ModelID

GROUP BY    GROUPING SETS ((MakeName, Color), ())

ORDER BY    MakeName, Color
```

Running this query gives the results that you can see in Figure 10-9.

FIGURE 10-9. CREATING TOTALS WITH GROUPING SETS

How It Works

Producing aggregations is something that you are now used to with SQL Server. So far, you have only seen how to deliver levels of aggregation or totals in *separate queries*; however, sometimes you need to see not just the subtotals, but also the grand total in a single query. This query extends the GROUP BY clause with an extension that is the GROUPING SETS clause. This new function allows you to specify exactly which totals and subtotals are returned in the final output.

First: You begin with a perfectly normal aggregation query. In this example, the Make, Model, and Stock tables are joined and the make name and color fields are output along with the total for the cost of vehicles purchased. Since this is an aggregation query, any fields that are not aggregated must be added to a GROUP BY clause. In this example, these are the Make, Name, and Color fields.

Then: The GROUPING SETS clause is added to the GROUP BY clause. This requires that you add parentheses that contain the fields that are to be aggregated. Each set of fields is inside its own parentheses. In this example, the make name and color fields are added so that the total for each combination of make and color will be calculated. Then, and separated with a comma, an empty pair of parentheses is added inside the outer grouping sets parentheses. This tells SQL Server to return the grand total for the dataset as well.

Reading the final result set is not completely intuitive, so we prefer to explain it. The total for each aggregated set of make and color is probably self-evident. However, the initial record without either a make or a color is probably less easy to understand. This is, in fact, the grand total. It is the record that is produced by the empty parentheses inside the GROUPING SETS clause. Since no fields are provided for the grand total in the GROUPING SETS clause, the grand total is represented by NULLs in the make name and color fields of the output.

Tricks and Traps

There is one fundamental point to remember when creating grouping sets:

- When adding a grouping sets clause, you have to be careful to respect the sets of parentheses in the clause. There is always an outer pair of parentheses and then an inner pair for each aggregation that you add.

5. Creating Subtotals and Totals in Aggregated Queries

This time it is the CEO herself who wants a quick report to see sales by make and color including subtotals for all possible combinations of makes and sales. Fortunately, it only takes only a few minutes to write the code that can deliver this list for her:

```
SELECT       MakeName, Color, SUM(Cost) AS Cost
FROM         Data.Make MK
INNER JOIN   Data.Model MD ON MK.MakeID = MD.MakeID
INNER JOIN   Data.Stock ST ON ST.ModelID = MD.ModelID
GROUP BY     GROUPING SETS ((MakeName, Color), (MakeName), (Color), ())
ORDER BY     MakeName, Color
```

Running this query gives the results that you can see in Figure 10-10. You might want to scroll down this list to see the subtotals for other makes.

FIGURE 10-10. ADDING SUBTOTALS WITH GROUPING SETS

How It Works

SQL does not limit you to displaying the grand total and the totals for each aggregation. It can also show any intermediate totals. In this way, SQL can help you see both the big picture and the interesting nuggets of detail.

The code that can deliver this mix of high-level aggregation and low-level details is, at its heart, a fairly simple aggregation query. It takes the Make, Model, and Stock tables and joins them before outputting the total cost for each make and color.

However, the GROUP BY clause is extended with a more complex GROUPING SETS clause that requests

A grand total	This is done by adding the empty parentheses inside the GROUPING SETS clause.
	Total for make This is done by adding (MakeName)—in its own parentheses—inside the GROUPING SETS clause.
Total for color	This is done by adding (Color)—in its own parentheses—inside the GROUPING SETS clause.
Aggregate totals	For make and color. These are requested just as you would request them in a standard GROUP BY clause—by adding the Make and Color fields separated by a comma. However, because this aggregation is a GROUPING SETS clause, these field names must be inside their own set of parentheses.

It can take a little practice to appreciate exactly what the GROUPING SETS query has delivered. More specifically, you have to look closely at the NULLs in the various columns to see how the subtotals are created when applying grouping sets to an aggregate query. Put simply

- If all columns except the value are NULL, then the row is the grand total.

- If a column contains a NULL alongside other elements, you are looking at the total for those elements. For instance, if the MakeName column is NULL and the Color column contains "British Racing Green," then the figure for that row is the total for the color "British Racing Green." Equally, if the MakeName column contains "Alfa Romeo" and the Color column contains NULL, then the figure shown in the record is the total for the make "Alfa Romeo."

Conceptually, the GROUPING SETS operator behaves in the way that is described in Figure 10-11.

FIGURE 10-11. ANATOMY OF A GROUPING SETS OPERATOR

Tricks and Traps

We have two comments at this point:

- You do not have to add an ORDER BY clause when using grouping sets; however, it does often make the final output easier to understand.

- You do not have to add the lowest level of aggregation to a GROUPING SETS clause if you do not want to see the subtotals for each combination of make and color. For instance, if you alter the GROUP BY clause in this example so that it reads

```
GROUP BY    GROUPING SETS ((MakeName), (Color), ())
```

you only see the totals for Make, Color, and the grand total, as you can see in Figure 10-12.

	MakeName	Color	Cost
1	NULL	NULL	19703564.00
2	NULL	Black	6101348.00
3	NULL	Blue	2097736.00
4	NULL	British Racing Green	1815580.00
5	NULL	Canary Yellow	904092.00
6	NULL	Dark Purple	1024212.00
7	NULL	Green	1592776.00
8	NULL	Night Blue	1343856.00
9	NULL	Pink	385800.00
10	NULL	Red	2277656.00
11	NULL	Silver	2160508.00
12	Alfa Romeo	NULL	207248.00
13	Aston Martin	NULL	4470956.00
14	Austin	NULL	51600.00
15	Bentley	NULL	1413392.00
16	BMW	NULL	48400.00
17	Bugatti	NULL	1524400.00
18	Citroen	NULL	80864.00
19	Delahaye	NULL	103720.00
20	Delorean	NULL	79600.00
21	Ferrari	NULL	5343440.00
22	Jaguar	NULL	887756.00
23	Lagonda	NULL	174400.00
24	Lamborghini	NULL	1381720.00
25	Maybach	NULL	340000.00
26	McLaren	NULL	236000.00
27	Mercedes	NULL	414452.00
28	Morgan	NULL	14800.00
29	Noble	NULL	197600.00
30	Peugeot	NULL	18636.00
31	Porsche	NULL	963752.00
32	Reliant	NULL	2720.00
33	Rolls Royce	NULL	1355192.00
34	Trabant	NULL	8028.00
35	Triumph	NULL	384888.00

FIGURE 10-12. DISPLAYING THE HIGHER AGGREGATION LEVELS USING A GROUPING SETS CLAUSE

6. Creating Clear Tables That Include Totals and Subtotals

The good news is that the speed with which you delivered the previous subquery impressed the CEO. The bad news is that she now wants the same information in a more comprehensible format so that the board of directors will understand it. She is worried that the top executives will not understand NULLs in columns and wants something more explicit.

After shaking your head in disbelief at the intellectual limitations of senior executives, you come up with the following code:

```
;

WITH GroupedSource_CTE

AS

(

SELECT

MakeName

,Color

,Count(*) AS NumberOfCarsBought


FROM         Data.Make MK

             INNER JOIN Data.Model MD ON MK.MakeID = MD.MakeID

             INNER JOIN Data.Stock ST ON ST.ModelID = MD.ModelID

WHERE        MakeName IS NOT NULL OR Color IS NOT NULL

GROUP BY     GROUPING SETS ((MakeName), (Color), ())

)
```

```
SELECT AggregationType
,Category
,NumberOfCarsBought

FROM
(
SELECT    'GrandTotal' AS AggregationType, NULL AS Category
          ,NumberOfCarsBought, 1 AS SortOrder
FROM      GroupedSource_CTE
WHERE     MakeName IS NULL and Color IS NULL
UNION
SELECT    'Make Subtotals', MakeName, NumberOfCarsBought , 2
FROM      GroupedSource_CTE
WHERE     MakeName IS NOT NULL and Color IS NULL
UNION
SELECT    'Color Subtotals', Color, NumberOfCarsBought , 3
FROM      GroupedSource_CTE
WHERE     MakeName IS NULL and Color IS NOT NULL
) SQ
ORDER BY SortOrder, NumberOfCarsBought DESC
```

Running this query gives the results that you can see in Figure 10-13.

	Aggregation Type	Category	NumberOfCarsBought
1	Grand Total	NULL	391
2	Make Subtotals	Aston Martin	87
3	Make Subtotals	Porsche	48
4	Make Subtotals	Triumph	44
5	Make Subtotals	Ferrari	35
6	Make Subtotals	Jaguar	31
7	Make Subtotals	Alfa Romeo	23
8	Make Subtotals	Bentley	21
9	Make Subtotals	Mercedes	16
10	Make Subtotals	Rolls Royce	15
11	Make Subtotals	Peugeot	11
12	Make Subtotals	Lamborghini	10
13	Make Subtotals	Noble	8
14	Make Subtotals	Austin	7
15	Make Subtotals	Bugatti	6

FIGURE 10-13. DISPLAYING SUBTOTALS AND GRAND TOTAL ONLY WITH GROUPING SETS

How It Works

Whatever the data that you are producing, it is essential that you and your audience are able to understand what you are looking at. Consequently, the next piece of SQL harnesses the power of grouping sets and adds some extra presentation tweaks to make the data easier to understand at first sight.

This query is essentially in three parts:

A CTE That aggregates the number of cars sold for each make, each color, and a grand total for all cars sold. This CTE uses the Make, Model, and Stock tables to isolate the cars that have been bought by Prestige Cars.

A subquery This is a derived table in the FROM clause of the main query. It isolates each type of aggregation (color, make, grand total) by filtering on the NULLs in the MakeName and Color columns. Each type of total is a separate query that also adds a column specifying the aggregation type as text. The three queries are then joined in a UNION query so that they all appear in the same table structure. This table has three columns: the aggregation type, the make or color, and finally, the metric.

An outer query   That selects the three columns from the derived table and adds a CASE clause to add some text (a string of equals signs in this case) to replace any NULLs in the output. This is purely decorative and has no value other than to highlight the grand total.

This query shows, then, how you can use CTEs, derived tables, and UNION queries all together in a practical and useful way. It also shows how you can create your own table output on the fly and combine different data elements (colors and makes of car in this example) in a single column using UNION queries.

7.   **Handling Hierarchical Data**

The CEO wants a list of staff and their managers that also displays each person's level in the company structure (with her at the top, obviously). A long time ago, you came across the Staff table, so you decide to use this data to display staff details along with their manager and the level of each manager and staff member in the corporate hierarchy. You use the following code to do this:

```
;

WITH HierarchyList_CTE

AS

(

SELECT       StaffID, StaffName, Department, ManagerID, 1 AS StaffLevel

FROM         Reference.Staff

WHERE        ManagerID IS NULL

UNION ALL
```

```
SELECT          ST.StaffID, ST.StaffName

                ,ST.Department, ST.ManagerID, StaffLevel + 1

FROM            Reference.Staff ST

INNER JOIN      HierarchyList_CTE CTE

                ON ST.ManagerID = CTE.StaffID

)


SELECT           STF.Department

                ,STF.StaffName

                ,CTE.StaffName AS ManagerName

                ,CTE.StaffLevel

FROM            HierarchyList_CTE CTE

INNER JOIN      Reference.Staff STF

                ON STF.ManagerID = CTE.StaffID
```

Running this code produces the output that you can see in Figure 10-14.

	Department	StaffName	ManagerName	StaffLevel
1	Finance	Gerard	Amelia	1
2	Marketing	Chloe	Amelia	1
3	Sales	Susan	Amelia	1
4	Finance	Jenny	Gerard	2
5	Finance	Chris	Gerard	2
6	Marketing	Megan	Chloe	2
7	Sales	Andy	Susan	2
8	Sales	Steve	Susan	2
9	Sales	Stan	Susan	2
10	Sales	Nathan	Susan	2
11	Sales	Maggie	Susan	2
12	Finance	Sandy	Chris	3

FIGURE 10-14. HIERARCHICAL OUTPUT

How It Works

This query shows the levels of the staff hierarchy, despite the fact that these levels are not given in the source data. It does this by using a technique known as *recursion*. This means that at some point, a process repeats itself and references itself in a loop that is repeated.

In the case of this particular query, the core is a piece of code called a *recursive CTE*. This means that the CTE runs repeatedly, starting at the highest level of the staff hierarchy and progressing down through the personnel pyramid until it stops when it reaches the bottom.

What the code does is this:

Define a root query   This is the starting point for the CTE. This is the first query inside the actual CTE. It defines the starting point for the hierarchy of numbers that define the level of each staff member. You can see the output from this query in Figure 10-15.

FIGURE 10-15. THE OUTPUT FROM THE ROOT QUERY IN A RECURSIVE CTE

Add a recursive query   This query is independent of the root query. It joins two datasets: the Staff table and the CTE itself. These are joined on the StaffID and the ManagerID so that the reference to each staff member's manager creates the hierarchy. It then increments the counter each time a new level is found in the Staff table, thus returning the depth of the staff hierarchy as a number. When a manager has no further lower levels of staff, the recursion stops.

To see this more clearly, take a look at Figure 10-16 where the recursive CTE is explained graphically. Specifically, you can see that the second query in the CTE refers to the name of the CTE. This means that the second query is repeated each time a match exists between the join fields. In other words, for every match between a manager ID and a staff member ID, the query runs again.

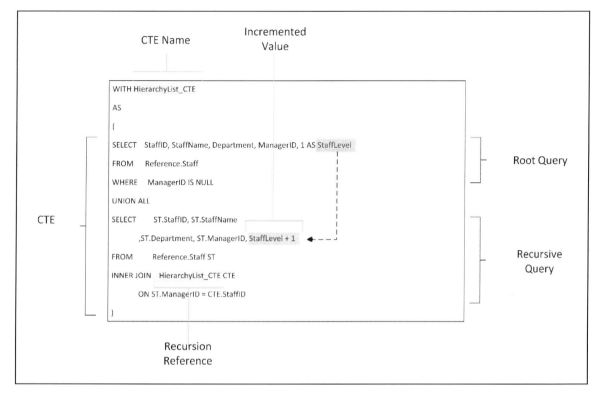

FIGURE 10-16. THE CONCEPT OF A RECURSIVE CTE

Finally, the output query takes the result from the CTE and joins it yet again to the staff table to obtain the manager of each staff member—just like you did in Chapter 3.

Tricks and Traps

There is one useful point to remember here:

- One cool use of this query is that you can easily extend it to show only the staff in a particular department if you add a final couple of lines of code like these:

```
WHERE        STF.Department = 'Finance'

ORDER BY     CTE.StaffLevel
```

Running the whole query now gives the result for the Finance department that you can see in Figure 10-17.

	Department	Staff Name	ManagerName	ManagerLevel	Staff Level
1	Finance	Gerard	Amelia	0	1
2	Finance	Jenny	Gerard	1	2
3	Finance	Chris	Gerard	1	2
4	Finance	Sandy	Chris	2	3

FIGURE 10-17. FILTERING HIERARCHICAL OUTPUT

8. Producing Indented Hierarchies

The CTO likes the staff hierarchy that you produced. Nonetheless, he wants you to add a fresh tweak. He wants the names of the staff to be indented so that the level in the hierarchy is more intuitively apparent. You can deliver this using the following piece of SQL.

```
;

WITH HierarchyList_CTE

AS

(

SELECT     StaffID, StaffName, Department, ManagerID, 1 AS StaffLevel

FROM       Reference.Staff

WHERE      ManagerID IS NULL

UNION ALL

SELECT       ST.StaffID, ST.StaffName

             ,ST.Department, ST.ManagerID, StaffLevel + 1

FROM         Reference.Staff ST

INNER JOIN   HierarchyList_CTE CTE

             ON ST.ManagerID = CTE.StaffID

)

SELECT       STF.Department
```

```
              ,REPLICATE(' ', StaffLevel * 2) + STF.StaffName

                  AS StaffMember

              ,CTE.StaffName AS ManagerName

              ,CTE.StaffLevel

FROM          HierarchyList_CTE CTE

INNER JOIN    Reference.Staff STF

              ON STF.ManagerID = CTE.StaffID

ORDER BY      Department, StaffLevel, CTE.StaffName
```

Running the modified code gives the output that you can see in Figure 10.18.

	Department	Staff Member	Manager Name	Staff Level
1	Finance	Gerard	Amelia	1
2	Finance	Jenny	Gerard	2
3	Finance	Chris	Gerard	2
4	Finance	Sandy	Chris	3
5	Marketing	Chloe	Amelia	1
6	Marketing	Megan	Chloe	2
7	Sales	Susan	Amelia	1
8	Sales	Andy	Susan	2
9	Sales	Steve	Susan	2
10	Sales	Stan	Susan	2
11	Sales	Nathan	Susan	2
12	Sales	Maggie	Susan	2

FIGURE 10-18. INDENTING OUTPUT

How It Works

As you have probably noticed by now, SQL is not very interested in the way that lists are presented. Delivering accurate output is what good SQL is all about. However, if you are concerned with the visual presentation of the output as we are in this example, you can trick SQL into producing indents in a column by forcing the code to add extra spaces before the data.

This is done using a new function—REPLICATE(). This function allows you to repeat one or more characters a specified number of times. When you use spaces as the characters to be repeated, this effectively indents the following text. REPLICATE() requires two parameters:

First:	The character (or sequence of characters) that you want to duplicate a number of times. In this example, we are using spaces.
Second:	A figure that tells the REPLICATE() function exactly how many times you want to reproduce the repeated text element.

The trick in this specific example is to make the indentation depend on the level in the hierarchy of each staff member. Here, we are using the StaffLevel field as the second parameter in the REPLICATE() function. This way, staff at level 1 are indented by one space, staff at level 2 are indented by two spaces, and so on. The end result is a series of indentations that correspond to each person's level in the corporate hierarchy.

Tricks and Traps

If you want to avoid annoying error messages, ne point is worth remembering when you are using the REPLICATE() function:

- The REPLICATE() function assumes that you are replicating text, and so it delivers its output as text. This means that if you are using REPLICATE() with data from a numeric column, you have to use, say, the CAST() function on the numeric column to convert its data to text.

9. Ordering a Hierarchy Using HierearchID

The HR director is very proud of her new personnel database, but, although she knows that it is in SQL Server, she does not know how to query it efficiently. She asks you to produce a list of staff that has all staff appear with their managers organized by department and that also respects the corporate structure. You can do this with a few lines of SQL.

```
SELECT        CAST(STF.HierarchyReference AS VARCHAR(50))
                    AS StaffHierarchy
              ,CAST(MGR.HierarchyReference AS VARCHAR(50))
                    AS ManagerHierarchy

              ,STF.StaffName AS ManagerName
              ,MGR.StaffName
FROM          Reference.StaffHierarchy STF
INNER JOIN    Reference.StaffHierarchy MGR
              ON STF.ManagerID = MGR.StaffID
ORDER BY      MGR.HierarchyReference
```

Running this short query produces the output that you can see in Figure 10-19.

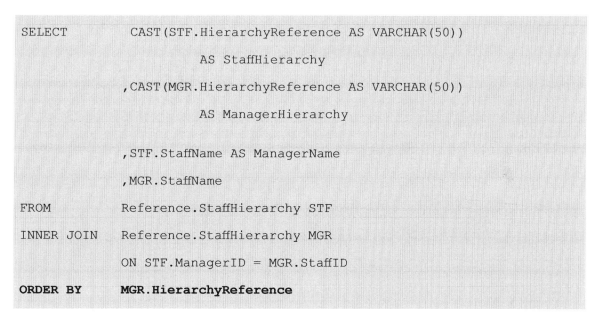

FIGURE 10-19. USING A HIERARCHYID TO ORDER HIERARCHICAL OUTPUT

How It Works

Organizing hierarchical data is not easy in databases because it can get complex tracking all the relationships between elements at the different levels. To help with the kinds of issues that hierarchy management has to face, SQL Server databases use a specific data type called *HierarchyID*. This data type indicates the level of a hierarchy for each record as well as the lineage of the record up to the top of the hierarchy.

Of course, if you are going to take advantage of a HierarchyID data type, then it must form part of the data that you are querying. Fortunately, the Prestige Cars database contains the table Reference.StaffHierarchy, which contains a field named HierarchyReference that is a HierarchyID data type. What is more, the contents of this field have been set up correctly to track the hierarchical position and relationships of each record in the table.

In this example, Amelia is the "root" of the hierarchy (the person at the top), so her HierarchyID is/1/. Her direct reports are Gerard, Cloe, and Susan. Their HierarchyIDs are, respectively, /1/1/, /1/2/, and /1/3/. As you can see, each person's HierarchyID— read from left to right—first indicates who they report to (the first figure) and then identifies them with a hierarchical reference. This reference is then used to indicate any staff who report to them further down the hierarchy. For example, Chris, who reports to Gerard, has a HierarchyID of /1/1/3/. This logic is then applied to every record in the table.

To better imagine the hierarchy as it is managed by a HierarchyID, take a look at Figure 10-20.

FIGURE 10-20. THE HIERARCHY MAINTAINED BY A HIERARCHYID

Once a correctly maintained HierarchyID field is in place, then querying the table and reflecting the hierarchy is not too hard. The join uses the Reference.StaffHierarchy table to itself so that it can output both the individual staff members and their supervisors. It does this by joining on the StaffManagerID and StaffID fields. Then it selects the HierarchyReference fields for both the staff member and the supervisor and converts these to text to make them readable. The really useful addition is sorting on the HierarchyID field (named HierarchyReference in this example). The result of the sort operation is a perfect hierarchical plan.

You need to be aware that you can *only* display the contents of the HierarchyReference field if you convert its contents to a VARCHAR (that is, a text) data type. This is necessary because the actual content of the HierarchyReference field is stored as binary (that is to say machine-readable) data. Indeed, if you add the HierarchyReference field to the SELECT clause without using CAST or CONVERT to transform it to text, you see something like Figure 10-21.

	HierarchyReference
1	0x58
2	0x5AD6
3	0x5AD6
4	0x5AD6D0
5	0x58
6	0x5ADA
7	0x58
8	0x5ADE
9	0x5ADE
10	0x5ADE
11	0x5ADE
12	0x5ADE

FIGURE 10-21. THE ACTUAL BINARY DATA IN A HIERARCHYID

We are sure that you agree that this is completely incomprehensible and that seeing the content converted to text is easier to understand.

Tricks and Traps

We have a few comments that are worth making here:

- In this query, we are assuming that a HierarchyID was not present in the previous two queries and so it could not be used in them.

- It is not necessary to add a HierarchyID field to a SELECT clause—doing so may even cause confusion. We only used it to show you the content of the field.

- There are many more ways to use HierarchyID fields to manage hierarchies; however, they are somewhat of a specialist area of SQL Server. Consequently, we advise you to check out the Microsoft documentation if you need more advice on this topic.

10. Replace Acronyms with Full Text in the Final Output

The sales manager needs a quick report of all the company's clients. However, he wants you to make the list more presentable by standardizing some of the output to compensate for some shortcomings in the source data. SQL makes this really easy, as the following code snippet shows:

```
SELECT      REPLACE(CustomerName, 'Ltd', 'Limited') AS NoAcronymName

FROM        Data.Customer

WHERE       LOWER(CustomerName) LIKE '%ltd%'
```

Running this query gives the results that you can see in Figure 10-22.

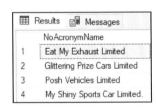

FIGURE 10-22. USING THE REPLACE() FUNCTION WHEN OUTPUTTING RESULTS

How It Works

Corporate data policies may prevent you from altering the data in a table; however, you may need to clean it up for presentation in some way. This is where the REPLACE() function becomes useful. It replaces specified text anywhere in a field with other text. All in all, it is a little like the search-and-replace function in a word processor. You can add some data cleansing at the query output stage without affecting the source data. This SQL snippet uses the Customer table and then applies the REPLACE() function to the data in the CustomerName field.

REPLACE() is another SQL function that needs you to specify three elements for it to work. Geeks call this *taking three arguments*. The arguments are

First:	The field whose data you want to modify
Second:	The text that you are looking for (Ltd in this example)
Third:	The text that you want to replace the search text with (Limited in this example)

As you can see from the code sample, these three arguments are separated by commas in the function.

You may have times when you want to replace multiple words with another word (or even with several words). In these cases, you need to nest several REPLACE() functions inside one another. The following example replaces Ltd with Limited, S.A. with Société Anonyme, and Corp with Corporation:

```
SELECT      REPLACE (

                  REPLACE (

                        REPLACE(CustomerName, 'Ltd', 'Limited')

                        ,'S.A.', 'Société Anonyme')

                  ,'Corp', 'Corporation')

FROM        Data.Customer
```

Although not difficult, this nesting of functions does require you to be attentive to the structure and to ensure that each opening parenthesis has a corresponding closing parenthesis.

Tricks and Traps

The REPLACE() function is really quite simple. Nonetheless, be aware of the following when you apply it:

- Since this technique only applies to a SELECT clause here, it has absolutely no effect on the underlying data, which is not altered in any way.

11. Replacing a Specified Number of Characters with Other Text

Sales personnel at Prestige Cars are having difficulty using the complicated stock codes that the system uses. You want to make the codes easier to use in practice. The following piece of SQL shows you how to display a revamped stock code when outputting vehicles:

```sql
SELECT

 STUFF(StockCode,1,23,'PrestigeCars-') AS NewStockCode

,Cost

,RepairsCost

,PartsCost

,TransportInCost

FROM Data.Stock
```

Running this query gives the results that you can see in Figure 10-23.

	NewStockCode	Cost	RepairsCost	PartsCost	TransportInCost
1	PrestigeCars--A7BC5F9CFB3F	52000.00	2175.00	1500.00	750.00
2	PrestigeCars--A7BC5F9CFB5F	176000.00	5500.00	2200.00	1950.00
3	PrestigeCars--A83FA9559C41	15600.00	660.00	0.00	150.00
4	PrestigeCars--0C47361DDE2D	9200.00	500.00	750.00	150.00
5	PrestigeCars--4053319E8E9D	15960.00	1360.00	500.00	150.00
6	PrestigeCars--49FA8E2C377F	176000.00	1000.00	3150.00	1950.00
7	PrestigeCars--38079BB4049B	23600.00	500.00	750.00	150.00
8	PrestigeCars--17F26B2B8DAF	39600.00	2500.00	1500.00	550.00
9	PrestigeCars--406D23940527	60800.00	3250.00	750.00	750.00
10	PrestigeCars--FD132C5E1BF2	172000.00	750.00	150.00	1950.00
11	PrestigeCars--61D919E64979	15680.00	890.00	500.00	150.00
12	PrestigeCars--6C6370812041	29200.00	1950.00	500.00	550.00
13	PrestigeCars--8A4CA195248D	6800.00	250.00	225.00	150.00
14	PrestigeCars--798431841575	36000.00	1250.00	750.00	550.00
15	PrestigeCars--A219D4C691C6	64400.00	500.00	750.00	750.00

FIGURE 10-23. USING THE STUFF() FUNCTION TO REPLACE A SPECIFIED NUMBER OF CHARACTERS WITH OTHER TEXT

How It Works

Occasionally you may need to tweak the output that a query returns so that the output is more comprehensible. In this example, you have decided that the first sets of letters and numbers that uniquely identify each vehicle in stock are superfluous (for the moment, anyway). You want to remove them from the invoices and lists that you produce and show something else instead.

This is where the STUFF() function can come in useful. It replaces a certain number of characters with another string of characters beginning at a specified position. So, unlike with the REPLACE() function, SQL is not looking for a specific character, but for *any character at a specific place in a field.*

In this example, the function is saying, "Take the Stock table then, starting at the first character in the StockCode field, replace the initial 23 characters with the text Prestige-Cars."

Tricks and Traps

You need to be aware of a couple of points when applying a STUFF() function to your SQL:

- You may be wondering why you need to use the STUFF() function when you also have the REPLACE() function. The two are, in fact, different. The STUFF() function does not look for a specific character or series of characters; it only looks at *where a character is inside a string.* It always replaces a character or characters at the *same position* inside a text field, no matter what the actual characters are. The REPLACE() function looks for a text to replace anywhere inside a string.

- The STUFF() function can replace one or more characters with any number of other characters. The replacement string can contain fewer or more characters than the initial string of characters that you are replacing.

12. Creating a Comma-Separated List from Multiple Records

As your final task for the day, you have been asked to produce a list of cars sold by color. However—and this is the potential problem—you need to show the colors for each make as a comma-separated list, and not as a list of elements over multiple rows. The following code snippet shows how you can do this:

```
;
WITH ConcatenateSource_CTE (MakeModel, Color)
AS
(
SELECT DISTINCT  MakeName + ' ' + ModelName, Color
FROM             Data.Make MK
                 INNER JOIN Data.Model MD ON MK.MakeID = MD.MakeID
                 INNER JOIN Data.Stock ST ON ST.ModelID = MD.ModelID
)


SELECT   MakeModel, STRING_AGG(Color, ',') AS ColorList
FROM     ConcatenateSource_CTE
GROUP BY MakeModel
```

Running this query gives the results that you can see in Figure 10-24.

	MakeModel	ColorList
1	Alfa Romeo 1750	Black,Blue
2	Alfa Romeo Giulia	Black,British Racing Green,Green,Red
3	Alfa Romeo Giulietta	Black,Blue,Dark Purple,Night Blue
4	Alfa Romeo Spider	Black,Blue,Green
5	Aston Martin DB2	Black,Blue,British Racing Green,Canary Yellow,Green,Night Blue,Red,Silver
6	Aston Martin DB4	Black,Canary Yellow,Green,Night Blue,Pink,Silver
7	Aston Martin DB5	Black,Blue,Night Blue,Red,Silver
8	Aston Martin DB6	Black,British Racing Green,Canary Yellow,Green,Night Blue,Red,Silver
9	Aston Martin DB9	Black,Blue,British Racing Green,Canary Yellow,Dark Purple,Green,Night Blue,Red,Silver
10	Aston Martin Rapide	Black,Night Blue,Red,Silver
11	Aston Martin Vanquish	Black,Dark Purple,Green,Night Blue,Red,Silver
12	Aston Martin Vantage	Black,British Racing Green,Green
13	Aston Martin Virage	Black,Blue,Dark Purple,Green,Night Blue,Pink,Red
14	Austin Cambridge	Black
15	Austin Lichfield	Night Blue,Pink

FIGURE 10-24. CONCATENATING TEXT USING THE STRING_AGG() FUNCTION

How It Works

Tables are not the only way that SQL Server can deliver its output. It can also join together a series of elements as a list separated by commas (or, indeed, any other character or characters). SQL "thinks" in terms of tables, and naturally it delivers its results in tabular form. Nonetheless, at times you may not want to see a long table of output, or even a pivot table, but instead a simpler list that shows all the data that interests you in a single column. This is what has been done with this particular query. It has output a single record for each individual model of vehicle and then added a second column that lists every color of car sold for the model in question. On this occasion, however, the colors are shown as a simple comma-separated list. This technique—joining together a string of values—is called *concatenating* a series of elements.

This code snippet is in two parts:

A CTE	That delivers a unique list of makes and models of car ever held in stock along with each individual color bought for each model.
A query	That takes the output from the CTE and tweaks it to return a comma-separated list of the colors of vehicle bought by make and model using the STRING_AGG() function.

The CTE is really quite simple. It is a standard SELECT query that returns the Make and Model amalgamated as a single field and then adds a second column containing the color of each vehicle bought. Since the query contains the DISTINCT keyword, only one record is output for each combination of make, model, and color.

Running the CTE gives the results that you can see in Figure 10-25.

FIGURE 10-25. THE OUTPUT FROM A CTE USED TO GENERATE A COMMA-SEPARATED LIST

The main query (shown in bold in the code) is simply a SELECT query that uses the CTE as its source. The query does the following:

Groups data	On the make and model and selects the field containing the make and model.
Creates a list	Of colors for each make and model. It does this using the STRING_AGG() function.

The STRING_AGG() function only needs two parameters:

First:	The field that you will use as the source for all the data that will be amalgamated into a list.
Second:	The separator character that will isolate each element in the list.

Just remember that you will need

An identification field	Which is similar to the list of makes and models of car that we are using here.

A list field	That will be used as the basis for the concatenated list of elements, which is similar to the color field that we are using here.
A list separator	Like the comma that is used in this example.

Tricks and Traps

The ability to create concatenated lists is extremely useful in practice. Just be sure to remember the following points:

- This technique can be slow when applied to large datasets; however, it is extremely useful and can be a valuable way of delivering the information that you need.

- You can use any character to separate the elements in the concatenated list, even spaces. Some character is necessary, though, or the list will be unreadable.

- If the source data is simple, you may not need a CTE to prepare the data, but you can query the source table(s) directly.

13. Creating Multiple Records from a List

The marketing director has, once again, found some external data that she wants you to handle for her. This data is a list of vehicle classifications, and it looks like the table in Figure 10-26.

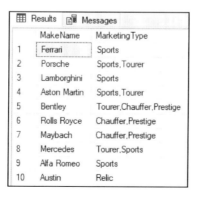

FIGURE 10-26. SOURCE DATA CONTAINING A COMMA-SEPARATED LIST

What you need to do is break down this list into a complete set of rows in which each element in the MarketingType column is on a separate row, even if this means each make of car appears on multiple rows.

After a few minutes, you come up with the following code to do this:

```
SELECT          MakeName, Value AS VehicleType

FROM            Reference.MarketingCategories

CROSS APPLY     STRING_SPLIT(MarketingType, ',')
```

Executing this code gives the result that you can see in Figure 10-27.

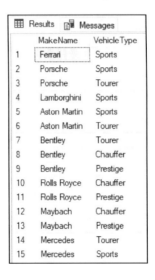

FIGURE 10-27. COMMA-SEPARATED DATA ORGANIZED AS SEPARATE RECORDS

How It Works

SQL Server (since version 2016) enables you to separate out delimited lists into multiple records simply and easily. You can do this using the STRING_SPLIT() function. This is how you use it:

First: Select the column that will contain the repeated elements in the output (MakeName in this example).

Second:	Add a comma and the word *Value*—which is the required field name for the split output from the column containing a separated list (MarketingType in this example).
Third:	Add an alias for the Value column (if you want to).
Fourth:	Define the source table in the FROM clause and add a CROSS APPLY function (this ensures that every record in the source data is processed).
Finally:	Enter the STRING_SPLIT() function. This takes two parameters: the column that contains the list of delimited elements to split and the *delimiter* (the character that separates each element in the list).

Once you have created a recordset of output like this, you can use it in other SQL queries, as required.

Tricks and Traps

We have a few points to make here:

- The delimiter character used in the STRING_SPLIT() function must be enclosed in single quotes.

- The delimiter character can be any character.

- The STRING_SPLIT() function does not exist in SQL Server versions prior to 2016.

14. Outputting Simple XML

The marketing director is in a bit of a panic. An external agency wants some data delivered in XML format, and naturally you are her first port of call to provide a solution. Fortunately, SQL Server can output query results as XML with incredible ease, so after a few minutes, you produce the following piece of code:

```
SELECT        MD.ModelName, ST.Color, ST.Cost

FROM          Data.Stock ST

INNER JOIN    Data.Model MD

              ON ST.ModelID = MD.ModelID

FOR XML PATH ('Stock'), ROOT ('PrestigeCars')
```

Running this code produces the result that you can see in Figure 10-28.

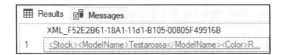

FIGURE 10-28. XML OUTPUT FROM A FOR XML QUERY

This output is, to say the least, a little cryptic. However, if you click on the XML itself, a new window opens displaying the entire result. You can see some sample output in Figure 10-29; however, you need to be aware that we have cut much of the data to show only the start and end of the XML that is produced.

```
XML_F52E2B61-18A...00805F49916B2.xml*    ⊐  ×   SQLQuery1.sql -...ADAM03\Adam (58))*
   <PrestigeCars>
     <Stock>
        <ModelName>Testarossa</ModelName>
        <Color>Red</Color>
        <Cost>52000.0000</Cost>
     </Stock>
     <Stock>
        <ModelName>355</ModelName>
        <Color>Blue</Color>
        <Cost>176000.0000</Cost>
     </Stock>

        ---------|

     <Stock>
        <ModelName>Robin</ModelName>
        <Color>Black</Color>
        <Cost>760.0000</Cost>
     </Stock>
     <Stock>
        <ModelName>Daytona</ModelName>
        <Color>Black</Color>
        <Cost>116000.0000</Cost>
     </Stock>
   </PrestigeCars>
```

FIGURE 10-29. FULL XML OUTPUT FROM A FOR XML QUERY

How It Works

XML (the acronym XML stands for e**X**tended **M**arkup **L**anguage) is, among other things, a standardized way of structuring data so that it can be transferred between different systems. It is particularly good for ensuring that data structures are respected when information is copied between databases. As you can see from Figure 10-28, it is also easy to read by humans (and most machines also find it easy to understand).

Producing XML from a SQL Server database can be as simple as adding the FOR XML PATH keywords at the end of an SQL query. This immediately transforms the output into XML rather than the standard list output that you have been using so far in this book.

In this example, the Stock and Model tables are joined so that you can select the model and color as well as various cost elements from the Stock table.

As an extra tweak, we have added two extra elements to the FOR XML PATH keywords:

('Element')	This is a row element that encloses each record in the output.
ROOT ('Element')	This adds a root element at the top and bottom of the entire output.

Unfortunately, it would take another small book to explain why, exactly, you might need a root element or when it is best to add row elements, which are both part of a more in-depth discussion of XML. Let's just say that when sending XML to third parties so that they can load them into their own systems, these two added elements often prove essential to a successful exchange of data.

Tricks and Traps

We have a few points to make here:

- You can extend the SQL query that produces XML using all the standard techniques that you have learned in this book. This includes a WHERE clause, GROUP BY elements, and so on.

- XML is a vast subject in its own right. Consequently, we are not able to explain how it is designed and how it works in this book.

15. Structuring XML Output

The marketing director has returned with another XML request. This time her agency needs the XML output presented in a specific way—some data needs to be presented as XML attributes and other elements need to be entities in a hierarchical structure. After a bit of work, you produce the following SQL:

```
SELECT          MD.ModelName AS "@Model"

                ,ST.Color

                ,ST.Cost AS "Costs/Purchase"
```

```
                    ,ST.PartsCost AS "Costs/Parts"

                    ,ST.RepairsCost AS "Costs/Repairs"

FROM          Data.Stock ST

INNER JOIN    Data.Model MD

              ON ST.ModelID = MD.ModelID

FOR XML PATH ('Stock')
```

Running this code produces the result that you can see in Figure 10-30—once you have clicked on the initial result in the query window.

```
XML_F52E2B61-18A...00805F49916B4.xml  ⊕ ✕  SQLQuery1.sql -...ADAM03\Adam (55))*
    <Stock Model="Testarossa">
      <Color>Red</Color>
      <Costs>
        <Purchase>52000.0000</Purchase>
        <Parts>1500.0000</Parts>
        <Repairs>2175.0000</Repairs>
      </Costs>
    </Stock>
    <Stock Model="355">
      <Color>Blue</Color>
      <Costs>
        <Purchase>176000.0000</Purchase>
        <Parts>2200.0000</Parts>
        <Repairs>5500.0000</Repairs>
      </Costs>
    </Stock>
    <Stock Model="911">
      <Color>British Racing Green</Color>
      <Costs>
        <Purchase>15600.0000</Purchase>
        <Parts>0.0000</Parts>
        <Repairs>660.0000</Repairs>
      </Costs>
    </Stock>
    <Stock Model="924">
      <Color>British Racing Green</Color>
      <Costs>
        <Purchase>9200.0000</Purchase>
        <Parts>750.0000</Parts>
        <Repairs>500.0000</Repairs>
      </Costs>
    </Stock>
```

FIGURE 10-30. STRUCTURED XML OUTPUT FROM A FOR XML QUERY

How It Works

XML allows you to define data as either attributes (like the model name in this example) or as elements (all the other data fields from the source query). Moreover, XML is very good at creating nested hierarchies of data. In this example, this means that all cost elements are grouped together as a subset of the data.

The XML query starts with the same SELECT query that you used in the previous example; however, this code is tweaked slightly to extend the XML structure.

As you saw in the previous section, XML defaults to displaying output as elements—that is, the data for each "field" is preceded by the element name inside < and >, and it is followed by the same name inside < and > with a backslash added before the element name. In some cases, however, you may want to display data as XML attributes—that is, the name of the element appears inside another element (and the data appears in double quotes).

Displaying XML output as an attribute is as simple as adding an alias to the field that you want to transform into an attribute; however, the alias *must*

- Be enclosed in quotes
- Start with an @

The ability to create a nested hierarchy of XML output is also added when you are using field aliases. In this case, the alias must contain each required level of the output hierarchy separated by a forward slash.

Tricks and Traps

At this juncture, you need to know that

- We specifically chose not to include a ROOT element in this XML so that you can see the difference in the output.

- You can format the output as you would "normal" SQL and define decimals, the way date are presented, and so on.

- The aliases can be placed in either double or single quotes.

There is much, much more that we could add on the subject of XML output from SQL queries. However, this can rapidly become a specialist subject, so we prefer to start you on your way with a couple of examples and advise you to consult more focused resources if you need further details on this particular subject.

16. Outputting JSON

Now it is the sales director's turn. She needs to send data from the Prestige Cars' database to a web designer in something called JSON. Fortunately, SQL Server makes this really simple, as the following code snippet shows.

```
SELECT TOP 3    MD.ModelName

                ,ST.Color

                ,ST.Cost

                ,ST.PartsCost

                ,ST.RepairsCost

FROM            Data.Stock ST

INNER JOIN      Data.Model MD

                ON ST.ModelID = MD.ModelID

FOR JSON PATH, ROOT ('Stock')
```

Executing this code produces the result that you can see in Figure 10-31.

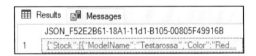

FIGURE 10-31. JSON OUTPUT FROM A FOR JSON QUERY

If you click on the output, you can see the result in a new query window. After a little formatting effort, it looks like the following code:

```
{

"Stock":

    [

        {

            "ModelName":"Testarossa",
```

```
      "Color":"Red",

      "Cost":52000.0000,

      "PartsCost":2200.0000,

      "RepairsCost":2175.0000

   }
,

   {

      "ModelName":"355",

      "Color":"Blue",

      "Cost":176000.0000,

      "PartsCost":2200.0000,

      "RepairsCost":5500.0000

   }
,

   {

      "ModelName":"911",

      "Color":"British Racing Green",

      "Cost":15600.0000,

      "PartsCost":0.0000,

      "RepairsCost":660.0000

   }
  ]

}
```

How It Works

Another structure that is frequently used to transfer data between heterogeneous systems is *JSON*. This stands for **J**ava**S**cript **O**bject **N**otation. Fortunately, SQL Server can generate JSON output extremely easily; all you have to do is add FOR JSON PATH to the initial SQL query.

In this example, the Stock and Model tables are joined so that you can select the model and color as well as various cost elements from the Stock table. Then you extend the query with FOR JSON PATH.

Generally, however, it is preferable also to add a ROOT element that then encloses the entire output. The complete line of SQL that converts a query into a JSON output query is

```
FOR JSON PATH, ROOT ('RootElement')
```

We realize that JSON is not intuitively comprehensible; however, it has become something of a lingua franca of the Internet age as far as sharing structured data between diverse systems is concerned. So, although a deep understanding of JSON structures may be overkill, understanding how to produce JSON datasets from SQL Server data is definitely not.

Tricks and Traps

We have a couple of points to make here:

- JSON is generally less easy to read by humans than XML.

- It is not necessary to reformat the JSON output. We have chosen to add some carriage returns and indents so that the structure of the data is a little easier to understand. In practice, the original JSON output from the SQL query can be used by any application that reads JSON without any manual intervention.

17. Defining JSON Output

Ten minutes after you produced the JSON data for the sales manager she sends you an email. The web designer wants the JSON data structured in a specific hierarchical way. After reading his definition of how the output should look you come up with the following SQL:

```
SELECT TOP 3    MD.ModelName

                ,ST.Color

                ,ST.Cost AS [Costs.Purchase]

                ,ST.PartsCost AS [Costs.Parts]

                ,ST.RepairsCost AS [Costs.Repairs]

FROM            Data.Stock ST

INNER JOIN      Data.Model MD

                ON ST.ModelID = MD.ModelID

FOR JSON PATH, ROOT ('Stock')
```

Once you have run the query, you can click on the output to get a closer look. We have formatted the result so that it looks like the JSON structure that you can see here:

```
{

    "Stock":

            [

                {

                    "ModelName":"Testarossa",

                    "Color":"Red",

                    "Costs":

                            {

                                "Purchase":52000.0000,

                                "Parts":1500.0000,

                                "Repairs":2175.0000

                            }

                }

            ,{
```

```
            "ModelName":"355",

            "Color":"Blue",

            "Costs":

                    {

                        "Purchase":176000.0000,

                        "Parts":2200.0000,

                        "Repairs":5500.0000

                    }

                }

        ,{

            "ModelName":"911",

            "Color":"British Racing Green",

            "Costs":

                    {

                        "Purchase":15600.0000,

                        "Parts":0.0000,

                        "Repairs":660.0000

                    }

                }

            ]

    }
```

How It Works

JSON is very good at structuring data. Specifically, it can contain many levels of nested hierarchies of data. In this example, the cost elements are contained at a sublevel in the final output. Once again, the Stock and Model tables are the basis for this query.

The extended JSON structure is attained by adding aliases to any source fields that need to be nested in the data hierarchy. More specifically, each level in the hierarchy is separated from other levels by a period, so defining an alias of "Costs.Purchase" creates a "Costs" sublevel containing a "Purchases" data element.

Tricks and Traps

There are a few points to make here on the subject of JSON formatting:

- When defining nested hierarchies of JSON data, you can enclose the alias in single quotes, double quotes, or square brackets.

- You can format the output as you would "normal" SQL and define decimals, the way dates are formatted, and so on, as you would for a standard SQL query.

We could add much, much more on the subject of JSON output from SQL queries, but since this requires an in-depth understanding of JSON, we instead advise you to consult more specialized resources if you need further details on this subject.

Conclusion

This chapter has taken you on a whirlwind tour of some of the SQL virtuoso techniques that you can use to hone your query output. From pivoting data via concatenated lists to adding complex subtotals in your reports or even replacing text in the final output, you have learned a useful variety of advanced ays to present data.

This chapter also concludes the book and your introduction to SQL Querying. We sincerely hope that you will put your learning to good use. Finally, we really hope that you have had fun learning SQL with SQL Server.

Core Knowledge Learned in This Chapter

The keywords and concepts that you have seen in this chapter are

Concept	Description
PIVOT	*This operator allows you to create pivot tables.*
GROUPING SETS	*This operator lets you add multiple subtotals to aggregate queries.*
STUFF()	*This function is used to replace text at a specified position in a field.*
STRING_AGG()	*This function can be used to create comma-separated lists from the data in a column.*
STRING_SPLIT()	*This function creates multiple rows from comma-separated lists.*
Recursion	*A programming technique that iterates several times through, referring to itself.*
Recursive CTE	*A common table expression that is joined to itself to loop through a hierarchy or sequence.*
FOR XML	*This operator outputs the results of the query as XML.*
FOR JSON	*This operator outputs the results of the query as JSON.*
PATH	*Used with FOR XML or FOR JSON, this operator allows you to shape the output.*
ROOT	*Used with FOR XML or FOR JSON, this operator lets you specify a root element for the output.*
HierarchyID	*This data type is used to structure hierarchies.*

Appendix A:
Installing SQL Server

The only way to learn SQL is to practice using it. Unless you already have a SQL database that is available for you to use, you will need your own SQL Server instance. In this appendix, you will see how to set up your own personal SQL Server on your laptop or personal workstation. Then, in Appendixes B and C, you will see how to install SQL Server Management Studio to query SQL Server as well as the sample database that is used in the examples in this book.

Installing SQL Server

Microsoft has, fortunately, made it easy for anyone to learn SQL on a current version of its database software. Not only that, but it has made the latest version of the database freely available for development use. This version is currently not time-limited and will allow you to test all the code that is available in this book. It is called SQL Server Developer.

Microsoft currently describes SQL Server Developer (also called SQL Server 2017 development edition) as "a full-featured free edition, licensed for use as a development and test database in a non-production environment." What this seems to mean is that you can use it to learn SQL as long as you do not use it in a business—or indeed anywhere—to run or manage data.

Note   We will describe only how to install SQL Server Developer on the Windows platform here. If you want to set up SQL Server Developer on Linux, then please consult the Microsoft website.

Here, then, is how to access, download, and install the database software:

1.   Browse to the Microsoft SQL Server downloads page. It is currently at https://www.microsoft.com/en-gb/sql-server/sql-server-downloads. It should look something like the one in Figure A-1.

Figure A-1. The Microsoft SQL Server downloads page

Note	If the URL has changed since this book was published, then use your preferred search engine and look for SQL Server development edition.

---

2. Click the Download Now button under Developer Edition.

3. After a few seconds, the executable that links to the full download will appear at the bottom of the browser window, or a pop-up window will ask you if you want to run the download. This will depend on the browser you are using.

4. Click the executable link or the Run button (depending on your browser).

5. Confirm (if asked) that you want this app to make admin-level changes to your system. The installation type dialog will appear. It should look something like the one in Figure A-2.

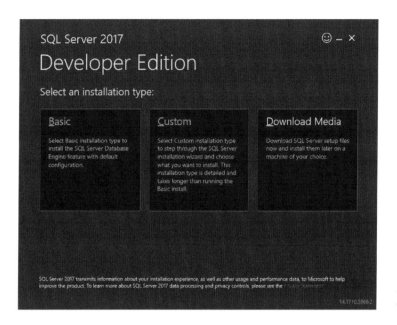

FIGURE A-2. THE INSTALLATION TYPE DIALOG

6. Click Basic. The license terms dialog will appear, looking like the one in Figure A-3.

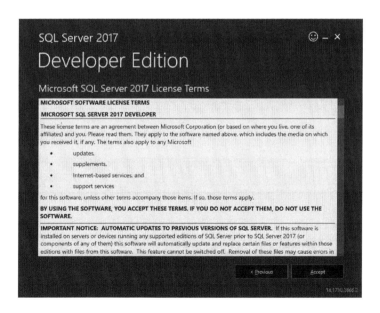

FIGURE A-3. THE LICENSE TERMS DIALOG

7.   Click Accept. The install location dialog will appear. It should look something like the one in Figure A-4.

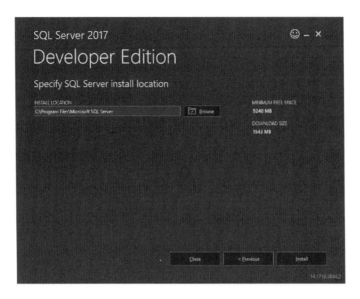

FIGURE A-4. THE INSTALL LOCATION DIALOG

8.   Leave the install location as is and click Install. The download will begin, and the dialog shown in Figure A-5 will appear while the download is carried out. Be warned that this can take a while, even with a fast Internet connection.

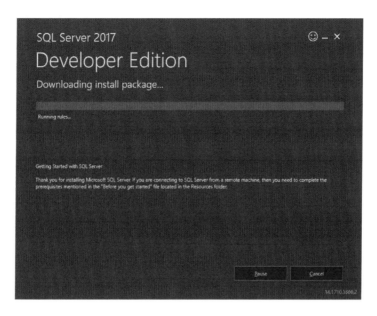

Figure A-5. The download dialog

9. The installation process will then extract the compressed files and begin the installation. You will see a dialog like the one in Figure A-6.

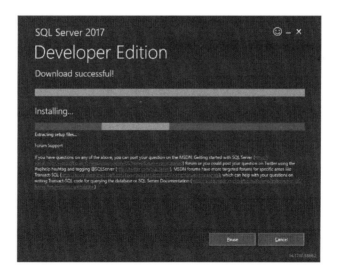

Figure A-6. The installation dialog

10. Once the installation is complete, you will see the successful completion dialog that is shown in Figure A-7.

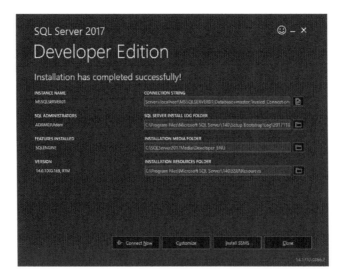

FIGURE A-7. THE SUCCESSFUL COMPLETION DIALOG

11. Click Close. A pop-up will ask if you really want to exit the SQL Server Installer. You can see this in Figure A-8.

FIGURE A-8. EXITING THE SQL SERVER INSTALLER

12. Click Yes.

Assuming that all ran smoothly, SQL Server 2017 is now installed on your computer. You can start using it to host databases.

Tricks and Traps

We have a couple of comments to make here.

- If there is already an older version of SQL Server installed on the destination computer, then a new instance (an independent version) of SQL Server 2017 will be installed as well. This will have no effect on the existing version of SQL Server.

- To install and run correctly, SQL Server 2017 requires a computer with at least the following:

  - 6 GB of available disk space

  - 1 GB of available memory

  - A 2.0 GHz processor

  - An 800 × 600 monitor

  In practice, however, you will probably need considerably more memory and a much faster processor to run any viable database application.

Appendix B:
Installing SQL Server
Management Studio

Having a version of SQL Server that you can access is a good start, but you will nonetheless need an application that you can use to enter queries and see the results. In this appendix, you will see how to install SQL Server Management Studio, the application that we recommend using to enter and run queries when you are learning SQL with SQL Server.

Installing SQL Server Management Studio

As we explained in Chapter 1, one widely used tool for querying SQL Server is SQL Server Management Studio. Here is how you can download and install this particular piece of software, which Microsoft has, fortunately, named free to download and use:

1.   Search for SQL Server Management Studio 2017 in your preferred search engine or click or use the following link: https://docs.microsoft.com/en-us/sql/ssms/download-sql-server-management-studio-ssms. You should see a dialog like the one shown in Figure B-1.

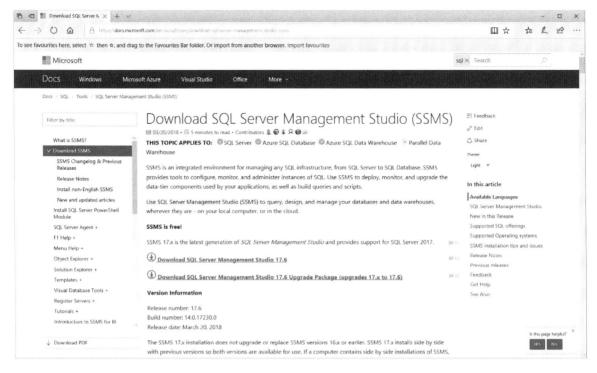

FIGURE B-1. THE SQL SERVER MANAGEMENT STUDIO 2017 DOWNLOAD PAGE

2.   Click Download SQL Server Management Studio 17.6 (or whatever the latest version currently is).

3.   Run the download (this will depend on the browser you are using). You will see the installation dialog shown in Figure B-2.

Figure B-2. The SQL Server Management Studio 2017 installation dialog

4. Click Install. SSMS will be installed while the progress dialog is displayed, as in Figure B-3.

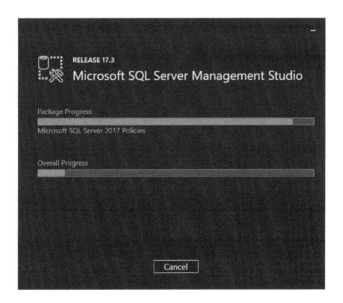

Figure B-3. Installation progress for SQL Server Management Studio 2017

5. Once the installation has finished, the Setup Completed dialog will be displayed, as shown in Figure B-4.

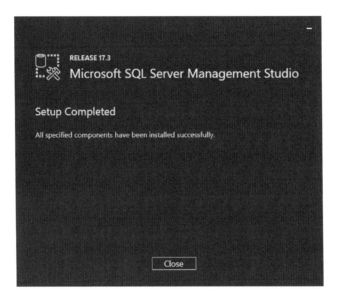

FIGURE B-4. THE SETUP COMPLETED DIALOG

6. Click Close.

You can now launch SQL Server Management Studio and connect to the server you installed previously.

Tricks and Traps

We have one comment to make here.

*   To launch SSMS, click the Start Menu button at the bottom left of the screen and scroll down the list of installed applications until you find Microsoft SQL Server Tools 2017. Expand this and you will see Microsoft SQL Server Management Studio, as shown in Figure B-5. Click on this to run SSMS.

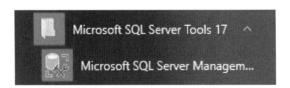

FIGURE B-5. RUNNING SQL SERVER MANAGEMENT STUDIO

Appendix C:
Setting Up the Sample Database

> *To practice the SQL examples that you have seen (or will discover) in the course of this book, you will need to download and install the sample database that is the basis for learning SQL with the aid of this book.*

This appendix will explain how to download the sample data, create the PrestigeCars database, and load the sample data into the PrestigeCars database so that you can practice your SQL.

1.   Downloading the Sample Data

First you will need to download the sample data to a local directory.

1.   In Windows Explorer, create a folder named
      C:\SQLQueriesSampleData.

2.   Download the sample data file (SQLQueriesSampleData.zip) from the
      Tetras Publishing website (www.tetraspublishing.com/sqlserver) .

3.   Extract the contents of the compressed file into the folder
      C:\SQLQueriesSampleData. The folder contents should look some-
      thing like Figure C-1.

Name	Date modified	Type	Size
Volume1	01/06/2018 08:46	File folder	
Volume2	01/06/2018 08:46	File folder	
SQLQueriesSampleData.sql	01/06/2018 08:49	Microsoft SQL Server Query File	1,703 KB

FIGURE C-1. THE SAMPLE DATA FOLDER CONTENTS

2. Creating the PrestigeCars Database

Now you will need to create a database into which you can load the sample data.

1. Run SQL Server Management Studio.

2. Right-click the Databases folder in SSMS and select New Database from the pop-up menu. You can see this in Figure C-2. The New Database dialog will appear.

FIGURE C-2. CREATING A NEW DATABASE.

3. Enter **PrestigeCars** as the database name. The New Database dialog will look something like the one in Figure C-3.

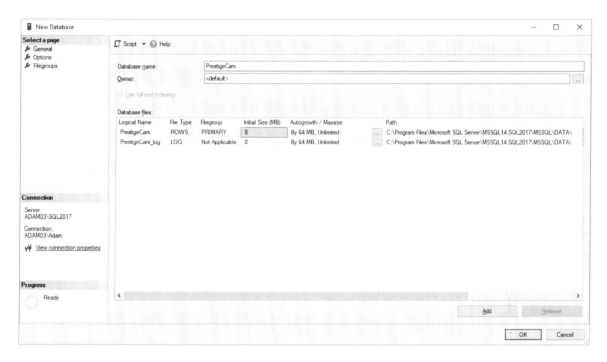

FIGURE C-3. CREATING A NEW DATABASE

    4.   Click OK. The PrestigeCars database will be created.

3.   Loading the Sample Data into the PrestigeCars Database

Finally, you need to load the sample data and all the database tables and views into the newly created PrestigeCars database.

    1.   In SQL Server Management Studio, click File⇨Open⇨File.

    2.   Browse to the file
C:\ SQLQueriesSampleData\SQLQueriesSampleData.sql.

    3.   Click Open. The script will appear in a new query window.

    4.   Press **F5** to run the script and load the data.

You can now start querying the sample data contained in the PrestigeCars database.

4.   Opening the Sample Queries

To save you having to type out all the sample queries in this book, hey are available in the download from the TetrasPublishing web site. If you have already downloaded the sample data as described in Section 1 of this Appendix, then you can jump directly to step 3.

1. In your web browser, navigate to www.tetraspublishing.com/sqlserver.

2. Download the sample data file (SQLQueriesSampleData.zip) from the Tetras Publishing website (www.tetraspublishing.com/sqlserver) and extract the contents into the folder C:\SQLQueriesSampleData.

3. Launch SQL Server Management Studio.

4. Click File⇨Open⇨File and navigate to C:\SQLQueriesSampleData\Volume2.

5. Double-click the file containing the sample queries for the chapter that you are working on.

Index

Symbols

A

B

C

F

G

H

I

J

Printed in Great Britain
by Amazon